good-carb
meals in minutes

linda gassenheimer

Kyle Books

good-carb

meals in minutes

a three-stage plan for permanent weight loss

linda gassenheimer

Kyle Books

To Harold – for his love, support and advice.

This edition is published by Kyle Books,
an imprint of Kyle Cathie Limited
www.kylecathie.com
general.enquiries@kyle-cathie.com

Distributed by National Book Network,
4501 Forbes Boulevard, Suite 200,
Lanham, MD 20706
Phone: (301) 459 3366
Fax: (301) 429 5746

First published in USA in 2000 as *Low-carb Meals in Minutes:*
The Busy Person's Guide to Low-carbohydrate Meals in as Little as Ten Minutes
by Bay Books, San Francisco, USA

ISBN 1 904920 25 X

A Cataloguing In Publication record for this title is available from the British Library.

Colour separations by Scanhouse Ltd.
Printed and bound by Rose Printing Company Inc.

contents

introduction

Good carbs, bad carbs, glycemic index, insulin resistance—terms for our 21st century. What do all of these words mean and more importantly what do they mean to us and our families? Added to these terms we hear experts tell us to eat a well-balanced meal and exercise. But what is a well-balanced meal? What should I eat and, how can I make that meal in minutes?

If you're confused about what to eat, you're not alone. I was interviewed by a food professional and she was confused by the amount of contradictory information that was available. Her question to me was, "isn't it calories in and calories out that matter. If you eat too much and don't use the calories, you gain weight?" My answer was, "does this mean I can have muffins for breakfast, cookies for lunch and cake for dinner up to 1200 calories worth and I'd lose weight?" Yes, I probably would lose weight, but obviously, it doesn't mean that. It's the type of calories that count.

These are the questions I answer in *Good-Carb Meals in Minutes*. It's not low-carb that counts, it's the good carbs. It's not low-fat to watch, it's the right fats. All foods fall into three categories, proteins, fats, and carbohydrates. For a balanced diet, we need to eat foods from all three categories. These easy-to-make meals use complex carbohydrates (the good carbs), are low in saturated fat (using lean proteins and the right fats such as olive oil and canola oil), and

contain between 1200 and 1500 calories for a day's balanced meals. With over 60 percent of our nation overweight, our government is concerned. Health and Human Services Secretary Tommy Thompson said when announcing new US government eating guidelines, "You lower your calorie intake, you lower your carbs, your fats. You eat more fruits and vegetables and you exercise."

My experience began 9 years ago. My husband came home from a visit to the cardiologist and said, "my doctor wants me to go on a low-carbohydrate diet." My first reactions was, "Why? We have always eaten well-balanced meals, and most diets are just fads." But he was determined. He had never had a weight problem before, but he found the few pounds gained during a holiday weren't coming off. His triglycerides were high and his cholesterol was creeping into an area of concern. As I struggled to put together good-carb meals, I realized this was a new challenge for me. I didn't want to go down the route of gimmick eating. No eating all the eggs and bacon you want, or eating at certain times of the day, or with certain food combinations. Bagels for breakfast and cans of sugary sodas after tennis were out. And, what could he substitute for crackers and chips with drinks? I wanted a real eating lifestyle that could fit our busy lives, our eating out, and our entertaining. Most of all I wanted good food that was good for us, too.

I worked with two cardiologists, an endocrinologist, and nutritionists to create an eating lifestyle that was healthy and balanced. What I found was that the doctors and nutritionists could readily explain why this approach worked, but they could not tell me what's for dinner. What foods can I pick up at the supermarket and assemble into meals that we wanted to eat. They couldn't answer the questions, what do I actually eat? I began writing articles and giving cooking classes. As I heard from readers and worked with participants in my classes, I was astounded by their weight-loss results. However, they were starved for additional recipes, techniques, and guidelines. They also wanted to know how to keep the weight off. The three stages in this book will put you on the right track for losing weight and most important of all—keeping it off. I was lost when I first tried to make low-carb meals. I had to fundamentally rethink my approach to shopping and cooking. I started by restocking the pantry and refrigerator. The changes were dramatic.

off the list were:

- Low-fat processed foods, such as fat-free cookies, cakes, and other sugary desserts.
- Fat-free mayonnaise, salad dressings, cream cheese, and soured cream.
- Condiments, sauces, and salsas where sugar is one of the first five ingredients.
- Jams and jellies.
- Pizza and platefuls of pasta as a main course.
- Garnished baked potato as a meal.
- Sugary sodas and fruit juices.
- Chips, pretzels, and popcorn.

on the list were:

- Eggs, as many as four a week. We hadn't eaten them for breakfast in 10 years.
- Egg substitute (which is basically egg whites), as a good source of protein.
- A well-stocked vegetable drawer, with cucumbers, lettuce, celery, bell peppers, mushrooms, and tomatoes.
- Low-fat deli meats, such as turkey breast, chicken, ham, and lean roast beef.
- Brown rice and whole wheat pasta, in place of the lower fiber, less nutritious white varieties.
- High-fiber, whole-grain breads that are relatively low in carbohydrate.
- No-sugar-added tomato sauce and salad dressings.
- Real mayonnaise made with soybean or olive oil
- High-fiber, no-sugar-added, bran breakfast cereal.
- Olive and canola oil.
- Walnuts, pecans, almonds, and peanuts.
- Eight glasses (64 ounces) of water per day.

With this list of dos and don'ts, I created recipes that are fast, fun, and delicious. My husband's response was enthusiastic: he lowered his cholesterol and triglyceride counts to healthy levels, lost his extra weight, and has kept it off for nine years.

Why is this lifestyle becoming mainstream? What are the principles behind it, and why is it working for so many people? The theory behind good-carbohydrate, high-protein diets is this: eating lots of carbohydrates could over-stimulate insulin production, causing peaks and valleys in blood sugar levels that might, in turn, create hunger pangs. On the other hand, protein is digested more slowly, promoting more even blood sugar levels. Eating more protein, fewer carbs and more mono-unsaturated fat promotes weight loss by decreasing fat storage, increasing fat burning and delaying the onset of hunger pangs.

Several cardiologists steered me away from diets that call for high levels of saturated fat. My experience has also been that many diets are based on gimmicks. My husband and I, as well as my readers, like to go out and enjoy our meals. We don't want to be oddities at the dinner table, especially in business situations. We want to be part of the mainstream, and we've found that special timing and food combination requirements are unnecessary. They're difficult to follow and stick to over a long period, and they're not necessary for a successful good-carb lifestyle.

So how do you get started? *Good-Carb Meals in Minutes* follows my *Dinner in Minutes* promise: attractive, delicious, fun, healthy, complete meals that are quick and easy to make.

The menus are designed to fit our fast-paced lives. After many years of juggling my family, career, and a desire for good food, I've learned to use classic techniques and familiar combinations to produce delicious results while cutting cooking time.

For many days of the week we eat breakfast on the run, if at all, and lunch at our desks or at a fast food restaurant, while dinner is take out, home-delivered or restaurant fare. So, I've included some recipes based on assembling prepared foods, as well as a guide to eating out and ordering in.

You will find a wide variety of meals that sample many ethnic flavors. Wherever I travel throughout the world, I go to street markets with chefs, taste their foods and bring back their flavors to add to the repertoire of simple, good-carb recipes.

Good Carb Meals in Minutes covers all aspects of food, from preparing to purchasing ingredients. It streamlines the organisation of your kitchen. An efficient kitchen with equipment in easy reach, uncluttered work surfaces and a clean sink can save 10–15 minutes of preparation time. The recipes use products you can readily buy with one-stop shopping in your local supermarket, and there's no need to think about how to cook a dish or what goes with it. Lastly, presentation is as important as preparation. If a dish doesn't look attractive, nothing else matters.

Consider *Dinner in Minutes*, an approach you can use for everyday meals, or dressed up for parties and special events. Each recipe works as a blueprint you can adapt to suit both your taste and the occasion:

- You can buy the freshest looking fish available rather than the variety called for in a recipe.

- You can use the best sirloin or tenderloin steak, or more economical cuts like flank and skirt steaks.

- Branching out to use the freshest and best ingredients, like a gourmet infused olive oil or aged balsamic vinegar, will add even more flavor.

- You can use the ingredients called for or change them within the blueprint guidelines.

- This flexible approach lets you choose whatever is in season, on sale, or just fits your mood.

shopping list

Each recipe contains a shopping list based on how most people buy food.

- The shopping list saves you both time and money since you buy only what you need.

- Ingredients are listed by supermarket sections to help you navigate the aisles with ease.

- I've included tips on how to get in and out of the supermarket fast and how to take advantage of today's timesaving prepared foods.

- Quick shopping is as important as quick cooking. You won't have to think about how many mushrooms to buy. I've given you the amount.

- The staples list helps you organise your cupboards, so that they are not filled with extraneous items. You will already have many of the ingredients for the recipes and will only need to buy a few fresh items.

helpful hints and countdown

Each meal contains helpful hints on shopping, cooking, and substitutions, as well as a countdown for getting the whole meal on the table at the same time.

- You can hit the kitchen on the run without having to plan or think about each step.

- In my home the dinner preparation starts the minute I turn on the light in the kitchen, and it does not end until the plates are brought to the table.

- The helpful hints tell you what to buy, how to buy it, and what you can substitute. They include tips on the best preparation method, quick-cooking techniques, and time-saving clean-up tips.

3-step good-carb eating plan

Good-Carb Meals in Minutes divided into three phases: an initial phase of significant carbohydrate reduction, an intermediate phase for reintroduction of carbs, and a maintenance phase of balanced eating.

1 quick start: reducing carbohydrate intake for maximum weight loss

The first step to successful eating in this plan calls for a reduction of carbohydrates. While differences exist, most proponents of lower carb levels advise an intake of about 30–40 grams of carbs a day. My Quick Start section maintains that level through healthy recipes containing vegetables and lean proteins. My students tell me breakfast presents the greatest challenge to adapting to good-carb eating. This 14-day meal plan gives you a variety of easy recipes, including some simple recipes for breakfast on the run, and others that can be completed in 15–20 minutes. Salads and wraps fit the bill for lunches. Try the Mozzarella Tomato Tower or Smoked Trout Salad. Many are available on restaurant menus, and you can use the recipes for proportion guidelines. Dinner can be Pecan-Crusted Fish or Pacific Rim Pork, both taking only minutes to make.

2 which carbs: reintroducing carbohydrates while continuing to lose weight

Two things usually happen at this point. You're losing weight and feel good, so you stay on the first phase until you get bored, or tempted. Or, you think, "Great, I've lost weight! Now I can have the foods I love and forget about the carb restrictions." The Which Carbs 14-day meal plan will help you sail through the second phase without having to question what you're eating. I reintroduce carbohydrates in the form of high-fiber, low-simple sugar carbs. Bran breakfast cereal helps start the day the good-carb way. Add to this dishes like Cheddar Scramble or a scrumptious Raspberry Smoothie. Tex-Mex Layered Salad or Roast Turkey and Tzatziki Sandwich are two tasty lunches. How does Chicken Provençal, Neapolitan Steak or Seared Sesame Tuna sound for dinner?

3 right carbs: permanent level with great food for a healthy lifestyle

So, what should you eat to maintain your weight loss? Right Carbs has the answers. Vietnamese Pancakes, Shrimp Caesar Wrap and Chicken with Parmesan and Tomato Sauce are a breakfast, lunch and dinner that are quick to make, fit the guidelines and, most important of all, taste fabulous!

Does it mean you can't have desserts? No. Some of the meals include a dessert. In addition, I have created a guilt-free Dessert chapter to satisfy your sweet tooth. When you want to take the time to make a special dessert try Strawberry Pecan Whip or Mocha Fudge Cake.

So how does my husband handle holidays and blow-out weekends? No need to worry here. Remember, balance is the key. We have found that you can splurge on special occasions without negative effects when you return to eating the Right Carbs. In other words, the low-carbohydrate approach is forgiving. Following the programme, even with some deviations, will produce a good result. My husband found that returning to the Right Carbs is easy because it takes so little effort and the menus are so appealing. Any time you want to restart weight loss, you can go back to Quick Start for a week or two and work yourself back up to Right Carbs.

The 14-day meal plans in each of the three sections are organised to provide a day-to-day guide to low-carb eating. The breakfasts, lunches, and dinners are presented as entire meals. While you can mix and match if you prefer a different side dish, the meals have been created to achieve the nutritional priorities of that phase. By all means, if you don't like or can't eat a particular food, simply replace that meal with a meal from the same section. Regardless of the section, feel free to substitute fish or chicken for each other.

Low-Carb Meals in Minutes is for all of you who want to eat healthily and be able to fit a low-carbohydrate weight-loss programme into your time-starved lives. The low-carb lifestyle has certainly changed our lives. My husband and I no longer think about what is and isn't low-carb – we just consider it good food that fits into our busy schedule.

Before starting a programme of this type, it is always best to check with your doctor first. This is especially true if you are taking any medication under a doctor's care – particularly if being treated for diabetes. It might be interesting to look at your cholesterol and related blood tests before and after to compare your results.

My goal in sharing these recipes with you is to help you enjoy good food for good health. My husband and I love good food. Now, with these recipes, we can live to eat and eat to live.

Bon Appétit.

smart shopping the good-carb way

When I was the Executive Director of a gourmet grocery chain, I used to hear people say, "I hate shopping. I'd cook more if I had the ingredients at home." Here are some tips that will help get you in and out of the shops quickly.

some advice

The adage of "don't go to the store hungry" is true. If I go to the market when I'm tired and hungry, I just get to a starving point and eat anything offered to me. Go after a meal, or have a snack before you go. This will help you concentrate on what you should be buying instead of what you shouldn't buy.

Try to go to the market when it isn't crowded or directly after a long day's work. Carry a cool box in your car so you can stop on the way to work, during lunch or at other times. Alternatively, if you have use of an office refrigerator, use it to store groceries. Here's a hint: there have been many times when I've accidentally left my shopping at work or at a friend's house. The best solution is to put your car keys in one of the bags. You won't be able to go anywhere without them.

Keep the foods from the staples list on hand. (See pages 13–15.) You will only need to pick up a few fresh items to complete your meal.

supermarket savvy
let the markets help you

Supermarkets are in a "meals solution" revolution. They are constantly updating their selection to help us get our meals on the table fast. Use them to your advantage.

dairy

Reduced-fat cheese has come a long way. Gone is the rubbery cheese that won't melt. Many producers have used new techniques to develop lower fat cheeses that melt well.

deli

Ask for roast chicken breast only. Look for new leaner cuts of cooked meats—Canadian bacon, roast beef and ham have been made leaner without the use of high carbs.

grocery aisles

There are many items that make our lives easier, with more coming out each day. Low-fat, no-sugar-added salad dressings and tomato-based pasta sauces are a few of the products. In fact, there are so many available, it's best to try a few and, when you find one you like, buy several bottles to keep on hand. Again, the most important advice is to read the nutritional labels and ingredients lists.

meat department

Look for lower fat or lean meats – many supermarkets now have separate sections for lean meats or mark them with special labels. There are many marinated or precooked meats available, but check their sugar, salt, and fat content.

produce department

Bags of washed, ready-to-eat salads are one of the best conveniences I've seen. Read the labels. If they don't say ready-to-eat or washed, then you will need to wash the ingredients prior to using.

Many supermarkets have ready-to-eat cubes of melon and pineapple.

salad bar

Great for picking up a quick salad or lunch and buying cut vegetables and fruits for cooking at home.

how to read the labels

It's worth spending a few minutes reading food labels, as many prepared foods have added salt and sugar. However, the terms used can be confusing:

- "Light" generally means that it contains 50 percent fewer calories from fat than a comparable product.
- "Low-fat" means 3 grams or less per serving.
- "Low-sodium" means 40mg or less per serving.
- "Reduced-fat" means at least 25 percent less fat per serving than the food it is being compared to.
- "Sugar Free" according to the FDA must mean less than 0.5 grams pers serving.

Check the serving size on the label. It can be misleading. If the serving size is 1 tablespoon, think if that is the amount you will actually eat.

staples

Keep these staples on hand and you'll only need to pick up a few fresh items to make quick meals.

canned or bottled goods

Dijon mustard

Fat-free, low-sodium chicken stock

Canned chickpeas, black beans, navy beans, cannellini

Mayonnaise made with olive or soybean oil

Low-sodium, no-sugar-added diced tomatoes and

   tomato sauce

Low-sodium tomato or V-8 juice

No-sugar-added oil and vinegar dressing

No-sugar-added tomato salsa

Hearts of Palm

Tuna packed in water

Canned water chestnuts

condiments

Hot pepper sauce

Low-sodium soy sauce

Worcestershire sauce

dairy

Eggs

Egg substitute (basically liquid egg whites)

Light yogurt

Parmesan cheese

Reduced-fat Swiss, Cheddar, mozzarella and

   Monterey Jack cheese

Reduced-fat cottage cheese

Skim milk

deli

Chicken breast

Lean ham (not honey-smoked or sugar-glazed)

Lean Canadian bacon

Lean roast beef

Turkey breast

dry goods

High-fiber, no-sugar-added, bran breakfast cereal

Oatmeal

Salt

Sugar substitute

Whole wheat flour

Whole wheat pasta

freezer goods

Frozen, diced green bell pepper

Frozen, diced onion

grains and breads

Barley

Brown rice

Lentils

Multi-grain bread

100% whole wheat bread

Rye bread

Whole wheat pita bread

Whole wheat tortillas

Wild rice

oils and vinegars

Balsamic vinegar

Distilled white vinegar

Olive oil

Olive oil spray

Canola oil

Red wine vinegar

Rice vinegar

produce department

Bell Peppers

Celery

Cucumbers

Garlic

Lemon

Red onions

Tomatoes

Yellow onions

spices and herbs

Black peppercorns

Cayenne pepper

Chili powder

Ground cinnamon

Ground cumin

Dried chives

Dried dill

Dried oregano

Dried rosemary

Dried tarragon

equipment

You really don't need a lot of special equipment to make these meals. However, the following items will speed your preparation time and make your life easier.

food processor

A food processor or mini-chop will quickly slice, chop, and blend foods together.

garlic press

Some of the newer ones allow you to crush garlic without peeling the cloves. I also use it to crush fresh ginger.

knives

Sharp knives are important for fast and accurate cutting. A dull knife can be dangerous. It can slip or slide when you are trying to slice. Three different types are all you really need for most cutting tasks: a 13-inch, 8-inch, and a serrated knife for fruits or tomatoes.

meat thermometer

I love the new style probe that uses a cord. The cord is connected to a dial that sits on the counter. With the cord, it works well for items on the stove, in the oven, or under the grill.

microwave oven

Use this fast-cooking tool. And remember, any dish that's microwave safe is dishwasher safe, too.

pots and pans

You can make most of the meals in this book using a medium 9 to10-inch non-stick skillet, a large 3 to 4-quart saucepan, and a wok. Nonstick skillets are essential, as these recipes are designed for cooking with small amounts of oil. If you follow the instructions, your food will not stick.

scale

A small kitchen scale is very handy and inexpensive.

vegetable peeler

For easy peeling, make sure yours is sharp. These are actually little knives and should be replaced as they start to dull.

quick cooking tips and helpful hints

Each recipe has a helpful hints section. Knowing what to substitute, how best to prepare ingredients or some other shortcut can make a big difference to the time it takes you to get your meal on the table.

chopping fresh herbs

To quickly chop herbs, dry and snip the leaves right off the stem with scissors.

crisp stir-fry

For crisp, not steamed, stir-fried vegetables, start with a very hot wok or skillet. Let the vegetables sit a minute before tossing to allow the wok to regain its heat.

dried spices and herbs

If using dried spices, make sure they are less than 6 months old. To bring out the flavor of dried herbs, chop them with fresh parsley. The juice from the parsley will help release the flavor of the herbs.

electric cooking

To get a quick high/low response from electric rings, heat two rings, one on medium-high and the other on low. Move the pan back and forth between them.

fluffy rice

I like to cook my rice like pasta, using a pot of boiling water that's large enough for the rice to roll freely. Use this method or follow the directions on the package of rice.

food processor

To use the food processor for a recipe without having to stop to wash the bowl, first chop the dry ingredients (such as nuts), and then the wet ones (such as onion). You won't have to stop in the middle of preparing the ingredients.

fresh ginger

To chop fresh ginger quickly, cut it into small cubes and press through a garlic press with large holes. If using a press with small holes, just capture the juice that is squeezed out; it will give enough flavor for the recipe.

parmesan cheese

Buy good quality Parmesan cheese and grate it by hand or in a food processor. Freeze extra for quick use later—simply spoon out what you need and leave the rest frozen.

shelling shrimp

Buying shelled shrimp saves time otherwise spent shelling them yourself, or ask for the shrimp to be shelled while you complete your shopping.

slices and weight

To determine the weight of sliced cheese or meat, divide the packet weight by the number of slices.

timely stir-fry

To keep from looking back at a recipe as you stir-fry the ingredients, line them up on a cutting board or plate in the order of use. You will know which ingredient comes next.

washing herbs

The quickest way to wash watercress, arugula, parsley, or basil is to place the bunch, head first, into a bowl of water. Leave for a minute, then lift out and shake dry. The dirt and sand will be left behind. Repeat if necessary.

washing mushrooms

To clean whole mushrooms, wipe them with a damp paper towel.

good-carb food guidelines

After you've cooked several recipes in this book, you will begin to understand the types of ingredients and proportions that are part of a good-carb lifestyle. Use these foods to help you create your own menus.

Vegetables are an important part of a healthy eating lifestyle. You may find it hard to believe that vegetables have carbohydrates. Some have more than others. Here's a list of vegetables that are low in carbohydrates versus those with high carbs that should be eaten in smaller quantities.

eat as many of these vegetables as you like:

Alfalfa sprouts

Artichokes

Asparagus

Beans, wax or green

Bok choy

Broccoli

Brussels sprouts

Cabbage

Cauliflower

Celery

Cucumber

Eggplant

Green beans

Herbs, all types

Kale

Leeks

Lettuce, all types: curly-leaved endive, escarole, chicory, romaine, iceberg, or round

Mushrooms, all types

Onions

Okra

Peppers: green, red, yellow bell peppers and all hot peppers

Radishes

Rutabagas

Scallions

Snow peas

Spinach

Swiss chard

Tomatoes

Turnips

Yellow squash

Zucchini

eat these vegetables in measured amounts (about 1/2 cup per serving):

Beets

Carrots

Corn

Hard squash, such as acorn or butternut

Potatoes

fruits

Fruits are often high in carbohydrates, and they should be avoided during the Quick Start phase. They are reintroduced in the Which Carb and Right Carb stages. The amounts given below are guidelines for how much should be eaten at a serving:

Apple (1 small)

Apricots (4)

Apricots, dried (7 halves)

Banana (½)

Berries: strawberries, raspberries, and blueberries (³/4 cup)

Cantaloupe (¼ whole cantaloupe)

Cherries (⅓ cup)

Grapes (⅓ cup)

Grapefruit (½)

Honeydew (¼ whole honeydew or 1 cup cubed)

Kiwi (1)

Lemon juice (¼ cup)

Lime juice (¼ cup)

Nectarine (1)

Orange (1)

Mango (½)

Peach (1)

Pear (1)

Pineapple (2 rings or ½ cup cubed)

Plums (2)

Tangerine (1)

Watermelon (1 cup cubed)

meats, poultry and seafood

From steak to shrimp and all of the meats in between, here's a list of the leaner cuts:

beef

Tenderloin (fillet mignon)

Ground sirloin

Top round

Eye round

Round tip

Top loin

poultry (skinless)

Chicken breast

Chicken legs

Cornish game hens

Low-fat turkey sausage (keep in freezer for a quick dinner, lunch, or breakfast)

Turkey breast

seafood

All types of shellfish. Tuna, salmon, sardines, mackerel, halibut, and trout are high in omega-3 fatty acids. Try to eat one of these on a regular basis.

pork

Pork tenderloin

Lean Canadian bacon

Lean ham (no honey-baked or sugar-glazed)

veal

Top round

Veal chop

Veal cutlet

lamb

Leg (preferred)

Chops with visible fat removed

easy ways to turn meals into "special events"

Presentation is as important as preparation. The appeal of a beautiful plate of food adds to our eating experience. Some meals are special with friends or when celebrating events and holidays, but all meals can have a special dimension if you follow these tips and utilize your own creativity.

Use attractive dinnerware (colorful plates with matching napkins) to create a warm and fun atmosphere. If possible, set your table with the theme of the meal in mind:

● Serve Asian dishes on Chinese-style plates and place chopsticks alongside the knives and forks.

● Mediterranean meals look great served in Italian pottery or presented on place mats and tablecloths using the blues, reds, and saffron yellows of Provence.

● Serve Southwestern dishes on earthenware plates that reflect the hot, earthy colors of the Southwest or Mexico.

● Set the table for tropical meals using tropical-colored place mats or arrange some hibiscus or tropical plants for a centerpiece.

For larger parties, dress up a buffet table by placing the platters of food on different levels. Simply use large mixing bowls turned upside down or small boxes. Place them on a table and cover with an attractive tablecloth. You can also create a sparkling atmosphere by placing votive candles around the centerpiece or at varying intervals on the table.

Day-to-day eating can be made special with minimal effort. For recipes that use the broiler or oven, use oven-to-table ware and bring the sizzling serving dish to the table. The sound and smell are part of the enjoyment. You can also serve omelettes and frittatas from a cast-iron pan.

Sprinkle soups with fresh green herbs, choosing a herb to complement the flavor of the dish: fresh basil or oregano for Italian meals, cilantro for a Southwestern or Caribbean touch, and chives or arugula for extra bite. When serving meat, fish, or poultry, make an attractive fan by slicing to one narrow point, then spreading the slices into a fan.

Add colored lettuce leaves as a garnish or base for

different dishes. For example, Grilled Cheddar and Chicken Salad can be served on a bed of red-leaf lettuce. Similarly, make salads with different colored leaves. Romaine, radicchio, arugula, or basil leaves add varied color and flavor. Or you can mix Belgian endive with spicy, deep green watercress.

Dress up salads with nasturtiums or other edible flowers. Arrange them attractively on the plate or cut the petals into strips and sprinkle them over the salad. Alternatively, you can create attractive salads by stacking the ingredients. Form them into a pyramid shape or create layers, with the salad greens as a base and the other ingredients in alternating colors. A layer of sliced red bell peppers, for instance, can be followed by a layer of sliced cucumbers, then topped with sliced or cherry tomatoes.

When serving wraps, cut them in half crosswise on the diagonal and lay one half on its side and lean the other half against it. This will make an attractive display on the plate and show the colorful layers inside the wrap.

When entertaining, serve Endive Filled with Ham and Cottage Cheese, arranged in a pretty star shape on a round serving platter, or Roast Beef and Watercress Wraps cut into small circles. Both can be prepared in advance.

The desserts in this book can be served with flavored decaffeinated coffee or herbal teas. My favorite dessert for a crowd is the Raspberry Parfait.

It's very pretty and takes only a few minutes to make. Best of all, it can be prepared ahead and refrigerated until needed.

The recipes in this book include tips on presentation, and have been planned with color and texture in mind. When creating your own meals, consider their appearance as well as their taste.

drinks

Regulating your intake of tea and coffee is important on the good-carb diet. One cup of either with each meal is fine—preferably decaffeinated. If you are drinking more than this, it really should be decaff. For the Quick Start programme, leave out the skim milk if you can bear it; once you move on to Which Carbs and Right Carbs, adding skim milk is OK. As far as alcohol is concerned, limit yourself to 1 glass of wine or 1 measure of spirits per day.

tips for eating out

One of the biggest challenges to eating a healthy diet is that many of our meals are prepared outside the home. We eat out, order in, and eat on the run. Use the recipes in this book as a guide to eating out, and you will be able to order from the menu with confidence. Here are some additional hints and tips to eat well in spite of your schedule.

● Avoid all deep-fried foods.

● Avoid sugary drinks. Opt for water, unsweetened iced tea, or diet soda.

● Plain, soft tacos or tortilla-filled wraps are fine as long as they aren't filled with rice and beans.

● Roasted or grilled meats are best. Make sure you include vegetables with your meal and avoid sugar-based sauces, especially barbecue sauce and most glazes.

● Many meals are loaded with carbs. If possible, order two vegetables instead of a starch.

● Ask for your salad dressing on the side. You'll be surprised at how far 1 tablespoon of dressing will go, or just dip your salad into the dressing.

● If you order dessert, share it with the table or make sure you don't have a starch during dinner. Better still, order a fresh fruit salad or berries.

● Have a low-carb snack (vegetables, a few nuts, a slice of low-fat cheese) before you go out to eat. This will help you avoid the basket of bread while you're waiting for your meal.

● Don't go out for drinks on an empty stomach. One drink will make you hungry, and you'll eat the first thing you can find. Have a healthy snack before you go out. If you think it will be a long night, start with sparkling water with a piece of lemon or lime or a diet soda first.

● Fast food can be fine. Order grilled chicken or fish and discard the bread. Or, eat it as an open sandwich using half a roll. Stay away from baked potatoes, chips, and french fries.

● Chinese food can be loaded with sugar. Order stir-fried meats and vegetables or skewered meats, and avoid soups with fried wontons, egg rolls, ribs in thick sauce, and noodles. Some restaurants now offer brown rice as an alternative to white.

● Italian food doesn't have to mean a plate of pasta. Order an antipasto platter or any of the meats, salads, or vegetables.

● French food can be very healthy. Order clear soups, salads, vegetables, meats, or seafood, but avoid heavy sauces and bread.

● Japanese sushi is based on rice —very often with sugar added to it. Try miso soup or any of the cooked meats and vegetables instead.

● Mexican food can be high in saturated fat and carbohydrates. Fajitas (1 tortilla) with garnishes, grilled meats, and salads are fine. Avoid rice, refried beans, and nachos.

Watch portion size when eating out. Here's a guide to help you size up what you should be eating.

3 ounces cooked meat, poultry, or fish	a deck of cards
1½ ounces cheese	6 dice
1 tortilla	a 7-inch plate
1 muffin	a large egg
1 teaspoon butter	a thumb tip
2 tablespoons peanut butter	a golf ball

sizing it up*

Snacks are important little meals that will help you through the day, especially during the Quick Start phase. They can prevent that sinking feeling at 4 or 5 p.m. when your energy is low, or the mid-morning, is-it-time-for-lunch clock watching.

Knowing what to snack on and how to have it handy can help prevent raids on the vending machine to satiate sweet cravings.

here are some ideas

● If you've had an extra large salad for lunch, take some back to the office or home and use the remainder as an afternoon snack.

● 1 ounce low-fat cheese (string cheese, stick cheese, small round individually packed wax-covered low-fat cheese).

● ¹/4 cup low-fat cottage cheese.

● 1 ounce nuts, such as almonds, pecans, and walnuts (¹/4 cup). Keep small packages of nuts in your drawer at work, pocketbook, or brief case.

● 2 ounces deli meats, such as lean ham, turkey, chicken, or roast beef.

● 1 hard-boiled egg. Keep a few hard-boiled eggs on hand for snacks. They need to be refrigerated.

● 1 ounce sunflower seeds

● 6 olives

● Any vegetables such as cucumber slices, celery sticks, broccoli or cauliflower florets, and bell pepper slices.

*Food Insight News published by IFIC
(International Food Information Council)

quick start

introduction

This two-week meal plan is designed to start you off on cutting carbs from your meals. When I give cooking classes and show these meals, the response always surprises me. "You mean I can eat all of that," is the usual response. Knowing the quantities of each type of food you can eat, will help you to build your own recipes to fit your lifestyle.

There is a range of recipes in this section, some of them quite easy, including involving only assembling ready-prepared foods from the supermarket. Another category involves cooking a few things to put the meal together. And still others involve cooking an entire meal in just minutes. This gives you a wide variety to choose from. Some you'll want to make on the weekend when you have more time while others will be grab-and-go for midweek.

I have organized the menus into a meal-at-a-glance chart with some easy and quick meals mid-week and those that take a little more time for the weekends. They are arranged to give variety throughout the day and over the days of the week. The meals are ordered in the chapter in the same sequence. Just follow the meals in the order given for an easy two-week plan.

breakfasts

There's plenty of variety in these breakfasts to fit all tastes from Cheesy Scrambled Eggs to Turkey Sausage and Veggie Saute. Pick the ones you like and use them for this two-week period.

mid-morning snack

When you first start reducing carbs, you will need to eat a mid-morning snack. I've included section with some suggestions (see page 23).

lunch

There's a lunch for any occasion here—quick grab lunches that can be eaten at home or taken with you and more elaborate lunches for when you have more time or friends stop by.

Enjoy a Chicken Caesar Salad, Greek Salad, and Shrimp Salad. These meals can be made at home and taken to work. They are commonly found on most lunch menus. If you are eating out, use these recipes as a guide for the portions you should eat. Make vinaigrette dressing according to the recipe given and keep refrigerated or buy a low carbohydrate dressing to keep on hand. Read the labels carefully.

I usually order my salads with the dressing on the side. Most salads come swimming in dressing. I find that 2 tablespoons of dressing gently coats the salad without overpowering it. So, I prefer to add the dressing to the salad myself.

mid-afternoon snack

When you first start reducing carbs, you will need to eat a mid-afternoon snack (see page 23).

dinner

Do you feel like Chinese, Tex-Mex, French, or American food tonight? There's something from each ethnic group—Pacific Rim Pork with Ginger Garlic Stir-fried Vegetables, Pecan Crusted Grouper with Vegetable Creole, Tex-Mex Meal Loaf, and Sirloin Burger with Coleslaw are some of the tempting meals.

Salsa Snapper with Parmesan Zucchini and Italian Salad is a 15 minute meal and there are several others. While Steak au Poivre (Steak in Pepper Sauce) with French Beans and Heart of Palm Salad, and Rosemary Roasted Pork with Gratinéed Fennel are meals for weekends or evenings when you have 30 minutes to make a dinner.

I've made dinner parties using these meals without telling anyone they were low carb. No one knew and the only questions asked was could they have the recipe.

How low is low carb? It's important to reduce carbohydrate intake low enough for a period of time so that you eliminate the peaks of insulin secretion. Following the Quick Start 14-day plan, you will consume an average of 30–40 grams of carbohydrates per day. Carbohydrates percentage is based on carbohydrates less fiber consumed which is the normal way of calculating carbohydrate consumption. The balance of these meals is 11 percent of calories from carbs, 38 percent of calories from low fat proteins, and 37 percent of calories from monounsaturated fat and 11 percent of calories from saturated fat.

To achieve the correct balance the recipes have been structured as complete meals. The nutritional analysis is given for the entire meal. Whatever meal you pick, it's best to stay with the entire menu given.

quick start 14-day menu plan

week 1	breakfast	lunch	dinner
sunday	Smoked Salmon Pinwheels 29	Mozzarella Tomato Tower 44	Shrimp Scampi with Roasted Asparagus 59–60
monday	Salsa and Sliced Eggs 30	Turkey Bundles 45	Asian Ginger Salmon 61–62
tuesday	Pesto Scramble 31	Tuna Salad Wraps 46	Glazed Balsamic Chicken 63–64
wednesday	Sunny Side Up Cheese Melts 32	Smoked Trout Salad 47	Tex-Mex Meat Loaf . . .65
thursday	Sautéed Ham and Tomatoes 33	Roast Beef and Watercress Wraps 48	Marsala Chicken . .66–67
friday	Florentiine Eggs and Ham 34	Crunchy Chicken Salad 49	Sirloin Burger with Fresh Slaw 68
saturday	Sausage and Vegetable Stir-fry 35	Curried Chicken–stuffed Tomatoes 50	Pacific Rim Pork . . .69–70

week 2	breakfast	lunch	dinner
sunday	Pepper and Turkey Omelette 36	Salmon Balsamico 51	Veal Escalopes with Garlic Greens 71
monday	Smoked Chicken Melt .37	Ham and Cucumber Parcels 52	Pecan-crusted Grouper with Vegetable Creole 72
tuesday	Devilish Eggs 38	Greek Salad 53	Sausage-pepper Sauté 73
wednesday	Swiss Scramble 39	Grilled Cheddar and Chicken Salad 54	Salsa-baked Snapper 74
thursday	Endive filled with Ham and Cottage Cheese 40	Shrimp Salad 55	Rosemary-roasted Pork 75–76
friday	Portobello Mushroom and Canadian Bacon Omelette 41	Herby Chicken Caesar Salad 56	Herb-stuffed Chicken 77–78
saturday	Cheddar and Sausage Frittata 42	Portobellos Stuffed with Smoked Trout and Sun-dried Tomatoes 57	Steak au Poivre . . .79–80

quick start
breakfasts

smoked salmon pinwheels

Smoked salmon spread with cream cheese makes an elegant, quick breakfast for midweek or the weekend.

smoked salmon pinwheels

¾ pound smoked salmon

½ cup (2 ounces) low-fat cream
   cheese

1 tablespoon skim milk

1 medium cucumber, sliced

2 medium tomatoes, sliced

Salt and freshly ground black
   pepper to taste

Place the salmon on a cutting board. Soften cream cheese with the milk and mix until smooth. Spread on the salmon. Roll up, slice crosswise into ½-inch pinwheels, and place on 2 plates. Season the cucumber and tomato slices with salt and pepper and divide between the plates

Makes 2 servings.

One serving: 324 calories, 37g protein, 11g carbohydrate, 14g fat (6g saturated), 61mg cholesterol, 1468mg sodium, 1g fiber

helpful hint

● *Buy good quality smoked salmon rather than lox, which can be very salty.*

countdown

● *Slice cucumber and tomatoes.*

● *Complete recipe.*

shopping list

TO BUY:

   1 small package low-fat cream cheese (2 ounces needed)

   ¾ pound sliced smoked salmon

   1 medium cucumber

   2 medium tomatoes

STAPLES:

   Skim milk

   Salt

   Black peppercorns

salsa and sliced eggs

Salsa makes an appetizing garnish for the eggs. Choose mild or hot, according to your taste. Keep hard-boiled eggs on hand, so this breakfast can be put together in minutes.

salsa and sliced eggs

4 eggs
1 medium cucumber, peeled
½ cup no-sugar-added tomato salsa

Place the eggs in a small saucepan and cover with cold water. Bring to a boil. Reduce the heat and gently simmer for 12 minutes. Drain and rinse the eggs under cold water. Peel and slice with an egg slicer or cut in half lengthwise.

Slice the cucumber in half crosswise; cut into 4 pieces lengthwise. Divide the egg slices between 2 plates and spoon with salsa. Arrange the cucumbers around the eggs and serve.
Makes 2 servings.

One serving: 201 calories, 15g protein, 12g carbohydrate, 11g fat (3g saturated), 426mg cholesterol, 511mg sodium, 3g fiber

helpful hint

- *Use an egg slicer to quickly slice the eggs.*

countdown

- *Hard boil the eggs.*
- *Slice cucumbers.*
- *Assemble dish.*

shopping list

TO BUY:

1 small jar no-sugar-added tomato salsa

1 medium cucumber

STAPLES:

Eggs

pesto scramble

Fresh basil, parsley, pine nuts, and Parmesan cheese are the ingredients of a good pesto.
● *Using a jar of pesto bought in the supermarket, you can make these scrambled eggs in just minutes. They can even be made in the microwave.* ● *There are many good varieties of pesto available—look for one made with olive oil.* ● *The eggs are served on a bed of wilted lettuce. Most people don't think of cooking lettuce. It develops a tasty, nutty flavor.*

pesto scramble

6 cups (5 ounces) washed, ready-to-eat, Italian-style salad leaves
1 cup egg substitute
1/4 cup prepared pesto
2 teaspoons olive oil
2 tablespoons freshly grated Parmesan cheese

Place the lettuce in a microwave-safe bowl and microwave on high for 3 minutes. Place on 2 plates. Mix the egg substitute and pesto together. Heat the oil in a medium-sized nonstick skillet over a high heat. Reduce the heat to low, or remove the pan from the heat, and add the egg mixture. Scramble for about 1 minute, or until set to desired consistency. Place over the lettuce and sprinkle with Parmesan cheese.
Makes 2 servings.

One serving: 279 calories, 18g protein, 10g carbohydrate, 18g fat (5g saturated), 236mg cholesterol, 147mg sodium, 1g fiber

helpful hints

● *If you don't have a microwave oven, sauté the lettuce for about 1 minute in a skillet, remove to a plate and scramble the egg in the same skillet.*
● *Buy good quality Parmesan cheese and grate it yourself. Freeze extra for quick use later—simply spoon out what you need and leave the rest frozen.*
● *Any type of washed, ready-to-eat lettuce can be used.*

countdown

● *Microwave lettuce.*
● *Make scrambled eggs.*

shopping list

TO BUY:
1 small container prepared pesto sauce (2 ounces needed)
1 bag washed, ready-to-eat, Italian-style salad leaves (5 ounces needed)
STAPLES:
Olive oil
Egg substitute
Parmesan cheese

helpful hints

- If you like your egg yolk cooked through, flip the egg over in the pan before adding the cheese.
- To determine the weight of each slice of cheese, divide the package weight by the number of slices.

countdown

- Microwave lettuce.
- Slice cucumber.
- Cook egg.

shopping list

TO BUY:

1 package sliced reduced-fat Swiss cheese (3 ounces needed)

1 package washed, ready-to-eat lettuce

1 medium cucumber

STAPLES:

Olive oil

Eggs

Salt

Black peppercorns

sunny-side-up cheese melts

Eggs sunny side up are an American tradition. Here's a variation on the theme.

sunny-side-up cheese melts

Several leaves washed, ready-to-eat lettuce (about 1 cup)

1 medium cucumber, peeled and sliced

2 teaspoons olive oil

2 large eggs

Salt and freshly ground black pepper to taste

4 slices reduced-fat Swiss cheese (about 3 ounces)

Place the lettuce on a plate and microwave on high for 1 minute. Divide the lettuce and cucumber between 2 plates, and heat the olive oil in a medium-sized nonstick skillet over a medium-high heat. Break the eggs into the skillet, and sprinkle with salt and pepper to taste. Cover, and cook for 2 minutes. Remove the lid and place the cheese over the egg yolks. Cover, and cook for 1 minute. Serve the eggs on the cooked lettuce.

Makes 2 servings.

One serving: 265 calories, 23g protein, 8g carbohydrate, 17g fat (6g saturated), 236mg cholesterol, 147mg sodium, 1g fiber

smoked salmon pinwheels **p29**

florentine eggs and ham p34

sautéed ham and tomatoes

This is a quick, 5-minute breakfast that can be made in a skillet, toaster oven, broiler, or microwave oven.

sautéed ham and tomatoes

1/2 pound sliced lean ham
2 small tomatoes, sliced
2 teaspoons olive oil
Salt and freshly ground black
*   pepper to taste*

Sauté the ham in a medium-sized nonstick skillet over a medium-high heat for 2 minutes, or until the ham begins to brown. Place the tomatoes on 2 plates and drizzle with olive oil. Sprinkle with salt and pepper to taste. Divide the ham between the plates and serve.
Makes 2 servings.

> **One serving:** 305 calories, 30g protein, 12g carbohydrate, 16g fat (5g saturated), 136mg cholesterol, 797mg sodium, 3g fiber

helpful hint

- *Look for low-fat ham. Stay away from honey-baked ham.*

countdown

- *Preheat broiler.*
- *Broil ham.*
- *Assemble dish.*

shopping list

TO BUY:
1/2 pound sliced lean ham
2 small tomatoes

staples:

Olive oil
Salt
Black peppercorns

florentine eggs and ham

Cooking the washed, ready-to-eat spinach in a microwave makes this a 15-minute breakfast.

florentine eggs and ham

8 cups (10 ounces) washed, ready-to-eat fresh spinach

2 tablespoons freshly grated Parmesan cheese

Salt and freshly ground black pepper to taste

1/2 pound (8 ounces) sliced lean ham (about 8 slices), cut into strips

1 tablespoon distilled white vinegar

2 eggs

Place the spinach in a microwave-safe bowl and microwave on high for 5 minutes. Sprinkle with the Parmesan cheese and season with salt and pepper to taste. Chop the cooked spinach into bite-sized pieces and divide between 2 plates.

Set a medium-sized nonstick skillet over a medium heat. Add the ham and sauté for 2 minutes, or until slightly browned. Divide evenly over the beds of spinach.

Next, add the vinegar to a pan of simmering water and create a whirlpool in its centre. Drop an egg into the whirlpool, turn off the heat and leave covered for 4 minutes, or until set. Repeat with the second egg. Serve the eggs over the ham and spinach.

Makes 2 servings.

One serving: 337 calories, 37g protein, 10g carbohydrate, 19g fat (5g saturated), 270mg cholesterol, 1501mg sodium, 7g fiber

helpful hints

- *Buy good quality Parmesan cheese and grate it yourself. Freeze extra for quick use later—simply spoon out what you need and leave the rest frozen.*
- *If you prefer fried eggs add the olive oil to the same pan used for the ham. Break the eggs into the pan and fry until set, about 1 minute. Using a spatula, gently turn the eggs over. Sprinkle with salt and pepper to taste.*

countdown

- *Make spinach.*
- *Make ham and eggs.*

shopping list

TO BUY:

1/2 pound sliced lean ham

1 bag washed, ready-to-eat fresh spinach (10 ounces needed)

STAPLES:

Eggs

Parmesan cheese

Olive oil

Salt

Black peppercorns

sausage and vegetable stir fry

Here's a tasty breakfast made without eggs. If you can find them, keep frozen, diced onions and a green bell pepper to use when really pressed for time. The flavor and texture are slightly different, but the results are good and saves chopping time.

sausage and vegetable stir fry

8 cups (10 ounces) washed, ready-
    to-eat fresh spinach

Salt and freshly ground black
    pepper to taste

2 teaspoons olive oil

2 low-fat turkey sausages, cut into
    ½-inch slices (6 ounces)

4 slices yellow onion

1 medium-sized green bell
    pepper, seeded and sliced

6 button mushrooms, sliced

Place the spinach in a microwave-safe bowl and microwave on high for 5 minutes. Add salt and pepper to taste. Divide the spinach between 2 plates. Heat the olive oil in a nonstick skillet over a medium-high heat. Add the sausages, onion, pepper, and mushrooms. Sauté for 5 minutes or until sausages are cooked through. Season with salt and pepper. Spoon over the spinach.
Makes 2 servings.

One serving: 271 calories, 22g protein,
18g carbohydrate, 13g fat (3g saturated),
45mg cholesterol, 715mg sodium, 7g fiber

helpful hints

- To determine the weight of each sausage, divide the package weight by the number of sausages.
- To save time, buy sliced mushrooms.
- If using whole mushrooms, clean them with a damp paper towel.

countdown

- Microwave spinach.
- Sauté sausages and vegetables.

shopping list

TO BUY:

    1 small package low-fat
        turkey sausages (6 ounces
        needed)

    1 small bag washed, ready-
        to-eat fresh spinach

    1 medium-sized green bell
        pepper

    1 small package button
        mushrooms

STAPLES:

    Yellow onion

    Olive oil

    Salt

    Black peppercorns

pepper and turkey omelette

Colorful, sweet peppers flavor this tasty omelette—and it takes only 20 minutes from start to finish. The recipe can easily be doubled, saving half for the next day. Simply rewarm in a microwave for about 2 minutes on high.

pepper and turkey omelette

1 cup egg substitute
¹/₄ cup chopped fresh parsley
Salt and freshly ground black
    pepper to taste
2 teaspoons olive oil
1 medium-sized red bell pepper,
    sliced (2cups)
1 medium-sized yellow bell
    pepper, sliced (2 cups)
6 ounces sliced smoked turkey
    breast, diced

Preheat the broiler. Combine the egg substitute and parsley. Add salt and pepper to taste. Place a medium-sized nonstick skillet over a medium-high heat and add the oil. Sauté the peppers for 5 minutes. Add the egg mixture and turkey and allow to set for 2 minutes. Place under the broiler for 3 minutes. Remove from the broiler, cut in half, slide out of the skillet and serve hot.
Makes 2 servings.

One serving: 289 calories, 39g protein,
13g carbohydrate, 8g fat (2g saturated),
60mg cholesterol, 295mg sodium, 0g fiber

helpful hints

● *To speed cook the peppers, place them in a microwave-safe bowl and microwave on high for 2 minutes and then sauté them with the turkey for a few seconds before adding the eggs.*

● *Any mixture of bell peppers can be used for a colorful effect: red, yellow, green, orange, or purple. Make sure you have at least 4 cups of sliced peppers.*

countdown

● *Preheat broiler.*
● *Prepare ingredients.*
● *Make omelette.*

shopping list

TO BUY:
  6 ounces sliced smoked turkey breast
  1 small bunch fresh parsley
  1 medium-sized red bell pepper
  1 medium-sized yellow bell pepper
STAPLES:
  Egg substitute
  Olive oil
  Salt
  Black peppercorns

smoked chicken melt

*This is an on-the-go breakfast that can be made in 5 minutes using a toaster oven or broiler.
Any type of lean or low-fat deli meat can be used.*

smoked chicken melt

*2 large cucumbers, peeled and
   sliced on the diagonal*

*2 tablespoons mayonnaise made
   with soybean or olive oil*

*6 ounces sliced roasted chicken
   breast*

*Salt and freshly ground black
   pepper to taste*

*2 slices reduced-fat Cheddar
   cheese (about 1¹/₂ ounces)*

Preheat the broiler. Place the cucumbers on a
foil-lined baking tray and spread the slices with
mayonnaise. Top with the chicken slices and
season with salt and pepper to taste. Tear the
cheese into pieces to cover the chicken. Place
under the broiler for 1 minute or until the cheese
melts. Divide between 2 plates and serve.
Makes 2 servings.

One serving: 351 calories, 34g protein,
9g carbohydrate, 20g fat (5g saturated),
92mg cholesterol, 329mg sodium, 2g fiber

helpful hints

● *Slice the cucumber on
the diagonal for a larger
surface area and oval-shaped
slice.*

● *To determine the weight
of each slice of cheese,
divide the package weight by
the number of slices.*

countdown

● *Preheat broiler or toaster
oven.*

● *Complete recipe.*

shopping list

TO BUY:

   *1 package sliced reduced-fat
      Cheddar cheese (1¹/₂
      ounces needed)*

   *6 ounces sliced roasted
      chicken breast*

   2 large cucumbers

STAPLES:

   *Mayonnaise made with
      soybean or olive oil*

   Salt

   Black peppercorns

devilish eggs

Devilled eggs are a classic comfort food. They can be made ahead, stored in the refrigerator and are easily carried with you for a breakfast or lunch on the run. In fact, it's a good idea to keep a few hard-boiled eggs on hand for quick meals or snacks.

devilish eggs

6 eggs (only 2 yolks used)

2 tablespoons mayonnaise made with soybean or olive oil

2 teaspoons Dijon mustard

Large pinch of cayenne pepper

2 tablespoons snipped fresh chives

Salt and freshly ground black pepper to taste

8 celery stalks, cut into 4-inch pieces

Place the eggs in a small saucepan and cover with cold water. Set over a medium-high heat and bring to a boil. Reduce the heat to low and gently simmer for 12 minutes. Drain, and then fill the pan with cold water. When the eggs are cool to the touch, peel and cut in half lengthwise. Remove and discard the yolks from 4 of the eggs. Set the egg whites on 2 plates. Place the remaining 2 whole eggs in the bowl of a food processor or mash with a fork in a mixing bowl. Add the mayonnaise, mustard, cayenne pepper, and chives. Season with salt and pepper to taste. Process until smooth. Fill the egg whites with the mixture. Serve with celery.

Makes 2 servings.

One serving: 251 calories, 16g protein, 14g carbohydrate, 18g fat (3g saturated), 218mg cholesterol, 653mg sodium, 4g fiber

swiss scramble

This breakfast can be made in 15 minutes or less. Swiss cheese, sweet peppers, and scallions add flavor and color to the light eggs.

swiss scramble

2 teaspoons olive oil

2 medium-sized green bell peppers, sliced (2 cups)

2 whole eggs

6 egg whites

2 cups scallions, sliced

4 slices reduced-fat Swiss cheese (about 3 ounces), torn into small pieces

Salt and freshly ground black pepper to taste

Heat the oil in a medium-sized nonstick skillet. Add the peppers and sauté for 3 minutes. Combine the whole eggs, egg whites, scallions, and cheese in a medium-sized bowl, and season with salt and pepper to taste. Add to the skillet and scramble for 2 minutes, or until cooked. Spoon onto 2 plates and serve.

Makes 2 servings.

One serving: 346 calories, 35g protein, 15g carbohydrate, 17g fat (6g saturated), 236mg cholesterol, 311mg sodium, 0g fiber

helpful hints

- *Egg substitute can be used instead of whole eggs.*
- *Any type of reduced-fat cheese can be used.*
- *To determine the weight of each slice of cheese, divide the package weight by the number of slices.*

countdown

- *Prepare all ingredients.*
- *Make spinach.*
- *Make eggs.*

shopping list

TO BUY:

1 package sliced reduced-fat Swiss cheese (3 ounces needed)

2 medium-sized green bell peppers

2 bunches scallions (16 scallions needed)

STAPLES:

Olive oil

Eggs

Salt

Black peppercorns

helpful hints

- *Buy large heads of endive. The larger leaves are easier to fill.*
- *The best way to clean endive is to wipe the outer leaves with damp paper towel. Try not to soak the leaves in water, as they tend to brown.*

countdown

- *Chop ham, walnuts and cheese.*
- *Fill endive.*

shopping list

TO BUY:

1 carton low-fat cottage cheese (8 ounces needed)

10 ounces sliced lean ham

1 small package walnut pieces (2 ounces needed)

2 medium heads Belgian endive

STAPLES:

Salt

Black peppercorns

endive filled with ham and cottage cheese

Walnuts, ham, and cottage cheese make a crunchy, flavorful stuffing for endive spears. It's also great as hors d'oeuvres or a quick snack. ● *This is a good on-the-go breakfast. It takes just seconds to blend the stuffing to a creamy consistency.*

endive filled with ham and cottage cheese

10 slices lean ham (about 10 ounces)

24 walnuts (2 ounces)

1/2 cup low-fat cottage cheese

Salt and freshly ground black pepper to taste

2 medium heads Belgian endive, leaves separated

Chop the ham, walnuts, and cottage cheese in a food processor. Add salt and pepper to taste. Spread the mixture into the wide base of each chicory leaf.

Makes 2 servings.

One serving: 432 calories, 39g protein, 11g carbohydrate, 27g fat (6g saturated), 72mg cholesterol, 1425mg sodium, 2g fiber

portobello mushroom and canadian bacon omelette

Canadian bacon, mushrooms, and scallions flavor this egg white omelette. ● *Look for lean or low-fat Canadian bacon. There are several brands available in the supermarket, and they are all packaged to keep for several weeks in the refrigerator. I always buy extra to have on hand for snacks or lunch.*

portobello mushroom and canadian bacon omelette

8 egg whites
1 cup scallions, sliced
Salt and freshly ground black
   pepper to taste
2 teaspoons olive oil
1/2 pound portobello mushrooms,
   sliced
1/2 pound sliced lean Canadian
   bacon, diced

Preheat the broiler. Combine the egg whites and scallions in a small mixing bowl, and season with salt and pepper to taste. Heat the oil in a medium-sized nonstick skillet over a medium-high heat. Add the mushrooms and Canadian bacon and sauté for 3 minutes. Add the egg mixture and allow to set for 2 minutes. Place under the broiler for 3 minutes, or until just cooked. Cut the omelette in half, slide out of the skillet and serve.

Makes 2 servings.

One serving: 297 calories, 40g protein, 7g carbohydrate, 11g fat (3g saturated), 53mg cholesterol, 1208mg sodium, 0g fiber

helpful hints

● *Any type of mushrooms can be used for this recipe.*
● *If you prefer, cover the omelette with a lid instead of finishing it under the broiler.*
● *To save time, use presliced portobello mushrooms. If the slices are too large, cut them in half.*
● *Use a skillet with an ovenproof handle to go under the broiler.*

countdown

● *Preheat broiler.*
● *Make omelette.*

shopping list

TO BUY:
   1/2 pound sliced lean
      Canadian bacon
   1 bunch scallions
      (8 needed)
   1/2 pound sliced portobello
      mushrooms
STAPLES:
   Eggs
   Olive oil
   Salt
   Black peppercorns

cheddar and sausage frittata

A frittata is a little like a crustless quiche and takes about 10 minutes to cook. It's great for breakfast, and when cooled and cut into squares, it's great for snacks.

cheddar and sausage frittata

2 teaspoons olive oil

1/4 cup red onion, sliced

1 medium-sized red bell pepper, sliced (2 cups)

2 celery stalks, sliced (1 cup)

2 low-fat turkey sausages, cut into 1/2-inch slices (6 ounces)

1 cup water chestnuts, drained and sliced

1 cup egg substitute

1 cup arugula, washed and sliced

1/2 cup (2 ounces) shredded, reduced-fat Cheddar cheese

Salt and freshly ground black pepper to taste

Preheat the oven to 400 degrees. Heat the olive oil in a medium-sized nonstick skillet over a medium-high heat. Sauté the onion, pepper, celery, sausages, and water chestnuts over a high heat for 3 minutes. Combine the egg substitute, arugula, and cheese in a medium-sized bowl and season with salt and pepper to taste. Reduce the heat to medium and pour the egg mixture into the skillet. Swirl in the skillet to cover the vegetables. Allow to set for 3 minutes. Transfer to the oven for 7 minutes, or until the eggs set to the desired consistency. Cut the frittata in half, slide out of the skillet onto 2 plates, and serve.

Makes 2 servings.

One serving: 396 calories, 36g protein, 20g carbohydrate, 19g fat (7g saturated), 65mg cholesterol, 1088mg sodium, 3g fiber

quick start
lunches

mozzarella tomato tower

This tower is made by alternating tomato slices, mozzarella, and fresh basil until the tomato is reformed. It's a modern version of a tomato-mozzarella plate that's fun to serve and delicious, too.

mozzarella tomato tower

helpful hint

- *Yellow tomatoes make an attractive alternative to red ones.*

countdown

- *Prepare ingredients.*
- *Assemble salad.*

shopping list

TO BUY:

1 small package reduced-fat mozzarella cheese (8 ounces needed)

1 small package pine nuts

2 medium tomatoes

1 small bunch fresh basil

1 bag washed, ready-to-eat mesclun or field greens

STAPLES:

Olive oil

No-sugar-added oil and vinegar dressing

Salt

Black peppercorns

4 teaspoons olive oil

2 medium tomatoes, cut into ½-inch slices

Salt and freshly ground black pepper to taste

½ pound shredded, reduced-fat mozzarella cheese

4 cups washed, ready-to-eat mesclun or field greens

2 tablespoons pine nuts

20 leaves fresh basil

2 tablespoons no-sugar-added oil and vinegar dressing

Drizzle 2 teaspoons of the olive oil over the tomato slices, and season with salt and pepper to taste. Drizzle the remaining 2 teaspoons of olive oil over the cheese, tossing to coat well. Divide the salad leaves between 2 plates. Sprinkle with the pine nuts. Place the stem slices of the tomatoes in the centre of the salad, skin-side down. Sprinkle a little mozzarella on top of each. Place a few basil leaves on the mozzarella. Continue layering the tomato slices, mozzarella, and basil leaves until the tomatoes are rebuilt, ending with a sprinkling of mozzarella on top. Gently press the slices together with the palm of your hand. Drizzle the tomatoes and salad leaves with the dressing and serve.
Makes 2 servings.

One serving: 427 calories, 35g protein, 12g carbohydrate, 24g fat (6g saturated), 16mg cholesterol, 971mg sodium, 4g fibre

turkey bundles

For the times when you don't have time to make a lunch, here is a dish you can make and eat in minutes.

turkey bundles

3/4 pound sliced turkey breast
18 to 20 leaves romaine or other lettuce
1/2 cup (3 1/2 ounces) deli coleslaw
2 small tomatoes, sliced

Place a slice of turkey on a lettuce leaf. Add a spoonful of coleslaw and a slice of tomato. Fold the lettuce. Continue with additional lettuce leaves until all the turkey is used.
Makes 2 servings.

One serving: 398 calories, 52g protein, 16g carbohydrate, 12g fat (3g saturated), 125mg cholesterol, 269mg sodium, 2g fibre

helpful hints

● *Check the ingredients of shop-bought coleslaw, as some prepared versions have added sugar.*
● *Drain the coleslaw before use.*

shopping list

TO BUY:
3/4 pound sliced turkey breast
3 1/2 ounces deli coleslaw
1 head romaine or other lettuce
2 small tomatoes

tuna salad wraps

You can find almost any type of food in wraps these days, including a whole dinner. I've used large lettuce leaves for the wrap in this recipe. ● These wraps are really portable and will last at least a day in the refrigerator. I take them out when we go sailing. They are great for a day outside—easy to serve and very delicious.

helpful hints

● *Use the tuna salad recipe given or use shop-bought tuna salad. If the shop-bought version is dripping in mayonnaise, drain it before using. Be sure to check the ingredients list of shop-bought tuna salad, as some have sugar added.*

● *The easiest way to snip chives is with scissors.*

countdown

● *Cut foil squares.*
● *Make tuna salad.*
● *Assemble wraps.*

shopping list

TO BUY:

9-ounce can tuna, packed in water
1 head romaine lettuce
1 small bunch chives
1 small bunch basil
12 ounces alfalfa sprouts

STAPLES:

Red onion
Mayonnaise made from soybean or olive oil
Foil
Salt
Black peppercorns

tuna salad wraps

12 or 14 large romaine lettuce leaves, washed and dried

9-ounce can tuna packed in water, rinsed and drained

1/4 cup mayonnaise made from soybean or olive oil

1/2 cup snipped chives

1/2 cup red onion, diced

Salt and freshly ground black pepper to taste

12 (11 x 4-inch) rectangles foil, parchment paper or wax paper

2 cups fresh basil leaves, washed and dried

2 cups alfalfa sprouts, tops only

Crush the stems of the lettuce leaves so they lie flat. In a small mixing bowl, break the tuna up with a fork and stir in the mayonnaise, chives, and onion. Add salt and pepper to taste. Spread the foil pieces on the countertop. Place a romaine leaf on each square. Spoon some of the tuna salad on each leaf and top with the basil. Spoon the remaining tuna salad on top and sprinkle with alfalfa sprouts. Roll up each leaf like a cigar, and wrap tightly in the foil. Seal the ends and slice in half crosswise. Use immediately or place in plastic bags and refrigerate until needed.

Makes 2 servings.

One serving: 421 calories, 37g protein, 12g carbohydrate, 25g fat (3g saturated), 66mg cholesterol, 738mg sodium, 1g fiber

smoked trout salad

It takes only a few minutes to put this tasty lunch together. A good quality smoked trout needs very little added to it to make a great meal.

smoked trout salad

6 cups (6 ounces) washed, ready-
   to-eat mesclun or field greens
3/4 pound smoked trout
2 1/2 tablespoons (1 ounce) walnut
   pieces
2 teaspoons olive oil
Salt and freshly ground black
   pepper to taste

Place the salad leaves on individual dishes. Flake trout into ½-inch pieces and place on top of the mesclun. Sprinkle with the walnuts and drizzle with the oil. Season with salt and pepper to taste and serve.
Makes 2 servings.

One serving: 342 calories, 31g protein, 5g carbohydrate, 22g fat (4g saturated), 77mg cholesterol, 60mg sodium, 2g fiber

helpful hints

- *Any type of smoked fish can be used.*
- *Any type of lettuce can be used.*

countdown

- *Prepare ingredients.*
- *Assemble salad.*

shopping list

TO BUY:
   3/4 pound smoked trout
   1 small package walnut
      pieces (1 ounce needed)
   1 bag washed, ready-to-eat
      mesclun or field greens
STAPLES:
   Olive oil
   Salt
   Black peppercorns

roast beef and watercress wraps

Arugula and horseradish give these roast beef wraps a spicy bite. Watercress adds a little crunch. Wraps are great finger food. This recipe uses large lettuce leaves instead of tortillas to wrap around the filling.

roast beef and watercress wraps

helpful hints

- *These travel well. Make them ahead, store in a plastic bag and refrigerate until needed.*
- *Any type of lettuce can be used. Large leaves are needed.*

countdown

- *Cut foil squares.*
- *Assemble recipe.*

shopping list

TO BUY:

³/₄ pound thinly sliced lean roast beef

1 jar white or red horseradish

1 head round lettuce

1 small bunch arugula

1 small bunch watercress

STAPLES:

Mayonnaise made with soybean or olive oil

Foil

12 large Boston lettuce leaves, washed and dried

12 x (11 x 4 -inch) rectangles foil, parchment paper or wax paper

2 tablespoons mayonnaise made with soybean or olive oil

2 tablespoons horseradish

³/₄ pound sliced lean roast beef

2 cups fresh arugula, washed and dried

12 small sprigs watercress, washed and dried

Crush the stems of the lettuce leaves so they lie flat. Place the foil pieces on the work surface. Place one lettuce leaf on each piece of foil. Combine the mayonnaise and horseradish in a small bowl, and spread on the leaves. Place one layer of roast beef on each leaf. Top with some arugula and a sprig of watercress. Roll up each leaf like a cigar, then wrap tightly in the foil. Seal the ends and slice in half crosswise to serve. Makes 2 servings.

One serving: 466 calories, 52g protein, 7g carbohydrate, 24g fat (6g saturated), 144mg cholesterol, 235mg sodium, 1g fiber

mozzarella tomato tower   **p44**

salmon balsamico p51

crunchy chicken salad

Here's a popular lunch or light dinner dish that appears on many restaurant menus.
● The secret to this salad is to cut all of the ingredients into small, even cubes. This way every bite contains different color and flavor combinations. ● This is a great way to use leftover chicken.

crunchy chicken salad

2 celery stalks, chopped into ¼-inch pieces (1 cup)

1 medium-sized green bell pepper, chopped into ¼-inch pieces (1 cup)

10 large red-leaf lettuce leaves, sliced into ¼-inch pieces (4 cups)

6–8 broccoli florets, chopped into ¼-inch pieces (1 cup)

¼ cup no-sugar-added oil and vinegar dressing

2 scallions, sliced (¼ cup)

½ pound roasted chicken breast, skinned and cut into ¼-inch cubes

Place the celery, sweet pepper, lettuce, and broccoli in a medium-sized bowl. Add the dressing and toss. Add the scallions and chicken, then toss again. Divide between 2 plates and serve.
Makes 2 servings.

One serving: 401 calories, 40g protein, 14g carbohydrate, 23g fat (4g saturated), 96mg cholesterol, 329mg sodium, 2g fiber

helpful hints

● Roasted, skinless chicken is available precut into small pieces. You can use it for this recipe, but read the label carefully to make sure there are no hidden carbs. Buy the original flavor rather than the honey-baked or barbecued variety.

● Any type of lean roasted meat can be used in the salad.

countdown

● Prepare ingredients.
● Assemble salad.

shopping list

TO BUY:
½ pound roasted chicken breast
1 medium green bell pepper
1 small head red-leaf lettuce
1 small package broccoli florets (6–8 florets needed)
1 small bunch scallions (2 needed)
STAPLES:
Celery
No-sugar-added oil and vinegar dressing

helpful hints

- Toasting ground spices before they are used releases their natural oils and flavors. This step can be omitted if you're pressed for time.
- To help the tomato halves sit straight, cut a thin slice from the rounded ends.

countdown

- Toast spices.
- Make recipe.

shopping list

TO BUY:

6 ounces cooked chicken breast
1 small package slivered almonds (1 ounce needed)
1 jar curry powder
2 large tomatoes
1 medium-sized red pepper
1 small head any type of lettuce (several leaves needed)

STAPLES:

Celery
Mayonnaise made with soybean or olive oil
Ground cumin
Salt
Black peppercorns

curried chicken–stuffed tomatoes

The pungent flavor of curry blends well with roasted chicken to make a tasty salad with a hint of India. ● *Authentic curries are made with a blend of about 15 spices. For this quick salad, I use curry powder, which loses its flavor quickly and should be not used if more than three to four months old.* ● *This recipe works for any type of leftover meat.* ● *Quick suggestion: Use chicken salad from the deli counter and add the other ingredients to it. Ask for the nutritional analysis, as some commercial chicken salads are made with sugar.*

curried chicken–stuffed tomatoes

1 tablespoon curry powder
2 teaspoons ground cumin
2 large tomatoes
2 tablespoons mayonnaise made with soybean or olive oil
Salt and freshly ground black pepper to taste
6 ounces cooked chicken breast, skinned and chopped
1 celery stalk, diced (1/2 cup)
Half a medium-sized red bell pepper, diced
2 1/2 tablespoons slivered almonds (1 ounce)
Several lettuce leaves, washed and torn into bite-sized pieces

Toast the curry powder and cumin in a small nonstick skillet for 1 minute or microwave on high for 30 seconds. Stem the tomatoes and slice in half crosswise. Scoop the pulp, seeds, and juice from the tomato halves into the bowl of a food processor, and blend until smooth. Alternatively, scoop the pulp onto a chopping board and the juice into a bowl. Chop the pulp by hand and add to the bowl. Set the tomato halves aside.

Add the spices and the mayonnaise to the bowl. Add salt and pepper to taste. Combine until smooth. Stir in the chicken, celery, bell pepper, and almonds. Taste for seasoning and add more if necessary. Divide the lettuce between 2 plates and place the tomato halves on the lettuce. Fill the tomatoes with the chicken salad and serve.

Makes 2 servings.

One serving: 381 calories, 34g protein, 15g carbohydrate, 23g fat (3g saturated), 77mg cholesterol, 197mg sodium, 2g fiber

salmon balsamico

Rich, flavorful salmon is easy to cook and very filling. The smooth, rich texture goes well with cool, crunchy salad leaves and vegetables.

salmon balsamico

2 teaspoons olive oil

$^1/_2$ pound salmon fillet

Salt and freshly ground black
    pepper to taste

$^1/_2$ pound sweet potatoes, peeled
    and cut into $^1/_2$-inch cubes

$^1/_2$ cup balsamic vinegar

4 cups washed, ready-to-eat
    mesclun or field greens

2 tablespoons no-sugar-added oil
    and vinegar dressing

Heat the oil in a small nonstick skillet over a medium-high heat. Rinse the salmon and pat dry with paper towel. Sauté the salmon for 3 minutes, then turn and brown for 3 more minutes, or longer if the salmon is more than 1 inch thick. Sprinkle the cooked salmon with salt and pepper to taste and set aside.

Fill another pan with water and bring to the boil. Add the sweet potato and cook for 5 minutes, then drain. Add the vinegar and sweet potatoes to the salmon, return to the heat and reduce for about 1 minute, or until the liquid is syrupy. Divide the salad leaves between 2 plates and toss with the salad dressing. Place the salmon on top of the salad leaves. Spoon the glaze and sweet potato cubes on top and serve.

Makes 2 servings.

One serving: 365 calories, 30g protein,
16g carbohydrate, 20g fat (3g saturated),
80mg cholesterol, 158mg sodium, 6g fiber

helpful hint

● *Any type of fish fillet can be used.*

countdown

● *Sauté salmon.*
● *Assemble salad.*

shopping list

TO BUY:

$^1/_2$ pound salmon fillet

$^1/_2$ pound sweet potatoes

1 bag washed, ready-to-eat
    mesclun or field greens

STAPLES:

Olive oil

No-sugar-added oil and
    vinegar dressing

Balsamic vinegar

Salt

Black peppercorns

ham and cucumber parcels

For the days when you don't have time to make a lunch, here is a dish you can prepare and eat in minutes.

ham and cucumber parcels

ham and cucumber parcels

3/4 pound sliced lean ham
18–20 leaves romaine or
   other lettuce
1/4 cup Dijon mustard
2 medium cucumbers, sliced

Place 1 slice of ham on a lettuce leaf. Spread the ham with Dijon mustard. Add a few slices of cucumber. Fold the lettuce. Continue with additional lettuce leaves until all the ham is used. Makes 2 servings.

One serving: 318 calories, 38g protein, 16g carbohydrate, 11g fat (3g saturated), 80mg cholesterol, 2218mg sodium, 3g fiber

helpful hints

- These travel well. Make them ahead, store in a plastic bag and refrigerate until needed.
- Any type of lettuce can be used. Large leaves are needed.

shopping list

TO BUY:
   3/4 pound sliced lean ham
   1 head romaine or other
     lettuce
   2 medium cucumbers
STAPLES:
   Dijon mustard

greek salad

With the help of the supermarket deli, you can make this salad in less than 5 minutes. A traditional Greek salad has olives, feta cheese, radishes, and good olive oil. You can also add sweet pimentos, caperberries, and anchovies, all of which can be found on the supermarket shelves. Use this recipe as the base and build your own salad with other fresh vegetables.

greek salad

2 tablespoons no-sugar-added oil
  and vinegar dressing

2 teaspoons dried oregano or
  2 tablespoons fresh

6 cups washed, ready-to-eat
  lettuce leaves

1 medium cucumber, peeled
  and sliced

12 black olives, chopped
  (preferably kalamata)

8 radishes, sliced (1/2 cup)

8 scallions, sliced (1 cup)

1/4 cup drained capers

1/2 pound medium-sliced lean deli
  turkey breast

3 ounces (2/3 cup) reduced-fat feta
  cheese, crumbled

Freshly ground black pepper
  to taste

Combine the oil and vinegar dressing and oregano together in a salad bowl. Add the lettuce, cucumber, olives, radishes, scallions, and capers. Toss well. Slice the turkey breast into 1/2-inch strips. Sprinkle on top of the salad with the crumbled feta cheese. Add pepper to taste. Divide between 2 plates and serve. *Makes 2 servings.*

One serving: 455 calories, 41g protein, 15g carbohydrate, 25g fat (9g saturated), 118mg cholesterol, 1639mg sodium, 2g fiber

helpful hints

● Dried oregano is called for in this recipe for speed. Fresh oregano (available in most supermarkets) will add a sweeter flavor to the salad. Use it if you have time.

● If using dried oregano, make sure it is less than six months old.

● Any type of washed, ready-to-eat lettuce can be used.

countdown

● Make salad dressing.
● Make salad.

shopping list

TO BUY:

1 package reduced-fat feta
  cheese (3 ounces needed)

1/2 pound medium-sliced
  lean deli turkey breast

1 jar capers

1 package black olives
  (preferably kalamata)

1 bag washed, ready-to-eat
  lettuce leaves

1 medium cucumber

1 small bunch radishes

1 bunch scallions (8 needed)

STAPLES:

No-sugar-added oil and
  vinegar dressing

Dried oregano

Black peppercorns

helpful hints

- Chop all ingredients in a food processor.
- To determine the weight of each slice of cheese, divide the package weight by the number of slices.

countdown

- Preheat broiler.
- Make chicken salad.
- Complete recipe.

shopping list

TO BUY:

1 package sliced, reduced-fat, aged Cheddar cheese (1½ ounces needed)

½ pound roasted chicken breast

1 medium-sized green bell pepper

1 small bunch fresh parsley

2 large tomatoes

STAPLES:

Yellow onion

Mayonnaise made with olive or soybean oil

Dijon mustard

Salt

Black peppercorns

grilled cheddar and chicken salad

This lunch can be made in 5 minutes by using either leftover chicken or roasted skinless chicken from the supermarket, but read the labels carefully to make sure there are no hidden carbs. Buy the original flavor rather than the honey-baked or barbecued variety. ● The cheese melts, providing a warm covering for the cool salad.

grilled cheddar and chicken salad

2 tablespoons mayonnaise made with olive or soybean oil

2 tablespoons warm water

2 tablespoons Dijon mustard

½ pound roasted chicken breast, chopped

1 medium-sized green bell pepper, seeded and chopped (1 cup)

½ cup yellow onion, diced

½ cup chopped fresh parsley

Salt and freshly ground black pepper to taste

2 large tomatoes, sliced

2 slices reduced-fat, aged Cheddar cheese (1½ ounces)

Preheat the broiler. Combine the mayonnaise, water, and mustard in a medium-sized bowl. Add the chicken, pepper, onion, and parsley. Add salt and pepper to taste and toss well. Place the tomato slices on an ovenproof dish or on a foil-lined baking tray and season with a little salt and pepper. Spread with chicken salad and tear cheese slices into small pieces to fit over the chicken salad. Grill for 2 minutes, or until the cheese melts, and serve.

Makes 2 servings.

One serving: 434 calories, 46g protein, 14g carbohydrate, 22g fat (6g saturated), 116mg cholesterol, 723mg sodium, 0g fiber

shrimp salad

Juicy shrimp, well seasoned, and crunchy celery make a delicious, quick lunch. Old Bay is a crab, shrimp seasoning from Maryland and is sold throughout the US. It's made with a blend of spices that go well with shellfish.

shrimp salad

1/4 cup mayonnaise made from
    soybean or olive oil
1 tablespoon Old Bay or Crab Boil
    seasoning
3/4 pound cooked shrimp, cut into
    1/2-inch pieces
8 celery stalks, finely chopped
    (4 cups)
Salt and freshly ground black
    pepper to taste
12–14 large romaine lettuce
    leaves, washed and dried

Combine the mayonnaise and fish seasoning in a medium-sized mixing bowl. Add the shrimp and celery and season with salt and pepper to taste. Mix well. Serve on a bed of lettuce leaves. *Makes 2 servings.*

One serving: 443 calories, 38g protein,
17g carbohydrate, 26g fat (3.6g saturated),
708mg cholesterol, 5mg sodium, 2g fiber

helpful hints

● *Any type of lettuce can be used.*
● *Buy cooked shrimp from the fish department in the supermarket or buy good quality frozen, cooked shrimp.*
● *Any type of crab or shrimp boil can be used.*

countdown

● *Prepare all ingredients.*
● *Assemble salad.*

shopping list

TO BUY:
    3/4 pound cooked shrimp
    1 small container Old Bay or
        Crab Boil seasoning
    1 head romaine lettuce
STAPLES:
    Celery
    Mayonnaise made from
        soybean or olive oil
    Salt
    Black peppercorns

herby chicken caesar salad

Caesar salads are one of the most popular American lunches. Crisp lettuce and smooth, tangy dressing provide an enjoyable, mouth-watering combination. This is a recipe that you can easily make at home. ● Here's a tip when ordering a Caesar salad at a restaurant: ask for the salad without the croûtons or remove them when the salad is served. Many salads come swimming in dressing, so ask for the dressing on the side, and use only 2 tablespoons on your salad.

helpful hints

- Use the recipe below or purchase a low-carbohydrate, Caesar-salad dressing.
- Toasting walnuts can be tricky, as they burn quickly. Watch them carefully.
- To save cleaning time, use the same baking tray to toast the walnuts and broil the chicken.
- Buy good quality Parmesan cheese and grate it yourself. Freeze extra for quick use later—simply spoon out what you need and leave the rest frozen.

countdown

- Preheat broiler.
- Make chicken.
- Make dressing.
- Assemble dish.

shopping list

TO BUY:
1/2 pound boneless, skinless chicken breast
1 small package walnut pieces (1/2 ounce needed)
1 tin anchovies
1 lemon
1 small head romaine lettuce
STAPLES:
Eggs
Parmesan cheese
Red onion
Olive oil
Olive oil spray
Garlic
Dried oregano
Worcestershire sauce
Salt
Black peppercorns

herby chicken caesar salad

2 tablespoons walnuts (1/2 ounce)
6 medium-sized garlic cloves, crushed
2 teaspoons dried oregano
1/4 teaspoon freshly ground black pepper
Pinch of salt
Grated rind from 1 lemon (1/2 tablespoon)
2 tablespoons freshly squeezed lemon juice (1 lemon)
2 egg whites
1/2 pound boneless, skinless chicken breast
Olive oil spray
4 anchovies, mashed
4 teaspoons Worcestershire sauce
4 teaspoons olive oil
1 small head romaine lettuce, washed and cut into pieces (about 6 cups)
4 slices red onion (1/2 cup)
2 tablespoons freshly grated Parmesan cheese

Preheat the broiler. Line a baking tray with foil. Place the walnuts on the tray and toast under the broiler for 1 minute, or until toasted. (Watch carefully to keep them from burning.) Combine 2 garlic cloves, the oregano, pepper, salt, grated lemon rind, and 1/2 tablespoon of the lemon juice in a small bowl. In a separate bowl, whisk the egg whites lightly until just frothy. Dip the chicken into the egg whites and then roll in the garlic-lemon mixture. Spray the foil-lined baking tray with olive oil. Place the coated chicken on the baking tray and broil about 5 inches from the heat for 5 minutes. Turn and grill for another 5 minutes. Remove from the oven.

To make the dressing, place the anchovies, remaining lemon juice, 4 crushed garlic cloves, Worcestershire sauce, and olive oil in the bowl of a food processor and blend thoroughly, scraping down the sides several times. Alternatively, mix the ingredients together by hand, mashing the anchovies and garlic to blend well. Place the lettuce in a salad bowl and toss with half the dressing. Divide the salad between 2 plates, add the walnuts and top with onion slices. Sprinkle with Parmesan cheese. Cut the chicken into thin slices and place on top. Spoon the remaining dressing over the top and serve. *Makes 2 servings.*

One serving: 442 calories, 48g protein, 11g carbohydrate, 24g fat (5g saturated), 101mg cholesterol, 708mg sodium, 1g fiber

portobellos stuffed with smoked trout and sun-dried tomatoes

Large portobello mushroom caps have an earthy flavor and meaty texture. They can be roasted, broiled, or sautéed. This dish can be eaten warm or at room temperature, and it only takes about 15 minutes to make. ● Curly endive has lacy, green-trimmed leaves, but any type of lettuce can be used for this recipe.

portobellos stuffed with smoked trout and sun-dried tomatoes

Olive oil spray

4 large portobello mushroom caps, washed (½ pound)

Salt and freshly ground black pepper to taste

2 tablespoons mayonnaise made with olive or soybean oil

1 tablespoon freshly squeezed lemon juice (about ½ lemon)

¼ cup horseradish

½ pound smoked trout or other smoked fish

1 cup sun-dried tomatoes, drained and diced

Several leaves curly endive

Preheat the oven to 450 degrees. Line a baking tray with foil and spray with olive oil. Place the mushrooms on the tray and spray both sides with olive oil until lightly coated. Bake for 5 minutes; turn and bake for 5 more minutes. Remove from the oven, and add salt and pepper to taste.

Combine the mayonnaise, lemon juice, and horseradish in a medium-sized mixing bowl. Flake the smoked trout into the mayonnaise mixture. Stir in the sun-dried tomatoes, blending well. Season with salt and pepper to taste. Spoon the mixture into the mushroom caps. Divide the lettuce between 2 plates, top with the stuffed mushroom caps, and serve.

Makes 2 servings.

One serving: 476 calories, 33g protein, 17g carbohydrate, 30g fat (5g saturated), 82mg cholesterol, 179mg sodium, 4g fiber

helpful hints

● *To clean whole mushrooms, wipe them gently with a damp paper towel.*

● *The smoked fish filling can be mixed in a food processor.*

countdown

● *Preheat oven to 450 degrees.*

● *Roast mushrooms.*

● *Assemble dish.*

shopping list

TO BUY:

½ pound smoked trout or other smoked fish

1 jar white horseradish

1 jar sun-dried tomatoes

4 large portobello mushrooms (½ pound)

1 lemon

1 head curly endive

STAPLES:

Olive oil spray

Mayonnaise made with olive or soybean oil

Salt

Black peppercorns

quick start
dinners

shrimp scampi with roasted asparagus

When I made this scampi for my husband, he couldn't believe it took only 5 minutes to make the sauce. The secret is red vermouth. It adds spice and depth to fresh tomatoes and goes perfectly with the shrimp. ● *Roasting intensifies the flavor of fresh vegetables. The roasted asparagus take only 15 minutes and are great with the simple leafy salad.*

shrimp scampi with roasted asparagus

2 teaspoons olive oil

6 medium-sized garlic cloves, crushed

$1/2$ cup dry red vermouth

1 cup diced tomatoes

$3/4$ pound large shrimp, shelled and deveined

$1/2$ cup chopped fresh parsley

Several drops hot pepper sauce

Salt and freshly ground black pepper to taste

Heat the olive oil in a medium-sized nonstick skillet over a medium-high heat. Sauté the garlic for a few seconds, then add the red vermouth and tomatoes. Cook for 5 minutes. Add the shrimp and parsley and cook for 2–3 minutes until the shrimp are pink. Season with hot pepper sauce, salt, and pepper to taste. Divide between 2 plates and serve.

Makes 2 servings.

One serving: 297 calories, 37g protein, 10g carbohydrate, 8g fat (1g saturated), 260mg cholesterol, 282mg sodium, 0g fiber

roasted asparagus

$1/2$ pound fresh asparagus

2 teaspoons olive oil

Salt and freshly ground black pepper to taste

Preheat the oven to 400 degrees. Cut or snap off any fibrous stems on the asparagus and discard. Slice the remaining asparagus into 2-inch pieces. Line a baking tray with foil and spoon the oil onto the foil. Sprinkle the oil with salt and pepper to taste. Add the asparagus and roll in oil, making sure all the spears are coated with the oil and seasoning. Spread the asparagus into a single layer and roast in the oven for 5 minutes. Roll the asparagus in the oil to recoat and roast, 10 more minutes for thick spears and 5 more minutes for thin ones. Remove from the oven and serve with the shrimp.

Makes 2 servings.

One serving: 55 calories, 2g protein, 3g carbohydrate, 5g fat (1g saturated), 0mg cholesterol, 3mg sodium, 2g fiber

helpful hints

● *To save roasting time, the asparagus can be cooked in a microwave oven on high: 3 minutes for thin asparagus and 5 minutes for thick spears.*

● *Buy shelled shrimp—it is well worth the time otherwise spent shelling them yourself.*

countdown

● *Preheat oven 400 degrees.*

● *Start asparagus.*

● *Make shrimp.*

● *Make Italian salad.*

shopping list

TO BUY:

$3/4$ pound large shrimp

1 small bottle dry red vermouth

1 small bunch fresh parsley

1 medium tomato

$1/2$ pound asparagus

1 bag washed, ready-to-eat, Italian-style lettuce

STAPLES:

Olive oil

No-sugar-added oil and vinegar dressing

Garlic

Hot pepper sauce

Salt

Black peppercorns

shrimp scampi with roasted asparagus continued

italian greens

4 cups washed, ready-to-eat, Italian-style lettuce

2 tablespoons no-sugar-added oil and vinegar dressing

Salt and freshly ground black pepper to taste

Place the salad in a small bowl and drizzle with the dressing. Season with salt and pepper to taste. Toss well and serve.

Makes 2 servings.

One serving: 84 calories, 1g protein, 2g carbohydrate, 8g fat (1g saturated), 0mg cholesterol, 81mg sodium, 0g fibre

asian ginger salmon

This is a very simple 15-minute dinner. It's a basic recipe that you can use as a blueprint to make other similar dinners. Boneless, skinless chicken breast can be used instead of salmon, cauliflower instead of broccoli, and green beans instead of yellow.

asian ginger salmon

Olive oil spray
3/4 pound salmon fillet
Salt and freshly ground black pepper to taste
2 tablespoons low-salt soy sauce
2 tablespoons water
2 tablespoons chopped fresh ginger

Heat a nonstick skillet over a medium-high heat and spray with olive oil. Add the salmon and brown for 2 minutes. Turn, season the cooked side, then brown the second side for 2 minutes. Lower the heat and sauté for 5 minutes. Combine the soy sauce, water, and ginger in a small bowl. Remove the salmon from the skillet, add the soy sauce mixture to the skillet and cook for several seconds. Divide the salmon between 2 plates and spoon the sauce over the salmon.
Makes 2 servings.

One serving: 310 calories, 43g protein, 2g carbohydrate, 12g fat (3g saturated), 120mg cholesterol, 714mg sodium, 0g fibre

sesame broccoli

1/4 pound (2 cups) broccoli florets
2 teaspoons olive oil
1/4 cup sesame seeds
Salt and freshly ground black pepper to taste

Place the broccoli in a microwave-safe bowl and microwave on high for 5 minutes. Alternatively, bring a pot of water to the boil and add the broccoli. Boil for 2 minutes and then drain. Heat the oil in a non-stick skillet over a medium-high heat. Sauté the broccoli and sesame seeds for 3-4 minutes, or until the sesame seeds are golden, and the broccoli is bright green, but crisp. Season with salt and pepper to taste. Serve with the salmon.
Makes 2 servings.

One serving: 158 calories, 7g protein, 6g carbohydrate, 14g fat (2g saturated), 0mg cholesterol, 79mg sodium, 2g fibre

helpful hints

● *Broccoli and beans can be microwaved at the same time for 3 minutes on high.*
● *To save washing an extra pan, prepare the salmon and cover with foil to keep warm. Use same skillet to sauté the broccoli.*
● *A washed, ready-to-eat salad can be substituted for one of the vegetables.*
● *To chop fresh ginger quickly, cut it into small cubes and press through a garlic press with large holes. If using a press with small holes, just capture the juice that is squeezed out; it will give enough flavor for the recipe.*

countdown

● *Make salmon.*
● *Make broccoli.*
● *Make beans.*

shopping list

TO BUY:
3/4 pound salmon fillet
1 small package sesame seeds
1/2 pound yellow wax beans
1/4 pound broccoli florets
1 small piece fresh ginger

asian ginger salmon continued

STAPLES:
   Olive oil
   Olive oil spray
   No-sugar-added olive oil and
      vinegar dressing
   Low-salt soy sauce
   Salt
   Black peppercorns

yellow bean salad

*¹/₂ pound yellow wax beans,
   trimmed and cut in half (2 cups)*
*2 tablespoons no-sugar-added
   olive oil and vinegar dressing*
*Salt and freshly ground black
   pepper to taste*

Place the beans in a microwave-safe bowl and microwave on high for 3 minutes. Alternatively, bring a pot of water to the boil and add the beans. Boil for 2 minutes, and then drain. Toss the cooked beans with the salad dressing. Season with salt and pepper to taste and serve. *Makes 2 servings.*

One serving: 119 calories, 2g protein,
10g carbohydrate, 9g fat (1g saturated),
0mg cholesterol, 79mg sodium, 2g fiber

glazed balsamic chicken

Balsamic vinegar makes a zesty glaze for chicken—and adds very few calories in the process.
● *Roasting or grilling intensifies the flavor of vegetables. The squash are left to cook while you prepare the chicken and snow peas.*

glazed balsamic chicken

Olive oil spray
³/₄ pound boneless, skinless
   chicken breast
Salt and freshly ground black
   pepper to taste
¹/₂ cup good quality balsamic
   vinegar
¹/₄ cup pine nuts
1 tablespoon Dijon mustard

Heat a medium-sized nonstick skillet over a medium-high heat and spray with olive oil. Brown the chicken for 3 minutes, turn and cook for another 3 minutes. Remove from the heat, cover with a lid, and let sit for 3 minutes. Remove the chicken to a plate, season with salt and pepper to taste, and cover with a plate or foil to keep warm. In the same skillet, add the vinegar and pine nuts. Cook over a medium-high heat to reduce, about 30 seconds, or until about half the amount of liquid remains. Add the mustard and mix well to make a smooth glaze. Return the chicken to the skillet, turning to coat both sides with the glaze. Cook for another minute, then divide between 2 plates to serve and spoon any remaining glaze on top.
Makes 2 servings.

One serving: 378 calories, 54g protein, 4g carbohydrate, 11g fat (2g saturated), 144mg cholesterol, 306mg sodium, 0g fiber

helpful hint

● *To save cleaning time, sauté the chicken and remove to a plate. Cover with another plate or foil to keep warm. Use the same skillet to sauté the snow peas.*

countdown

● *Preheat grill.*
● *Start zucchinis.*
● *Make chicken.*
● *Sauté mange tout.*

shopping list

TO BUY:
   ³/₄ pound boneless, skinless
      chicken breast
   1 small package pine nuts
   ¹/₂ pound fresh snow peas
   ¹/₂ pound small yellow
      squash
   1 medium-sized red pepper
STAPLES:
   Olive oil
   Olive oil spray
   Balsamic vinegar
   Dijon mustard
   Garlic
   Salt
   Black peppercorns

glazed balsamic chicken continued

roasted squash

Olive oil spray

2 teaspoons olive oil

2 medium-sized garlic cloves, crushed

1 tablespoon water

$1/2$ pound small yellow squash, cut into 1-inch pieces (2 cups)

1 medium-sized red bell pepper, cut into 1-inch pieces (2 cups)

Salt and freshly ground black pepper to taste

Preheat the broiler. Line a baking sheet with foil and spray with olive oil. Place the foil-lined sheet under the broiler 5 inches from the heat. Combine the olive oil with garlic and water in a small mixing bowl. Remove the baking sheet from the grill and place the vegetables on the sheet. Spoon half of the olive oil mixture over the vegetables and toss well. Spread the vegetables out to form a single layer. Broil for 10 minutes. Turn the vegetables over and spoon with the remaining olive oil mixture. Broil for another 10 minutes. The vegetables should be cooked through, but not black. Sprinkle with salt and pepper to taste. Serve with the chicken. *Makes 2 servings.*

One serving: 104 calories, 3g protein, 11g carbohydrate, 7g fat (1g saturated), 0mg cholesterol, 4mg sodium, 1g fiber

sautéed snow peas

2 teaspoons olive oil

$1/2$ pound snow peas (about 2 cups)

Salt and freshly ground black pepper to taste

Heat the olive oil in a nonstick skillet over a medium-high heat. Add the snow peas and sauté for 2 minutes, tossing continuously. Season with salt and pepper to taste. Serve with the chicken.
Makes 2 servings.

One serving: 66 calories, 2g protein, 5g carbohydrate, 5g fat (1g saturated), 0mg cholesterol, 3mg sodium, 2g fiber

tex-mex meat loaf

This moist, well-seasoned meat loaf smothered in spicy salsa makes a great, homely meal. By forming the meat into small loaves instead of one large loaf, it takes only 20 minutes to cook, rather than the usual 45–60 minutes.● The heat circulates more quickly around the loaves. The cooked loaves will keep a day in the refrigerator. If you have time, double the recipe and form 4 loaves. Save the other two for another quick meal.

tex-mex meat loaf

Olive oil spray
1/4 cup red onion, thinly sliced
1 cup mushrooms, thinly sliced
10 ounces ground veal
2 egg whites
Salt and freshly ground
    black pepper to taste

1 large tomato, diced
1/2 cup chopped fresh cilantro
1 small jalapeño pepper, seeded
    and chopped (1 tablespoon)
1/2 teaspoon ground cumin
1 tablespoon freshly squeezed
    lime juice

Preheat the oven to 400 degrees. Line a baking tray with foil and spray with olive oil. Heat a nonstick skillet over a medium-high heat and spray with olive oil. Add the onion and mushrooms and sauté for 5 minutes. Combine the vegetables with the ground veal and egg whites in a medium-sized mixing bowl. Add salt and pepper to taste. Place the meat directly on the foil-lined baking tray and shape into 2 loaves about 6 x 3 inches each. Bake for 20 minutes.

While the loaves bake, combine the diced tomato, cilantro, jalapeño, cumin and lime juice in a small bowl. Season with salt and pepper to taste. Spoon the salsa over the baked meat loaves and serve on 2 plates with the avocado.
Makes 2 servings.

One serving: 407 calories, 45g protein, 13g carbohydrate, 17g fat (10g saturated), 125mg cholesterol, 164mg sodium, 2g fiber

sliced avocado

1/2 small avocado, pitted, peeled,
    and sliced
1 tablespoon no-sugar-added oil
    and vinegar dressing
Salt and freshly ground black
    pepper to taste

Arrange the avocado slices next to the meat loaves and drizzle with dressing. Season with salt and pepper to taste. Serve with the meat loaf.
Makes 2 servings.

One serving: 114 calories, 1g protein, 3g carbohydrate, 12g fat (2g saturated), 0mg cholesterol, 43mg sodium, 2g fiber

helpful hint
● *Use the salsa recipe given or purchase a no-sugar-added version.*

countdown
● *Preheat oven to 400 degrees.*
● *Make meat loaf.*
● *Prepare avocado.*

shopping list
TO BUY:
    10 ounces ground veal
    1 small avocado
    1 small package sliced
        mushrooms (2 ounces
        needed)
    2 limes
    1 large tomato
    1 small bunch cilantro
    1 small jalapeño pepper
STAPLES:
    Olive oil spray
    Red onion
    Eggs
    No-sugar-added oil and
        vinegar dressing
    Ground cumin
    Salt
    Black peppercorns

helpful hints

- To save cleaning a second skillet, use the same one to cook the chicken and spinach.
- Buy an inexpensive Marsala wine for this recipe. It also goes well with veal, pork, and turkey.

countdown

- Make salad and set aside.
- Make chicken.
- Make spinach.

shopping list

TO BUY:

1 small carton heavy whipping cream

10 ounces boneless, skinless chicken breast

1 bottle medium-dry Marsala wine

1 small head radicchio lettuce

1 small bunch radishes

1 bag washed, ready-to-eat fresh spinach (10 ounces needed)

STAPLES:

Olive oil

No-sugar-added oil and vinegar dressing

Garlic

Salt

Black peppercorns

marsala chicken

The rich, smoky flavor of Sicily's Marsala wine makes a quick glaze for this chicken. To help cook the chicken faster, I flatten the chicken breast to about ½-inch thick. This also enlarges the surface area available to absorb the glaze.

marsala chicken

10 ounces boneless, skinless chicken breasts

2 teaspoons olive oil

Salt and freshly ground black pepper to taste

½ cup medium-dry Marsala wine

1 tablespoon heavy whipping cream

Remove all visible fat from the chicken. Pound with the palm of your hand to flatten to about ½ inch thick. Heat the oil in a nonstick skillet over a medium-high heat. Brown the chicken, about 2 minutes on each side. Season each cooked side with salt and pepper to taste. Add the Marsala wine to the pan and continue to cook for 2–3 minutes. Remove the chicken to 2 plates. Continue to simmer the sauce for about 1 minute to reduce. Add the cream and season with salt and pepper to taste. Spoon the sauce over the chicken and cover with foil to keep warm before serving.

Makes 2 servings.

One serving: 394 calories, 45g protein, 7g carbohydrate, 14g fat (4g saturated), 131mg cholesterol, 113mg sodium, 0g fiber

roman spinach

8 cups (10 ounces) washed, ready-to-eat fresh spinach

2 teaspoons olive oil

4 medium-sized garlic cloves, crushed

Salt and freshly ground black pepper to taste

Place the spinach in a large saucepan (do not add water). Cover and cook for 5 minutes, tossing once or twice, then drain. Alternatively, place in a microwave-safe bowl and microwave on high for 5 minutes. Heat the olive oil in the same saucepan over a medium heat and add the garlic. Stir for about 30 seconds. Return the spinach to the pan. Season with salt and pepper to taste. Serve with the chicken.

Makes 2 servings.

One serving: 97 calories, 7g protein, 10g carbohydrate, 5g fat (1g saturated), 0mg cholesterol, 172mg sodium, 7g fiber

radicchio salad

1 small head radicchio, torn into bite-sized pieces (3 cups)

12 radishes

1 tablespoon no-sugar-added oil and vinegar dressing

Salt and freshly ground black pepper to taste

Divide the radicchio leaves between 2 plates and grate the radishes on top. Alternatively, grate the radishes in a food processor fitted with a grating blade. Spoon the dressing over the salad and season with salt and pepper to taste before serving.

Makes 2 servings.

One serving: 103 calories, 1g protein, 6g carbohydrate, 9g fat (1g saturated), 0mg cholesterol, 96mg sodium, 1g fiber

sirloin burger with fresh slaw

In the mood for a burger? Here's a quick one made with lean sirloin and accompanied by slaw. Sliced, ready-to-use cabbage and carrot can be found in the produce section of the supermarket, making homemade coleslaw a breeze.

helpful hints

- If pressed for time, use a shop-bought coleslaw instead of the recipe given. Check the nutritional analysis of shop-bought coleslaw, as some prepared versions have added sugar.
- To determine the weight of each slice of cheese, divide the package weight by the number of slices.

countdown

- Make coleslaw.
- Make burger.

shopping list

TO BUY:

  1 package sliced reduced-fat
    Cheddar cheese
    (1½ ounces needed)

  ½ pound ground lean sirloin

  1 bag presliced coleslaw mix

  2 medium tomatoes

STAPLES:

  Red onion

  Olive oil spray

  Mayonnaise made with
    soybean or olive oil

  Dijon mustard

  Distilled white vinegar

  Sugar substitute

  Salt

  Black peppercorns

sirloin burger

¼ cup red onion, chopped

½ pound ground lean sirloin

Salt and freshly ground black
    pepper to taste

Olive oil spray

2 slices reduced-fat Cheddar
    cheese (about 1½ ounces)

4 teaspoons Dijon mustard

Combine the onion and ground sirloin in a medium-sized bowl. Season with salt and pepper to taste. Form into 2 patties. Set a medium-sized nonstick skillet over medium-high heat and spray with olive oil. Cook the sirloin burgers for 5 minutes. Turn and top each burger with a slice of cheese. Continue cooking for 3 more minutes. Top the cheese with mustard and serve.

Makes 2 servings.

One serving: 338 calories, 46g protein, 2g carbohydrate, 17g fat (8g saturated), 117mg cholesterol, 496mg sodium, 0g fiber

fresh slaw

2 tablespoons mayonnaise made
    with soybean or olive oil

2 tablespoons distilled white
    vinegar

4 teaspoons Dijon mustard

2 (.035-ounce) envelopes sugar
    substitute

Salt and freshly ground black
    pepper to taste

4 slices red onion (½ cup)

4 cups presliced coleslaw mix

2 medium tomatoes, sliced

Combine the mayonnaise, vinegar, mustard and sugar substitute in a medium-sized bowl. Season with salt and pepper to taste. Add the coleslaw mix and onion and toss well. Add more salt and pepper, if needed. Divide between 2 plates, and arrange the tomato slices on the side.

Makes 2 servings.

One serving: 191 calories, 5g protein, 18g carbohydrate, 12g fat (2g saturated), 5mg cholesterol, 355mg sodium, 2g fiber

pacific rim pork

Spicy, Pacific Rim flavors add zest to this easy-to-prepare dinner. ● *The pickled vegetable salad makes a great snack. Make extra and store in a plastic bag. Serve it on its own, or add it to chicken or tuna salads.*

pacific rim pork

³/₄ pound pork tenderloin, visible fat removed

For marinade:
¹/₄ cup low-salt soy sauce
¹/₄ cup distilled white vinegar
4 medium-sized garlic cloves, crushed
4 teaspoons Dijon mustard
2 teaspoons ground ginger
Dash of freshly ground black pepper

Preheat the broiler and place the rack on the top rung of the oven. Line a baking sheet with foil. Cut the pork almost in half lengthwise and open like a book. Do not cut all of the way through. Combine the marinade ingredients in a small bowl. Add the pork and allow to marinate for 20 minutes. Remove from the marinade and place the pork on the foil-lined baking sheet. Broil for 5 minutes, turn and broil for 3 more minutes. The pork is done when a meat thermometer inserted in the centre registers 160 degrees. Slice and serve with the salad and vegetables. *Makes 2 servings.*

One serving: 293 calories, 50g protein, 2g carbohydrate, 8g fat (3g saturated), 159mg cholesterol, 478mg sodium, 0g fiber

pickled radish salad

1 cup water
¹/₂ cup plus 2 tablespoons distilled white vinegar
8 (.035-ounce) envelopes sugar substitute
1 teaspoon crushed red pepper
1 teaspoon salt
1 medium cucumber, peeled and sliced
2 cups Daikon (white) radish, peeled and sliced
2 tablespoons yellow onion, chopped

Mix the water, vinegar, sugar substitute, crushed red pepper, and salt together in a medium-sized bowl. Add the cucumber, radish, and onion and marinate for 15 minutes. Drain and serve. *Makes 2 servings.*

One serving: 34 calories, 1g protein, 9g carbohydrate, 0g fat (0g saturated), 0mg cholesterol, 276mg sodium, 1g fiber

helpful hints

● *If possible use white radish in the salad. Daikon radish is a white, Oriental radish with a sweet, fresh flavor. Otherwise, red radishes can be used.*

● *To keep from having to look back at the recipe as you stir-fry the ingredients, line them up on a chopping board or plate in the order of use so you know which ingredient comes next.*

● *For crisp, not steamed, stir-fried vegetables, start with a very hot wok or skillet. Let the vegetables sit for a minute before tossing to allow the wok to regain its heat.*

countdown

● *Preheat broiler.*
● *Marinate pork.*
● *Make salad.*
● *Prepare stir-fry vegetable ingredients.*
● *Broil pork.*
● *While pork cooks, make stir-fry vegetables.*

shopping list

TO BUY:
³/₄ pound pork tenderloin
1 small jar ground ginger
1 bottle sesame oil
1 small head Chinese lettuce (napa cabbage)
1 package fresh bean sprouts
1 jar crushed red pepper
1 medium cucumber
1 Daikon (white) radish

pacific rim pork continued

ginger-garlic stir-fry vegetables

STAPLES:
Garlic
Yellow onion
Dijon mustard
Low-salt soy sauce
Distilled white vinegar
Sugar substitute
Salt
Black peppercorns

2 teaspoons sesame oil

2 teaspoons ground ginger

4 cups Chinese lettuce (napa cabbage), washed and sliced

2 cups fresh bean sprouts

4 medium-sized garlic cloves, crushed

Pour the oil into a wok or nonstick skillet and place over a high heat. When the oil begins to smoke, add the ginger, lettuce, bean sprouts, and garlic. Stir-fry for 6 minutes and then serve. *Makes 2 servings.*

One serving: 92 calories, 4g protein, 10g carbohydrate, 5g fat (1g saturated), 0mg cholesterol, 13mg sodium, 2g fiber

veal escalopes with garlic greens

In this dish, romaine and radicchio leaves are just wilted in a skillet and flavored with garlic to form a crunchy, colorful topping for the veal escalopes. ● Veal escalopes take only a few minutes to cook. The secret to keeping them juicy is to brown them in a hot skillet for 1 minute on each side, then remove them to a plate and cover to keep warm. Boneless, skinless chicken breasts can be substituted, though they will need to cook longer. ● Saffron is the stigmas from a saffron crocus. It is pricy because it is harvested by hand. Fortunately, a little goes a long way.

veal escalopes with garlic greens

Olive oil spray

3/4 pound veal escalopes pounded to 1/8–1/16-inch thick

Salt and freshly ground black pepper to taste

4 medium-sized garlic cloves, crushed

4 cups romaine and radicchio leaves torn into bite-sized pieces

Set a medium-sized nonstick skillet over a high heat and spray with olive oil. Brown the veal for 1 minute on each side. Season the cooked sides and remove to 2 plates. Add the garlic and salad leaves to the pan. Toss for 1 minute, or until the leaves just start to wilt. Season with salt and pepper to taste. Serve the salad leaves over the veal escalopes.

Makes 2 servings.

One serving: 398 calories, 46g protein, 3g carbohydrate, 20g fat (12g saturated), 150mg cholesterol, 114mg sodium, 0g fiber

saffron cauliflower

1/2 pound (4 cups) cauliflower florets

4 teaspoons olive oil

1/4 teaspoon saffron strands

Salt and freshly ground black pepper to taste

Place the cauliflower in a vegetable steamer set over boiling water. Steam for 6–7 minutes, or until tender. Alternatively, place in a microwave-safe dish—do not add water—and microwave on high for 5 minutes. Spoon the olive oil into a large serving bowl and add the saffron. Microwave on high for 10 seconds. Add the cauliflower to the oil, season with salt and pepper to taste, and toss well before serving.

Makes 2 servings.

One serving: 130 calories, 4g protein, 10g carbohydrate, 9g fat (1g saturated), 0mg cholesterol, 60mg sodium, 5g fiber

helpful hints

● Turmeric or bijol can be used instead of the saffron.
● Buy cauliflower already cut into florets.
● Washed, ready-to-eat salad can be used. Make sure the leaves are firm. A mesclun or field greens salad will be too soft to work in this recipe.

countdown

● Make cauliflower, cover to keep warm.
● Prepare veal and garlic greens.

shopping list

TO BUY:

3/4 pound veal escalopes
1 small package saffron strands
1/2 pound cauliflower florets
1 small head romaine lettuce
1 small head radicchio lettuce

STAPLES:

Olive oil
Olive oil spray
Garlic
Salt
Black peppercorns

pecan-crusted grouper with vegetable creole

Pecan-flavored grouper and vegetable creole are updated versions of Southern comfort food. ● *To cook fish fast, preheat the baking tray in the oven. The hot tray will help to cook the fish on the underside without having to turn the fish.*

pecan-crusted grouper

1/4 teaspoon salt
1/4 teaspoon freshly ground black pepper
1/4 teaspoon cayenne pepper
2 egg whites, lightly beaten
1/2 cup (2 ounces) pecans, finely chopped
3/4 pound grouper fillet
2 teaspoons olive oil
Olive oil spray

Preheat the oven to 400 degrees. Line a baking tray with foil and place in the oven to heat. Combine the salt, black pepper, and cayenne on a plate. Line up the spice mixture, the beaten egg whites, and the pecans in a row on the countertop for easy coating of the fish. First, roll the fish in the spice mixture, coating both sides. Next, dip the fish into the egg whites and then roll in the pecans.

Heat the olive oil in a nonstick skillet over a medium-high heat. When the oil is hot, brown the fish for 2 minutes. Turn and brown the other side for 1 minute. Remove the baking tray from the oven and spray with olive oil. Place the fish on the tray and return the tray to the oven for 5 minutes to finish cooking. Serve with the creole. *Makes 2 servings.*

One serving: 399 calories, 39g protein, 4g carbohydrate, 26g fat (3g saturated), 62mg cholesterol, 412mg sodium, 3g fiber

vegetable creole

2 teaspoons olive oil
1/2 cup yellow onion, sliced
1 medium-sized green bell pepper, sliced (1cup)
1 zucchini, sliced (2 cups)
4 medium-size garlic cloves, crushed
2 cups canned no-sugar-added, diced tomatoes
1 tablespoon Worcestershire sauce
2 (.035-ounce) envelopes sugar substitute

Heat the olive oil in a nonstick skillet over a medium-high heat. Add the onion, pepper, zucchini, and garlic and sauté for 5 minutes. Lower the heat to medium. Add the tomatoes, Worcestershire sauce, and sugar substitute. Cover with a lid and cook for 5 minutes. Serve hot with the grouper. *Makes 2 servings.*

One serving: 156 calories, 6g protein, 22g carbohydrate, 5g fat (1g saturated), 0mg cholesterol, 378mg sodium, 7g fiber

sausage-pepper sauté

This is a 15-minute meal. I keep low-fat turkey sausages in my freezer for emergency meals and use whatever is in my vegetable drawer to go with it—peppers, celery, mushrooms, broccoli, or cauliflower. Use this recipe as a base and create your own sausage meal. ● A jar of marinated artichokes or hearts of palm from the pantry can be made into an instant salad to complete a great, quick meal.

sausage-pepper sauté

Olive oil spray
4 low-fat turkey sausages (3/4 pound), cut into 1-inch slices
1 medium-sized red bell pepper, sliced (2 cups)
2 garlic cloves, crushed
Salt and freshly ground black pepper to taste
1/2 cup fresh basil leaves, torn into small pieces

Set a medium-sized nonstick skillet over a medium-high heat and spray with olive oil. Add the sausage, pepper, and garlic, and sauté for 10 minutes. Season with salt and pepper to taste. Sprinkle with the basil and serve.
Makes 2 servings.

One serving: 344 calories, 30g protein, 14g carbohydrate, 18g fat (5g saturated), 90mg cholesterol, 1084mg sodium, 0g fiber

marinated artichoke salad

2 (6-ounce) jars marinated artichoke hearts, drained
2 cups washed, ready-to-eat, Italian-style salad leaves
2 tablespoons no-sugar-added oil and vinegar dressing
Salt and freshly ground black pepper to taste

Cut the artichoke hearts in half. Place the salad leaves in a small bowl and toss with the dressing. Season with salt and pepper to taste. Place the artichoke hearts on top and serve.
Makes 2 servings.

One serving: 229 calories, 3g protein, 13g carbohydrate, 17g fat (1g saturated), 0mg cholesterol, 618mg sodium, 3g fiber

helpful hints

● Most supermarkets sell marinated artichoke hearts in a jar or can.
● To determine the weight of each sausage, divide the package weight by the number of sausages.

countdown

● Make sausage and peppers.
● Make artichoke salad.

shopping list

TO BUY:
1 package low-fat turkey sausages (3/4 pound needed)
2 jars marinated artichoke hearts (12 ounces needed)
1 medium-sized red bell pepper
1 bag washed, ready-to-eat, Italian-style salad leaves
1 small bunch basil
STAPLES:
Olive oil spray
No-sugar-added oil and vinegar dressing
Garlic
Salt
Black peppercorns

salsa-baked snapper

This is a great meal for those evenings you need to get a tasty dinner on the table in 15 minutes. Fresh fish is the original fast food. Simply cover the fish with salsa, broil, and serve.

salsa-baked snapper

Olive oil spray
3/4 pound snapper fillet
Salt and freshly ground black pepper to taste
1 cup no-sugar-added tomato salsa

Preheat the oven to 400 degrees. Line a baking tray with foil and spray with olive oil. Place the fish on the baking sheet, spray with olive oil and season with salt and pepper to taste. Bake for 10 minutes. Spoon the salsa over the fish and bake for 5 more minutes before serving.
Makes 2 servings.

One serving: 244 calories, 39g protein, 10g carbohydrate, 4g fat (1g saturated), 62mg cholesterol, 872mg sodium, 4g fiber

parmesan zucchini

1/2 pound zucchini, sliced (2 cups)
4 teaspoons olive oil
Salt and freshly ground black pepper to taste
2 tablespoons freshly grated Parmesan cheese

Place the zucchini in a microwave-safe bowl and heat on high for 5 minutes. Alternatively, bring a medium saucepan of water to a boil and add the zucchini. Boil for 3 minutes and drain. Toss with the olive oil and season with salt and pepper to taste. Sprinkle with Parmesan cheese and serve.
Makes 2 servings.

One serving: 123 calories, 4g protein, 4g carbohydrate, 11g fat (2g saturated), 4mg cholesterol, 110mg sodium, 1g fiber

italian greens

2 tablespoons no-sugar-added oil and vinegar dressing
2 teaspoons dried oregano
4 cups washed, ready-to-eat, Italian-style salad leaves

Spoon the dressing into a salad bowl and stir in the oregano. Add the salad, toss well and serve.
Makes 2 servings.

One serving: 88 calories, 1g protein, 3g carbohydrate, 9g fat (1g saturated), 0mg cholesterol, 81mg sodium, 1g fiber

rosemary-roasted pork

Northern Italy inspired this roasted pork dinner served with fennel gratin and Brussels sprouts. The secret to roasting the pork in only 15 minutes is to butterfly it by cutting it in half lengthwise. ● Pecorino cheese is an alternative to using Parmesan cheese, but with a sharper flavor. It's made from sheep's milk and the most popular kinds are hard and perfect for grating. ● Fennel has a pale green bulb and stalk with feathery leaves. It has a slight anise or liquorice flavor when raw that becomes even milder when cooked.

rosemary-roasted pork

Olive oil spray

³/₄ pound pork tenderloin

2 teaspoons olive oil

2 tablespoons chopped fresh rosemary or 2 teaspoons dried

Salt and freshly ground black pepper to taste

Preheat the oven to 400 degrees. Line a baking tray with foil, spray with olive oil and place in the oven to heat. Remove all visible fat from the pork and cut the loin nearly in half lengthwise. Open the pork and lay flat like a book. Pound it flat with the palm of your hand or with the bottom of a pan. Rub the pork with olive oil and sprinkle with rosemary on both sides. Place the pork on the hot baking tray. Roast for 15 minutes. Remove from the oven, cover with foil and let the meat rest for 5 minutes. Season with salt and pepper to taste. Slice and serve. *Makes 2 servings.*

One serving: 345 calories, 49g protein, 0g carbohydrate, 15g fat (4g saturated), 159mg cholesterol, 115mg sodium, 0g fiber

helpful hints

- Parmesan cheese can be used instead of pecorino cheese.
- A quick way to chop fresh rosemary is to snip it right from the stem with scissors.
- Celery can be substituted for the fennel in the recipe.

countdown

- Preheat oven to 400 degrees.
- Start pork.
- Make fennel.
- Steam Brussels sprouts.

shopping list

TO BUY:

  1 small piece pecorino cheese

  ³/₄ pound pork tenderloin

  1 small bunch fresh rosemary or 1 jar dried

  1 medium bulb fennel

  ¹/₄ pound Brussels sprouts

STAPLES:

  Olive oil spray

  Olive oil

  Salt

  Black peppercorns

rosemary-roasted pork continued

fennel gratin

4 teaspoons olive oil

1/2 medium bulb fennel, stalks and
    leaves removed, thinly sliced
    (2 cups)

Salt and freshly ground black
    pepper to taste

2 tablespoons grated pecorino
    cheese

Heat the olive oil in a nonstick skillet over a
medium-high heat. Add the fennel and toss in the
oil. Cover with a lid and cook for 2 minutes.
Alternatively, place in a microwave-safe bowl, add
the oil, and toss to coat. Cover and microwave on
high for 8 minutes. Season the cooked fennel
with salt and pepper to taste and toss well.
Sprinkle with the cheese and place in the oven
with the pork for 5 minutes, or until the cheese
starts to melt. Use the same baking tray as the
pork to save clean-up time. Serve with the pork.
Makes 2 servings.

One serving: 135 calories, 2g protein,
0g carbohydrate, 11g fat (2g saturated),
4mg cholesterol, 106mg sodium, 0g fiber

brussels sprouts

1/4 pound Brussels sprouts,
    damaged outer leaves removed
    and sprouts halved (2 cups)

2 teaspoons olive oil

Salt and freshly ground black
    pepper to taste

Place the Brussels sprouts in the basket of a
vegetable steamer. Place over boiling water and
steam for 6–7 minutes. Alternatively, microwave
on high for 5 minutes. Transfer the cooked
Brussels sprouts to a serving bowl. Add the olive
oil and season with salt and pepper to taste. Toss
well before serving.
Makes 2 servings.

One serving: 60 calories, 1g protein,
4g carbohydrate, 5g fat (1g saturated),
0mg cholesterol, 12mg sodium, 1g fiber

herb-stuffed chicken

This fresh herb stuffing gives a fragrant flavor to the chicken and keeps it moist during cooking. The stuffing, a combination of chopped fresh tarragon, scallions, and mushrooms, is so simple, it really only takes minutes to make. The herbs and mushrooms can be chopped in a food processor to save even more time. ● Small, baby turnips are sweet and need only a little sautéing to bring out their flavor and keep their crunchy texture.

herb-stuffed chicken

2 (6-ounce) boneless, skinless
  chicken breasts
2 tablespoons fresh tarragon
  or 2 teaspoons dried
2 scallions, sliced
2 medium-sized button
  mushrooms
2 tablespoons non-fat plain yogurt
Salt and freshly ground black
  pepper to taste
Olive oil spray

Holding the chicken breast flat with the palm of your hand, make a horizontal slit in each breast. It should be deep enough to form a pocket the length of the chicken breast. In a food processor or by hand, chop the tarragon, scallions, and mushrooms together. Add the yogurt and blend well. Season with salt and pepper to taste. Season the inside slits of the chicken. Spoon the herb stuffing into the slit. Gently press the chicken breast together to close the slits. Set a medium-sized nonstick skillet over a medium-high heat, and spray with olive oil. Brown the chicken breasts for 2 minutes on each side, seasoning each cooked side with salt and pepper. Lower the heat to medium, cover with a lid, and cook for 6 more minutes. Serve hot. *Makes 2 servings.*

One serving: 309 calories, 55g protein, 2g carbohydrate, 10g fat (2g saturated), 144mg cholesterol, 138mg sodium, 0g fiber

helpful hint

● *Dried tarragon can be substituted for fresh. Make sure the dried leaves are green. If they have started to turn brown, it's time to buy a new jar.*

countdown

● *Prepare all ingredients.*
● *Start chicken.*
● *While chicken cooks, make asparagus and turnips.*

shopping list

TO BUY:
  1 small pot non-fat plain
    yogurt
  2 (6-ounce) boneless,
    skinless chicken breasts
  1/2 pound fresh asparagus
  1/2 pound baby turnips
  1 small bunch fresh tarragon
    or 1 jar dried
  1 small package button
    mushrooms
  1 small bunch scallions
    (2 needed)
STAPLES:
  Olive oil
  Olive oil spray
  Garlic
  Salt
  Black peppercorns

herb-stuffed chicken continued

pan-roasted asparagus and baby turnips

1/2 pound fresh asparagus

4 teaspoons olive oil

1/2 pound baby turnips, peeled and cut into 1-inch cubes (about 2 cups)

1 medium-sized garlic clove, crushed

Salt and freshly ground black pepper to taste

Cut or snap off the 1-inch fibrous stems on the asparagus and discard. Slice the remaining asparagus into 2-inch pieces. Heat the olive oil in a medium-sized nonstick skillet over a medium-high heat and add the turnips. Sauté for 5 minutes, turning to make sure all sides are browned. Add the asparagus and garlic and continue to sauté, 5 minutes for thin asparagus, and 10 minutes for thick. Season with salt and pepper to taste. Serve with the chicken.
Makes 2 servings.

One serving: 134 calories, 3g protein, 12g carbohydrate, 9g fat (1g saturated), 0mg cholesterol, 90mg sodium, 5g fiber

steak au poivre

Here's a meal that's perfect for those evenings when you want something a little special.
● *Steak au Poivre, or black pepper steak, is a very simple, very French dish. This recipe calls for cracked or coarsely broken black peppercorns, which are available in the spice section of the supermarket.* ● *Crème fraîche adds a tangy flavor and creamy texture to the sauce. Use it instead of the heavy whipping cream if at all possible.* ● *Brandy is the generic name for cognac or Armagnac. You can buy brandy in small splits at many markets and most liquor stores.* ● *Hearts of palm are the tender heart of the Sabal palm tree.*

steak au poivre

2 (5-ounce) beef tenderloin steaks

1 tablespoon cracked black pepper

4 teaspoons canola oil

Salt to taste

2 tablespoons cognac or brandy

1 tablespoon crème fraîche (or heavy whipping cream)

Cover the steaks with the cracked pepper, pressing it into the meat with the palm of your hand. Heat the oil in a nonstick skillet over a medium-high heat. Brown the steaks for 4 minutes. If the steaks are browning too quickly, reduce the heat to medium. Turn and salt the cooked sides to taste. Brown the second side for 2 minutes, or until a meat thermometer registers 140 degrees. Remove the steaks to 2 plates.

Add the cognac to the hot pan, scraping up the brown bits as it cooks. Add the crème fraîche and mix well. Taste for salt and adjust the seasoning if necessary. Spoon the sauce on top of the steaks and serve.

Makes 2 servings.

One serving: 376 calories, 30g protein, 2g carbohydrate, 24g fat (8g saturated), 98mg cholesterol, 81mg sodium, 0g fiber

helpful hints

● *If pressed for time, use a bottled, no-sugar-added oil and vinegar dressing instead of the recipe provided here.*
● *Strip, flank, or skirt can be substituted instead of the beef tenderloin steak.*
● *Any type of lettuce leaves can be used instead of red lettuce.*
● *Regular green beans can be used instead of French green beans and cut in half.*
● *To save cleaning an extra skillet, prepare the steaks and green beans in the same skillet.*

countdown

● *Make the hearts of palm salad.*
● *Blanch the green beans.*
● *Make the steak.*
● *Sauté the green beans.*

shopping list

TO BUY:

*1 small carton crème fraîche
(or heavy whipping cream)*

2 (5-ounce) beef fillets

1 jar cracked black pepper

*1 small bottle brandy,
preferably cognac*

*1 jar or can hearts of palm
(10 ounces needed)*

*1/2 pound French green beans
(haricots verts)*

1 small head red lettuce

STAPLES:

Garlic

Canola oil

Red wine vinegar

Dijon mustard

Salt

Black peppercorns

steak au poivre continued

french green beans

*1/2 pound French green beans
(haricots verts), trimmed*

4 teaspoons canola oil

*2 medium-sized garlic cloves,
crushed*

*Salt and freshly ground black
pepper to taste*

Bring a medium saucepan full of water to a boil. Add the beans. As soon as the water comes back to a boil, drain the beans. Return the beans to the pan and fill the pan with iced water to stop the cooking. Drain the beans. In the same saucepan, heat the oil over a high heat. Add the beans and garlic, and sauté for 2–3 minutes until the beans are crisp. Season with salt and pepper to taste and serve with the steak.
Makes 2 servings.

One serving: 88 calories, 3g protein, 11g carbohydrate, 5g fat (1g saturated), 0mg cholesterol, 4mg sodium, 2g fiber

hearts of palm salad

1 tablespoon red wine vinegar

4 teaspoons Dijon mustard

*Salt and freshly ground black
pepper to taste*

2 teaspoons canola oil

*2 cups hearts of palm, drained and
cut into 1/2-inch slices
(10 ounces)*

Several red lettuce leaves

In a salad bowl, whisk the vinegar and mustard together until smooth. Season with salt and pepper to taste. Whisk in the oil and adjust for seasoning as necessary. Add the hearts of palm to the dressing. Toss well. Place the lettuce on 2 small plates, spoon the hearts of palm on top and serve.
Makes 2 servings.

One serving: 100 calories, 5g protein, 9g carbohydrate, 6g fat (1g saturated), 0mg cholesterol, 868mg sodium, 4g fiber

rosemary-roasted pork   **p75**

endive filled with cheese and roasted peppers   **p96**

which carbs

introduction

When I teach classes, I find that this is the most important section. My students are afraid to start reintroducing carbs for fear they will negate all of the benefits they've achieved. This section shows you how to start bringing carbs back into your life without gaining weight. I have carefully chosen these recipes to reincorporate high-fiber, low simple-sugar carbohydrates. Organised into a meal-at-a-glance chart, these recipes include some easy and quick meals for busy mid-week schedules and some more elaborate recipes suited to a relaxed weekend pace. They are arranged to give variety throughout the day and over the course of the week. For an overview see the 14-day meal plan. Otherwise, the meals appear in the same sequence within the chapter, so just follow the meals in the order given.

breakfast

You can choose from a variety of breakfasts. Quick ideas like Cheddar Scramble and Dijon Ham and Cheddar Melt can be made in less than 5 minutes. You can also enjoy Pecan Ham Roll-Ups or Shrimp, Red Pepper, and Tomato Frittata.

lunch

Chicken Salad Amandine and Salad Niçoise from the French Riviera are two tempting choices.

dinner

Neapolitan Steak, Spicy Chicken Legs, and Whisky Pork Chops are some of the meals that have been carefully planned to slowly reintroduce carbohydrates.

During the Which Carb 14-day meal plan, you will consume an average of 75–85 grams of carbohydrate per day. This percentage is based on carbohydrates less fiber consumed—the normal way of calculating carbohydrate consumption. The balance of these meals is 23 percent of calories from carbohydrates, 38 percent of calories from lean protein, 27 percent of calories from mono-unsaturated fat and 8 percent of calories from saturated fat.

quick carbs 14-day menu plan

week 1	breakfast	lunch	dinner
sunday	Sausage and Mushroom Egg Pizzetta 85	Tex-Mex Layered Salad 100	Thai Peanut-Rub Pork 115
monday	Arugula and Ham Scramble 86	Smoked Whitefish Salad 101	Pesto Chicken . .116–117
tuesday	Turkey and Cottage Cheese 87	Salad Niçoise 102	Grilled Scallops Parmigiana 118–119
wednesday	Dijon Ham and Cheddar Melt 88	Chicken Salad Amandine 103	Breaded Veal Cutlets 120
thursday	Quick Herb Omelette 89	Turkey and Sadziki Sandwich . . .104	Garlic Shrimp Stir Fry 121–122
friday	Smoked Turkey Roll-ups 90	California Chef's Salad 105	Sole Amandine 123
saturday	Shrimp, Red Pepper, and Tomato Frittata 91	Turkey, Salsa, and Citrus Salad 106	Smothered Steak with Caramelized Onions 124–125

week 2	breakfast	lunch	dinner
sunday	Asian Omelette 92	Jerk Chicken with Hearts of Palm 107	Whisky Pork Chops 126–127
monday	Tuna-stuffed Sweet Peppers 93	Deli Salad 108	Seared Sesame Tuna 128–129
tuesday	Pecan Ham Roll-ups 94	Egg Salad 109	Chicken Provençal 130–131
wednesday	Cheddar Scramble 95	Balsamic and Dill Salmon Salad 110	Mussels Marinière . . .132
thursday	Endive Filled with Cheese and Roasted Red Peppers 96	Hollywood Cobb Salad 111	Spicy Crab and Vegetable Stir-Fry 133–134
friday	Spanish Omelette 97	Black Bean and Salsa Wraps 112	Neapolitan Steak 135–136
saturday	Raspberry Smoothie with Toasted Walnut Oatmeal 98	Chili Chicken 113	Spicy Chicken Legs 137–138

which carbs
breakfasts

sausage and mushroom egg pizzetta

Sausage, mushrooms, onion, and tomato sauce form the topping for an egg pizza base. This is a fun breakfast that takes about 15 minutes to make. It's great for a weekday or weekend treat, breakfast, lunch, or dinner.

sausage and mushroom egg pizzetta

2 cups egg substitute

Freshly ground black pepper

Olive oil spray

1/2 cup low-fat, no-sugar-added tomato sauce for pasta

2 small low-fat turkey sausages, cut into 1-inch slices (6 ounces)

6 button mushrooms, sliced (1 cup)

1 tablespoon diced red onion

4 slices reduced-fat mozzarella cheese (3 ounces)

Preheat the broiler. Season the egg substitute with pepper to taste. Set a small 8-inch skillet over a medium-high heat. Spray with olive oil and pour in half the egg substitute. Swirl in the pan to make a thin layer. Allow to cook for 2 minutes, turn over for 1 minute, and remove from the heat. Spread the tomato sauce on top. Add the sausage, mushrooms, onion, and mozzarella cheese. Place under the broiler about 10 inches from the heat. Broil for 10 minutes. Carefully slide onto a plate and serve. Repeat for the second serving.

Makes 2 servings.

bran cereal

1 cup high-fiber, no-sugar-added bran cereal

1 cup skim milk

Divide between 2 cereal bowls.

Makes 2 servings.

Total breakfast one serving: 387 calories, 38g protein, 39g carbohydrate, 13g fat (5g saturated), 55mg cholesterol, 1189mg sodium, 15g fiber

helpful hints

● Sliced mushrooms can be found in the produce section or salad bar of the supermarket.

● To determine the weight of each sausage or slice of cheese, divide the package weight by the number of sausages or slices.

countdown

● Preheat broiler.
● Make egg pizza base.
● Complete pizza.

shopping list

TO BUY:

1 small package reduced-fat mozzarella cheese (3 ounces needed)

1 package low-fat turkey sausages (6 ounces needed)

1 jar low fat, no sugar added tomato sauce for pasta (4 ounces needed)

1 package button mushrooms (6 mushrooms needed)

STAPLES:

Red onion

Olive oil spray

Egg substitute

High-fiber, no-sugar-added bran cereal

Skim milk

Black peppercorns

arugula and ham scramble

Ham blends well with savory arugula in this simple-to-make scrambled egg dish.

arugula and ham scramble

helpful hints

- *To quickly wash arugula, place it in a bowl of cold water, and then lift it out of the bowl. The sand will be left behind.*
- *To quickly chop or slice the arugula for this dish, place the leaves on top of each other and slice them all at the same time.*
- *Use spinach if arugula is unavailable.*

countdown

- *Prepare all ingredients.*
- *Make eggs.*
- *Make oatmeal.*

shopping list

TO BUY:
- *1/2 pound sliced lean ham*
- *1 small bunch arugula*

STAPLES:
- *Egg substitute*
- *Olive oil*
- *Oatmeal*
- *Skim milk*
- *Sugar substitute*
- *Black peppercorns*

1 cup egg substitute
2 cups arugula, coarsely chopped or sliced
Freshly ground black pepper to taste
2 teaspoons olive oil
1/2 pound sliced lean ham, cubed (about 8 slices)

Combine the egg substitute and arugula, seasoning with pepper to taste. Heat the oil in a medium-sized nonstick skillet over a medium-high heat. Add the ham and sauté for 2 minutes. Add the arugula and egg mixture. Scramble for 1 minute, or until the egg is set to desired consistency. Serve.
Makes 2 servings.

oatmeal

1 cup oatmeal
2 cups water
1 cup skim milk
2 (.035 ounce) envelopes sugar substitute (optional)

To prepare in the microwave, combine the oatmeal and water in a microwave-safe bowl. Microwave on high for 4 minutes. Stir in the milk and sugar substitute, divide between 2 bowls, and serve warm.

Alternatively, to prepare on the hob, combine the oatmeal and water in a small saucepan over a medium-high heat, and bring to a boil. Reduce the heat to medium and cook for about 5 more minutes, stirring occasionally. Stir in the milk and sugar substitute, divide between 2 bowls and serve warm.
Makes 2 servings.

Total breakfast one serving: 427 calories, 41g protein, 42g carbohydrate, 11g fat (2g saturated), 54mg cholesterol, 1274mg sodium, 4g fiber

turkey and cottage cheese

This breakfast is ideal when you're on the go, as it takes only a few minutes to make.
- *The addition of a few pecans to the oatmeal gives it a crunchy texture and nutty flavor.*

turkey and cottage cheese

1 cup low-fat cottage cheese
2 tablespoons freeze-dried chives
¹/₂ pound sliced roast turkey breast

Combine the cottage cheese and chives in a small bowl. Place the turkey slices on 2 plates and spoon the cottage cheese mixture on the slices. Fold the turkey slices in half and serve. *Makes 2 servings.*

pecan oatmeal

1 cup oatmeal
2 cups water
¹/₄ cup (1 ounce) pecan pieces
1 cup skim milk
2 (.035 ounce) envelopes sugar substitute (optional)

To prepare in the microwave, combine the oatmeal and water in a microwave-safe bowl. Microwave on high for 4 minutes.

Alternatively, to prepare on the hob, combine the oatmeal and water in a small saucepan over a medium-high heat and bring to a boil. Reduce the heat to medium and cook about 5 more minutes, stirring occasionally.

Place the pecans on a foil-lined tray and toast in a toaster oven or under the broiler for 1 minute, or until golden. Stir the milk, sugar substitute, and toasted pecans into the oatmeal. Divide between 2 bowls and serve. *Makes 2 servings.*

Total breakfast one serving: 473 calories, 40g protein, 40g carbohydrate, 17g fat (4g saturated), 52mg cholesterol, 439mg sodium, 5g fiber

helpful hints
- *Other types of fresh herbs such as dill, parsley, or basil can be used in place of chives.*
- *Toasting pecans can be tricky, as they burn quickly. Watch them carefully.*

countdown
- *Make turkey.*
- *Make oatmeal.*

shopping list

TO BUY:
1 small carton low-fat cottage cheese (8 ounces needed)
¹/₂ pound sliced roast turkey breast
1 package pecan pieces (1 ounce needed)
1 jar freeze-dried chives
STAPLES:
Oatmeal
Skim milk
Sugar substitute

dijon ham and cheddar melt

For those mornings when you don't feel like eggs, try this quick cheese and ham melt.
If you like spicy food, adjust the amount of cayenne accordingly.

dijon ham and cheddar melt

*¹/₂ pound sliced lean smoked ham
(about 8 slices)*

*4 slices (3 ounces) reduced-fat,
aged Cheddar cheese*

2 tablespoons Dijon mustard

Pinch cayenne pepper

*1 medium tomato, cut into
¹/₂-inch slices*

Line a baking tray with foil. Place the ham on foil and cheese on top. Spread the cheese with mustard and sprinkle with cayenne. Place in the toaster oven or under the broiler for 4 minutes, or until the cheese melts. Place the tomato slices on 2 plates with the ham and cheese to serve.
Makes 2 servings.

cinnamon oatmeal

1 cup oatmeal

2 cups water

1 cup skim milk

¹/₂ teaspoon ground cinnamon

*2 (.035 ounce) envelopes sugar
substitute (optional)*

To prepare in the microwave, combine the oatmeal and water in a microwave-safe bowl. Microwave on high for 4 minutes. Stir in the milk, cinnamon, and sugar substitute, divide between 2 bowls and serve warm.

Alternatively, to prepare on the hob, combine the oatmeal and water in a small saucepan over a medium-high heat and bring to a boil. Reduce the heat to medium and cook for about 5 more minutes, stirring occasionally. Stir in the milk, cinnamon, and sugar substitute, divide between 2 bowls and serve warm.
Makes 2 servings.

Total breakfast one serving: 484 calories,
40g protein, 43g carbohydrate, 16g fat (8g saturated),
84mg cholesterol, 1773mg sodium, 4g fiber

helpful hints

● *To determine the weight of each slice of cheese or ham, divide the package weight by the number of slices.*
● *No-sugar-added instant oatmeal can be used.*

countdown

● *Preheat broiler or toaster oven.*
● *Make cheese and ham melt.*
● *Make oatmeal.*

shopping list

TO BUY:

1 package sliced reduced-fat, aged Cheddar cheese (3 ounces needed)

¹/₂ pound sliced lean smoked ham

1 medium tomato

STAPLES:

Oatmeal

Skim milk

Ground cinnamon

Dijon mustard

Cayenne pepper

Sugar substitute

quick herb omelette

Omelette aux Fines Herbes is on almost every French bistro menu. This is a quick version of this very French dish. ● The secret here is to chop the dried herbs with the fresh parsley. The moisture from the parsley helps to release the juices from the dried herbs.

quick herb omelette

1 tablespoon dried chives
1/2 tablespoon dried tarragon
1 cup fresh parsley leaves
2 eggs
6 egg whites
Salt and freshly ground black
   pepper to taste
2 teaspoons olive oil
1 1/2 ounces sliced reduced-fat
   Swiss cheese (about 2 slices)

Chop the chives, tarragon, and parsley together. Whisk the eggs and egg whites together in a medium-sized bowl. Stir in the herbs and add salt and pepper to taste. Heat the oil in a medium-sized nonstick skillet over a medium-high heat. Pour in the egg mixture and allow to set for 1 minute. Cover with a lid and cook 2–3 minutes more, or until the egg is almost set. Turn the omelette over, place the cheese slices on top, and cover. Cook for 1 more minute. Slide a knife under the omelette and fold in half. Cut the folded omelette in half and serve on 2 plates. *Makes 2 servings*

bran cereal

1 cup skim milk
1 cup high-fiber, no-sugar-added
   bran cereal

Divide the milk and cereal between 2 bowls. *Makes 2 servings.*

> Total breakfast one serving: 343 calories, 33g protein, 36g carbohydrate, 15g fat (4g saturated), 226mg cholesterol, 488mg sodium, 13g fiber

helpful hints

● To determine the weight of each slice of cheese, divide the package weight by the number of slices.
● Make sure the dried chives and tarragon are less than 6 months old.
● Parsley, chives, and tarragon can be chopped together in a food processor or mini chop.

countdown

● Prepare all ingredients.
● Make omelette.
● Assemble bran cereal.

shopping list

TO BUY:
   1 small package sliced
      reduced-fat Swiss cheese
      (1 1/2 ounces needed)
   1 jar freeze-dried chives
   1 large bunch fresh parsley
STAPLES:
   Eggs
   Skim milk
   High-fiber, no-sugar-added
      bran cereal
   Olive oil
   Dried tarragon
   Salt
   Black peppercorns

smoked turkey roll-ups

helpful hints

- Fresh basil or parsley can be substituted for the arugula.
- Any type of sprouting bean can be used.

countdown

- Make turkey roll-ups.
- Make oatmeal.

shopping list

TO BUY:

1/2 pound sliced lean smoked turkey breast
1 small bunch arugula
1 container alfalfa sprouts

STAPLES:

Mayonnaise made with olive or soybean oil
Oatmeal
Skim milk
Ground nutmeg
Sugar substitute

Turkey slices filled with nutty-flavored arugula and alfalfa sprouts provide a quick-grab breakfast. The roll-ups can be made the night before and eaten on the run.

smoked turkey roll-ups

1/2 pound sliced lean smoked turkey breast
2 tablespoons mayonnaise made with olive or soybean oil
Several arugula leaves
2 cups alfalfa sprouts

Place the turkey slices on a work surface or plate. Spread the turkey with mayonnaise. Top with arugula leaves and sprouts. Roll up, divide between 2 plates, and serve.
Makes 2 servings.

spiced oatmeal

1 cup oatmeal
2 cups water
2 (.035 ounce) envelopes sugar substitute (optional)
1/2 teaspoon ground nutmeg
1 cup skim milk

To prepare in the microwave, combine the oatmeal and water in a microwave-safe bowl. Microwave on high for 4 minutes. Stir in the sugar substitute and nutmeg. Stir in the milk, divide between 2 bowls and serve warm.

Alternatively, to prepare on the hob, combine the oatmeal and water in a small saucepan over a medium-high heat and bring to a boil. Reduce the heat to medium and cook for about 5 more minutes, stirring occasionally. Stir in the sugar substitute and nutmeg. Stir in the milk, divide between 2 bowls and serve warm.
Makes 2 servings.

Total breakfast one serving: 484 calories, 43g protein, 36g carbohydrate, 18g fat (3g saturated), 87mg cholesterol, 218mg sodium, 5g fiber

shrimp, red pepper, and tomato frittata

This is an unusual frittata topped with sliced tomatoes and melted cheese.

shrimp, red pepper, and tomato frittata

2 whole eggs

6 egg whites

Salt and freshly ground black pepper to taste

2 teaspoons olive oil

1 medium-sized red bell pepper, sliced (2 cups)

1/2 pound cooked shrimp, cut in half crosswise

1 medium-sized tomato, sliced

1/4 cup grated, reduced-fat Cheddar cheese (1 ounce)

Preheat the oven to 400 degrees. Lightly beat the whole eggs and egg whites together in a medium-sized bowl and season with salt and pepper to taste.

Pour the oil into a medium-sized nonstick skillet and place over a medium heat. Add the pepper and sauté for 3 minutes. Add the shrimp and pour the egg mixture into the pan, swirling in the pan to cover the pepper. Allow to set for 1 minute. Place the tomato slices on top and sprinkle with the cheese.

Place in the oven for 5 minutes, or until the eggs are set to the desired consistency. Divide the frittata between 2 plates and serve.
Makes 2 servings.

yogurt bran cup

1 cup light strawberry-banana flavored yogurt

1 cup high-fiber, no-sugar-added bran cereal

Divide the yogurt between 2 bowls and sprinkle with the bran.
Makes 2 servings.

> Total breakfast one serving: 467 calories, 53g protein, 41g carbohydrate, 17g fat (5g saturated), 399mg cholesterol, 716mg sodium, 13g fiber

helpful hints

● *Use a skillet with an ovenproof handle, and be careful when removing the skillet from the oven.*

● *Buy cooked shrimp in the seafood section of the supermarket, or look for good quality, large, frozen cooked shrimp.*

● *To determine the weight of each slice of cheese, divide the package weight by the number of slices.*

countdown

■ *Preheat oven to 400 degrees.*

● *Make frittata.*

● *Assemble bran cup.*

shopping list

TO BUY:

1 package grated, reduced-fat Cheddar cheese (1 ounce needed)

1 carton light strawberry-banana flavored yogurt

1/2 pound cooked shrimp

1 medium-sized red bell pepper

1 medium-sized tomato

STAPLES:

Eggs

Olive oil

High-fiber, no-sugar-added bran cereal

Salt

Black peppercorns

asian omelette

Crisp water chestnuts and bean sprouts give an Oriental flavor to this omelette. It's adapted from the popular Chinese dish, Egg Foo Yong.

asian omelette

2 teaspoons olive oil

½ cup fresh bean sprouts

½ cup water chestnuts, drained and sliced

Freshly ground black pepper to taste

1 cup egg substitute

¼ pound sliced lean ham, chopped (about 4 slices)

Heat the oil in a nonstick skillet over a medium-high heat. Add the bean sprouts and water chestnuts, and sauté for 1 minute. Season the egg substitute with pepper to taste and pour into the pan, swirling to cover the vegetables. Allow to set for 1 minute. Sprinkle the ham on top, cover, and cook 2–3 minutes longer, or until the egg sets to desired consistency. Cut the omelette in half, slide out of the pan and serve. *Makes 2 servings.*

bran cereal

1 cup skim milk

1 cup high-fiber, no-sugar-added bran cereal

Divide the milk and cereal between 2 bowls. *Makes 2 servings.*

Total breakfast one serving: 369 calories, 42g protein, 44g carbohydrate, 8g fat (1g saturated), 28mg cholesterol, 1146mg sodium, 15g fiber

tuna-stuffed sweet peppers

This popular combination of tuna salad and melted cheese works well for breakfast.

tuna–stuffed sweet peppers

1 (6-ounce) can tuna packed in
water, drained, and rinsed

2 tablespoons mayonnaise made
from soybean or olive oil

6 to 8 fresh basil leaves, torn into
bite-sized pieces (about 4
tablespoons)

Salt and freshly ground black
pepper to taste

2 small red bell peppers, seeded
and halved

4 slices reduced-fat Monterey jack
cheese (3 ounces)

Preheat the broiler. Line a baking tray with foil. In a small bowl, flake the tuna with a fork. Stir in the mayonnaise and basil and season with salt and pepper to taste. Spoon the tuna salad into the bell pepper halves, and top with the cheese. Grill for 2 minutes, or until the cheese has melted. Divide between 2 plates and serve. *Makes 2 servings.*

bran cereal

1 cup skim milk

1 cup high-fiber, no-sugar-added
bran cereal

Divide the milk and cereal between 2 bowls. *Makes 2 servings.*

Total breakfast one serving: 455 calories,
43g protein, 39g carbohydrate, 21g fat (6g saturated),
60mg cholesterol, 957mg sodium, 13g fiber

helpful hint

- *Any reduced-fat Mexican cheese can be substituted for Monterey jack cheese.*

countdown

- *Preheat broiler.*
- *Make tuna melt.*
- *Assemble cereal.*

shopping list

TO BUY:

1 package reduced-fat
Monterey jack cheese
(3 ounces needed)

1 (6-ounce) can tuna packed
in water

1 small bunch fresh basil

2 small red bell peppers

STAPLES:

Mayonnaise made from
soybean or olive oil

High-fiber, no-sugar-added
bran cereal

Skim milk

Salt

Black peppercorns

pecan ham roll-ups

Cream cheese and pecans make a quick filling for sliced ham. These can be made a day ahead and used for a quick-take breakfast.

helpful hints

- *To determine the weight of each slice of ham, divide the package weight by the number of slices.*
- *Warm water can be used instead of skim milk to soften the cream cheese.*

countdown

- *Make ham roll-ups.*
- *Make oatmeal.*

shopping list

TO BUY:

1/2 cup reduced-fat cream cheese

1/2 pound sliced lean ham

1 small package pecan pieces (1/2 ounce needed)

STAPLES:

Oatmeal

Skim milk

Ground cinnamon

Sugar substitute

pecan ham roll-ups

1/4 cup reduced-fat cream cheese
2 tablespoons skim milk
6 pecans, chopped (2 tablespoons)
1/2 pound sliced lean ham (about 8 slices)

Blend the cream cheese, milk, and pecans in a food processor. Or, chop the pecans by hand and combine with the cream cheese and milk. Lay the ham slices on the countertop or plate and spread with the cream cheese mixture. Roll up, divide between 2 plates, and serve.
Makes 2 servings.

cinnamon oatmeal

1 cup oatmeal
2 cups water
1 cup skim milk
1/2 teaspoon ground cinnamon
2 (.035 ounce) envelopes sugar substitute (optional)

To prepare in the microwave, combine the oatmeal and water in a microwave-safe bowl. Microwave on high for 4 minutes: Stir in the milk, cinnamon, and sugar substitute, divide between 2 bowls, and serve warm.

Alternatively, to prepare on the hob, combine the oatmeal and water in a small saucepan over a medium-high heat and bring to a boil. Reduce the heat to medium and cook for about 5 more minutes, stirring occasionally. Stir in the milk, cinnamon, and sugar substitute. Divide between 2 bowls and serve warm.
Makes 2 servings.

Total breakfast one serving: 449 calories, 32g protein, 42g carbohydrate, 18g fat (6g saturated), 76mg cholesterol, 1169mg sodium, 5g fiber

cheddar scramble

This is a breakfast you can make on the run. The eggs take 1¹/₂ minutes to cook and, best of all, there's no pan to wash.

cheddar scramble

2 cups egg substitute

4 slices reduced-fat Cheddar cheese (3 ounces)

Freshly ground black pepper to taste

Combine half of the egg substitute with 2 slices of the cheese in a microwave-safe bowl. Season with pepper to taste. Microwave on high for 1½ minutes. Stir and then heat for another 30 seconds. Repeat for the second serving. Serve hot.

Makes 2 servings.

bran cereal

1 cup skim milk

1 cup high-fiber, no-sugar-added bran cereal

Divide the milk and cereal between 2 bowls. *Makes 2 servings.*

Total breakfast one serving: 358 calories, 41g protein, 35g carbohydrate, 10g fat (6g saturated), 32mg cholesterol, 998mg sodium, 13g fiber

helpful hint

● *To determine the weight of each slice of cheese, divide the package weight by the number of slices.*

countdown

● *Make eggs.*

● *Assemble cereal.*

shopping list

TO BUY:

1 small package sliced reduced-fat Cheddar cheese (3 ounces needed)

STAPLES:

Egg substitute

Skim milk

High-fiber, no-sugar-added bran cereal

Black peppercorns

endive filled with cheese and roasted red peppers

helpful hints

- *Buy a large Belgian endive if available. The leaves will hold more filling.*
- *Be sure to drain the roasted red bell peppers to make a drier filling.*
- *Ordinary green basil can be substituted for purple basil.*

countdown

- *Make stuffed endive.*
- *Assemble cereal.*

shopping list

TO BUY:

1 small package low-fat cream cheese

1 carton low-fat cottage cheese (1 pound needed)

1 small can or jar roasted red bell peppers

1 small bunch purple basil

2 large Belgian endives

STAPLES:

Skim milk

High-fiber, no-sugar-added bran cereal

Salt

Black peppercorns

This is a quick breakfast that you can put together in minutes. In fact, it's also a good snack. Keep the mixture in the refrigerator and use it as a dip or spread with other vegetables.

endive filled with cheese and roasted red peppers

2 cups low-fat cottage cheese

¹/₄ cup low-fat cream cheese (2 ounces)

2 cups roasted red bell peppers, drained and diced

1 cup purple basil, chopped

Salt and freshly ground black pepper to taste

2 large heads Belgian endive

Combine the cottage cheese, cream cheese, roasted red bell pepper, and purple basil by hand in a medium-sized bowl or in a food processor. Season with salt and pepper to taste. Remove any damaged outer leaves from the chicory, break off leaves, and divide between 2 plates. Spoon the filling onto the wide end of each leaf and serve.

Makes 2 servings.

bran cereal

1 cup skim milk

1 cup high-fiber, no-sugar-added bran cereal

Divide the milk and cereal between 2 bowls.

Makes 2 servings.

Total breakfast one serving: 394 calories, 36g protein, 47g carbohydrate, 11g fat (8g saturated), 44mg cholesterol, 1005mg sodium, 13g fiber

turkey and sadziki sandwich **p104**

black bean and salsa wraps **p112**

spanish omelette

This zesty breakfast classic is updated here to make a quick meal. You can add chiles, garlic, and peppers for variety and additional spice. Just use this recipe as a guideline.

spanish omelette

2 whole eggs
4 egg whites
1/2 pound sliced turkey breast, chopped
8 scallions, sliced (1 cup)
Salt and freshly ground black pepper to taste
2 teaspoons olive oil
1 medium tomato, cubed

Preheat the broiler. Whisk the whole eggs and egg whites together in a medium-sized mixing bowl. Stir in the turkey and scallions, and season with salt and pepper to taste. Heat the oil in a medium-sized nonstick skillet over a medium-high heat. Add the tomato and sauté for 3 minutes. Add the egg mixture, swirling to cover the tomato. Allow to set for 1 minute and then place under the broiler for 5 minutes. Divide the omelette in half, slide out of the skillet and serve on 2 plates.
Makes 2 servings.

bran cereal

1 cup skim milk
1 cup high-fiber, no-sugar-added bran cereal

Divide the milk and cereal between 2 bowls.
Makes 2 servings.

Total breakfast one serving: 465 calories, 54g protein, 39g carbohydrate, 16g fat (4g saturated), 295mg cholesterol, 455mg sodium, 13g fiber

helpful hint

● Use a skillet with an ovenproof handle, but be careful with the hot handle when removing the skillet from the oven.

countdown

● Preheat broiler.
● Make omelette.
● Assemble cereal.

shopping list

TO BUY:
1/4 pound sliced turkey breast
1 small bunch scallions (8 needed)
1 medium tomato
STAPLES:
Eggs
Skim milk
Olive oil
High-fiber, no-sugar-added bran cereal
Salt
Black peppercorns

raspberry smoothie with toasted walnut oatmeal

When I did some research into smoothies, I was astounded at their high carbohydrate content. But the cool, smooth, frozen drinks are so good that I decided to create one that was quick, easy, delicious—and good for us too. My family proclaimed this one a winner. ● *Use a microwave to make the oatmeal, and this breakfast will take only 10 minutes to make.*

raspberry-red smoothie

1 cup fresh or frozen raspberries

1/2 cup light raspberry-flavored yogurt

2 teaspoons vanilla extract

2 (0.035 ounce) envelopes sugar substitute (optional)

2 cups ice cubes

Place the raspberries, yogurt, vanilla extract, and sugar substitute in a blender. Blend until smooth. Add the ice cubes, and blend until thick. Pour into 2 glasses and serve cold. *Makes 2 servings.*

toasted walnut oatmeal

1 cup oatmeal

2 cups water

1/4 cup walnuts

1 cup skim milk

2 (.035 ounce) envelopes sugar substitute (optional)

To prepare in the microwave, combine the oatmeal and water in a microwave-safe bowl. Microwave on high for 4 minutes.

Alternatively, to prepare on the stove, combine the oatmeal and water in a small saucepan over a medium-high heat and bring to a boil. Reduce the heat to medium and cook for about 5 more minutes, stirring occasionally.

Place the walnuts on a foil-lined tray and toast in a toaster oven or under the broiler for 1 minute, or until lightly toasted. Stir the milk, sugar substitute, and walnuts into the oatmeal. Divide between 2 bowls and serve warm. *Makes 2 servings.*

smoked turkey breast

6 ounces sliced smoked turkey breast, cubed

Several lettuce leaves

Place lettuce on 2 plates with the turkey cubes on top, and serve. *Makes 2 servings.*

Total breakfast one serving: 492 calories, 38g protein, 49g carbohydrate, 16g fat (2g saturated), 63mg cholesterol, 149mg sodium, 8g fiber

which carbs
lunches

tex-mex layered salad

This is a very pretty salad that will impress guests. Arrange the salad in a large glass bowl so that the layers of colors show through. The salad can be made several hours in advance. Keep covered and refrigerated, and add the dressing just before serving.

tex-mex layered salad

1 medium tomato

1/4 cup red onion, chopped

1 jalapeño pepper, seeded and chopped

1/2 teaspoon ground cumin

Salt and freshly ground black pepper to taste

2/3 cup canned black beans, rinsed and drained

4 cups iceberg lettuce, washed and shredded

1 medium-sized green bell pepper, chopped (1 cup)

1/2 pound sliced smoked lean turkey breast, cut into 1/2-inch strips

1/4 cup no-sugar-added oil and vinegar dressing

Chop half of the tomato and slice the remaining half. Combine the chopped tomato with the onion and jalapeño in a medium-sized bowl. Stir in the ground cumin. (These steps can be done in a food processor or by hand.) Season with salt and pepper to taste. Gently stir in the black beans. Layer the lettuce, bell pepper, half the black bean mixture, and turkey in a medium glass bowl. Arrange the tomato slices on the turkey and spoon the remaining black beans over the tomatoes. Pour the dressing over the salad and serve.

Makes 2 servings.

One serving: 467 calories, 41g protein, 27g carbohydrate, 21g fat (4g saturated), 80mg cholesterol, 238mg sodium, 3g fiber

smoked whitefish salad

Whitefish is a mild-flavored member of the salmon family. Its high fat content makes it perfect for smoking, and the delicate white flesh makes a light, smoked salad.

smoked whitefish salad

2 tablespoons mayonnaise made
   with olive or soybean oil

2 tablespoons non-fat, plain yogurt

$1/4$ cup snipped fresh dill or
   1 teaspoon dried

$1/2$ pound smoked whitefish,
   flaked

4 scallions, sliced ($1/2$ cup)

2 celery stalks, sliced (1 cup)

Salt and freshly ground black
   pepper to taste

Several Boston lettuce leaves

2 medium tomatoes, sliced

2 slices rye bread

Combine the mayonnaise, yogurt and dill in a medium-sized bowl. Add the whitefish, scallions, and celery. Season with salt and pepper to taste. Toss well. Serve on 2 plates over the lettuce with sliced tomatoes and bread. *Makes 2 servings.*

One serving: 327 calories, 34g protein, 22g carbohydrate, 14g fat (2g saturated), 43mg cholesterol, 1447mg sodium, 4g fiber

helpful hints

- If using fresh dill, simply snip the leaves with scissors.
- Make sure dried dill is less than 6 months old. It should be green, not brown or gray.

countdown

- Prepare ingredients.
- Make salad.

shopping list

TO BUY:

1 carton non-fat, plain yogurt

$1/2$ pound smoked haddock

1 bunch fresh dill or 1 jar
   dried

1 small bunch scallions
   (4 needed)

1 small head Boston lettuce

2 medium tomatoes

STAPLES:

Celery

Mayonnaise made with olive
   or soybean oil

Rye bread

Salt

Black peppercorns

salad niçoise

helpful hint

● Use the dressing recipe provided here or buy a no-sugar-added oil and vinegar dressing, and add diced red onion.

countdown

● Make dressing.
● Blanch asparagus.
● Assemble salad.

shopping list

TO BUY:

2 (6-ounce) cans low-salt, solid white tuna, packed in water
1 jar or can pitted black olives
1/2 pound fresh asparagus
1 bag washed, ready-to-eat field greens or French-style salad
2 medium tomatoes
2 medium oranges

STAPLES:

Red onion
Dijon mustard
Red wine vinegar
Olive oil
Salt
Black peppercorns

This quick salad from the French Riviera is filled with olives, tomatoes, asparagus, and tuna. These ingredients were chosen to give a variety of textures, colors, and flavors: crisp, pale green lettuce; ripe red tomatoes; soft, pink tuna; and dark green asparagus. Use this recipe as a base and create your own version of this classic, using other ingredients or leftovers.

salad niçoise

1/4 cup red wine vinegar
2 tablespoons Dijon mustard
1/4 cup red onion, diced
2 tablespoons water
2 tablespoons olive oil
Salt and freshly ground black pepper to taste
2 (6-ounce) low-salt, solid white tuna, drained and rinsed
1/2 pound fresh asparagus
4 cups washed, ready-to-eat field greens or French-style salad
2 medium tomatoes, cut into wedges
8 pitted black olives, quartered

To prepare the vinaigrette dressing, whisk the vinegar and mustard together in a large bowl with the onion and water. Whisk in the oil to a smooth consistency. Season with salt and pepper to taste. Flake the tuna into the vinaigrette.

Cut or snap off the 1-inch fibrous stems on the asparagus and discard. Slice the remaining asparagus into 2-inch pieces. Bring a medium-sized saucepan of water to a boil. Add the asparagus. As soon as the water comes back to a boil, drain the asparagus, and refresh in cold water. (If using thick asparagus boil for 5 minutes.) To microwave the asparagus instead, place asparagus in a microwave-safe bowl and microwave on high for 4 minutes. Add the asparagus to the tuna mixture and toss gently. Divide the lettuce between 2 plates. Spoon the tuna-asparagus mixture over the lettuce. Arrange the tomato wedges around the plate, sprinkle the olives over the top and serve. *Makes 2 servings.*

One serving: 424 calories, 51g protein, 14g carbohydrate, 20g fat (2g saturated), 75mg cholesterol, 1283mg sodium, 3g fiber

citrus

2 medium oranges

Divide the oranges between 2 plates and serve. *Makes 2 servings.*

One serving: 62 calories, 1g protein, 15g carbohydrate, 0g fat (0g saturated), 0mg cholesterol, 0mg sodium, 3g fiber

chicken salad amandine

Almonds and apples add a crunchy texture and varied flavors to this chicken salad. Use leftover roasted chicken or shop-bought rotisserie chicken for a fast meal.

chicken salad amandine

2 tablespoons slivered almonds

2 tablespoons mayonnaise made
   with olive or soybean oil

1/4 cup non-fat, plain yogurt

4 teaspoons dried tarragon

Salt and freshly ground black
   pepper to taste

1/2 pound roast chicken breast,
   skin removed and cut into
   1-inch pieces

2 celery stalks, sliced (1 cup)

1 Golden Delicious apple, cored
   and cut into 1/2-inch cubes

1 small head radicchio

Place the almonds on a foil-lined tray and toast in a toaster oven or under the broiler for 1 minute. Alternatively, toast in a nonstick skillet over a medium heat for 1 minute, or until golden. Combine the mayonnaise, yogurt, and tarragon in a medium-size bowl. Season with salt and pepper to taste. Add the chicken, celery, toasted almonds, and apple. Toss well and adjust seasonings if necessary. Carefully remove the leaves from the radicchio, making them into small cups. Spoon the chicken salad into the radicchio leaves. Serve on 2 plates.
Makes 2 servings.

One serving: 457 calories, 43g protein, 24g carbohydrate, 23g fat (3g saturated), 101mg cholesterol, 282mg sodium, 5g fiber

helpful hints

● *Make sure the bottle of dried tarragon is less than 6 months old. It should be a green color, not brown or gray. This freshness will make a marked difference to the flavor of the salad.*

● *Any type of lettuce can be used.*

● *Toasting almonds intensifies their flavor, but can be tricky. Watch them carefully, as they burn easily. This step can be omitted.*

countdown

● *Toast almonds.*

● *Make salad.*

shopping list

TO BUY:

   1 carton non-fat, plain yogurt

   1/2 pound roast chicken
      breast

   1 small package slivered
      almonds (1 ounce needed)

   1 Golden Delicious apple

   1 small head radicchio

STAPLES:

   Celery

   Mayonnaise made with olive
      or soybean oil

   Dried tarragon

   Salt

   Black peppercorns

helpful hint

- *Buy ready-to-eat shredded lettuce.*

countdown

- *Make sadziki.*
- *Make sandwich.*

shopping list

TO BUY:

1 carton non-fat plain yogurt

1/2 pound sliced roast turkey breast

1 small package pistachio nuts (1 1/2 ounces needed)

1 cucumber

1 bunch fresh mint

1 bag washed, ready-to-eat, shredded lettuce

STAPLES:

Garlic

Red onion

Whole wheat bread

Salt

Black peppercorns

turkey and sadziki sandwich

The refreshing flavor of mint and cucumber mingle with roasted turkey in this grilled Middle Eastern sandwich. Sadziki is a yogurt sauce that can also be used as a vegetable dip. It takes only seconds to make in a food processor.

turkey and sadziki sandwich

1 medium cucumber, peeled and seeded (about 1 1/2 cups)

1/2 cup non-fat, plain yogurt

2 medium-sized garlic cloves, crushed

2 tablespoons chopped fresh mint

1/4 cup red onion, chopped

Salt and freshly ground black pepper to taste

2 slices whole wheat bread, toasted

1/2 pound sliced roast turkey breast, skinned and cut into 1-inch pieces

2 cups washed, ready-to-eat, shredded lettuce

Chop the cucumber in the bowl of a food processor and drain. Stir the yogurt, garlic, mint, and onion into the food processor bowl with the drained cucumber. Season with salt and pepper to taste.

Place a slice of toasted bread on each plate. Top with roast turkey and shredded lettuce. Spoon a little sadziki over the lettuce. Serve any extra lettuce and sauce on the side.

Makes 2 servings.

One serving: 302 calories, 40g protein, 23g carbohydrate, 6g fat (1g saturated), 81mg cholesterol, 241mg sodium, 6g fiber

pistachios

1/4 cup shelled pistachio nuts

Divide the pistachios between 2 plates and serve.

Makes 2 servings.

One serving: 131 calories, 5g protein, 6g carbohydrate, 11g fat (1g saturated), 0mg cholesterol, 2mg sodium, 0g fiber

california chef's salad

Julienned slices of ham, turkey, roast beef, and cheese alongside an array of fresh vegetables are the basis for this American favorite. The addition of alfalfa sprouts gives this dish a modern 'California' touch. • Traditionally, the ingredients in a Chef's Salad are cut in julienne strips (large match sticks). However, if you are pressed for time, you can slice them in a food processor fitted with a thick slicing blade. • You can use whatever lean cold meats and vegetables you have on hand, referring to the proportions given in the recipe as a guideline.

california chef's salad

1/4 cup balsamic vinegar

1 tablespoon Dijon mustard

2 tablespoons water

2 tablespoons canola oil

Salt and freshly ground black
   pepper to taste

8 large romaine lettuce leaves,
   washed, dried and sliced

2 small cucumbers, peeled and
   julienned

1 medium-sized red bell pepper,
   julienned (2 cups)

1 1/2 ounces reduced-fat
   Swiss cheese, julienned (about
   2 slices)

2 ounces sliced smoked deli
   chicken breast, julienned
   (1/3 cup)

2 ounces sliced lean deli roast
   beef, julienned (1/2 cup)

2 ounces sliced lean deli ham,
   julienned (1/2 cup)

1 cup alfalfa sprouts

Mix the vinegar and mustard together in a small bowl until smooth. Add the water and oil, blending well. Season with salt and pepper to taste. Divide the lettuce leaves between 2 plates. Place the remaining ingredients on the leaves in pie-shaped segments, like the spokes of a wheel. Spoon the dressing over the top and serve.

Makes 2 servings.

One serving: 400 calories, 34g protein,
19g carbohydrate, 22g fat (5g saturated),
71mg cholesterol, 519mg sodium, 2g fiber

helpful hints

● Ask the deli to cut the meat in 1/2-inch slices. You can then easily cut the slices into 1/2-inch julienne strips.

● Use any type of sprouts.

● If making salad in advance, add dressing just before serving.

● Any type of no-sugar-added dressing can be used instead of the dressing recipe given.

● To determine the weight of each slice of cheese, divide the package weight by the number of slices.

countdown

● Make dressing.
● Prepare ingredients.
● Assemble salad.

shopping list

TO BUY:

   1 small package reduced-fat
      Swiss cheese (1 1/2 ounces
      needed)
   2 ounces sliced smoked deli
      chicken breast
   2 ounces sliced lean roast beef
   2 ounces sliced lean deli ham
   1 head romaine lettuce
   2 small cucumbers
   1 medium-sized red bell
      pepper
   1 container alfalfa sprouts

STAPLES:

   Canola oil
   Dijon mustard
   Balsamic vinegar
   Salt
   Black pepper

turkey, salsa, and citrus salad

helpful hint

- Any type of lettuce can be used.

countdown

- Prepare ingredients.
- Assemble salad.

shopping list

TO BUY:

1/2 pound sliced lean smoked turkey breast

1 jar no-sugar-added tomato salsa (8 ounces needed)

1 ripe small avocado

2 small oranges

1 container alfalfa sprouts

1 small head curly endive

2 medium plums

STAPLES:

Salt

Black peppercorns

The nutty flavor and creamy texture of ripe avocado blends well with sweet orange and smoky turkey in this quick salad—only 5 minutes from start to finish. • Ask the produce manager for a ripe avocado if you don't find one displayed. Sometimes they don't display ones that will ripen within a day. A quick way to help avocados ripen is to remove the stem, place the avocado in a paper bag and leave in a warm spot. • Curly endive has a loose head with lacy, green-rimmed leaves that curl at the pointed tips.

turkey, salsa, and citrus salad

1/2 pound sliced lean smoked turkey breast, cut into 1-inch cubes (1 1/2 cups)

1 ripe small avocado, pitted and cut into 1-inch cubes (1/2 cup)

1 cup no-sugar-added tomato salsa

2 small oranges, peeled and cut into 1-inch cubes (about 2 cups)

1 cup handful alfalfa sprouts

Salt and freshly ground black pepper to taste

Several curly endive leaves

Combine the turkey, avocado, and salsa in a medium-sized bowl, tossing well. Gently stir in the orange cubes and sprouts. Season with salt and pepper to taste. Place the curly endive on 2 plates, spoon the turkey-avocado mixture on top and serve.

Makes 2 servings.

One serving: 464 calories, 40g protein, 33g carbohydrate, 19g fat (3g saturated), 80mg cholesterol, 850mg sodium, 12g fiber

plum plate

2 medium plums, halved and pitted

Slice the plums. Divide between 2 plates and serve.

Makes 2 servings.

One serving: 36 calories, 1g protein, 9g carbohydrate, 0g fat (0g saturated), 0mg cholesterol, 0mg sodium, 0.5g fiber

jerk chicken with hearts of palm

'Jerking' is an old Jamaican method for preserving and cooking meat. It's a long process that involves marinating the meat and then slowly cooking it over a pimento (allspice) wood fire. For this recipe, I adapted the flavors and inspiration of jerk cooking to create an exotic, quick meal.

jerk chicken with hearts of palm

1 tablespoon chopped yellow
   onion

2 teaspoons dried thyme

Pinch of salt

½ teaspoon ground nutmeg

2 (0.035 ounce) envelopes sugar
   substitute (optional)

1 teaspoon freshly ground black
   pepper

¾ pound boneless, skinless
   chicken breast

Olive oil spray

Half a small head cos lettuce, torn
   into bite-sized pieces

2 cups sliced hearts of palm

2 tablespoons no-sugar-added oil
   and vinegar dressing

In a food processor or by hand, combine the onion, thyme, salt, nutmeg, sugar substitute, and black pepper. The juice from the onion will bind the ingredients together. Remove any visible fat from the chicken breast and poke several holes in the meat with a knife or fork. Spoon the jerk seasoning over both sides of the chicken and let marinate for 15 minutes before cooking. Set a nonstick skillet over a medium heat and spray with olive oil. Sauté the chicken for 5 minutes, then turn and sauté for 5 more minutes, or until a meat thermometer registers 160 degrees. Divide the lettuce between 2 plates. Scatter the hearts of palm slices over the lettuce. Drizzle the dressing over the lettuce. Slice the chicken into strips and arrange on the lettuce to serve.

Makes 2 servings.

One serving: 437 calories, 60g protein, 15g carbohydrate, 18g fat (3g saturated), 144mg cholesterol, 981mg sodium, 5g fiber

tangerine

2 medium tangerines

Divide the tangerines between 2 plates.
Makes 2 servings.

One serving: 37 calories, 1g protein, 9g carbohydrate, 0g fat (0g saturated), 0mg cholesterol, 1mg sodium, 0g fiber

helpful hints

● *Use the jerk recipe provided or purchase a jerk seasoning or marinade. Make sure it does not have added sugar.*
● *Make sure the dried thyme is less than 6 months old.*
● *This jerk chicken will keep 1 to 2 days in the refrigerator. Double the recipe and save half for another lunch.*

countdown

● *Prepare ingredients.*
● *Make chicken.*
● *While chicken cooks, arrange hearts of palm and lettuce on plate.*

shopping list

TO BUY:
   ¾ pound boneless, skinless
      chicken breast
   1 jar or can hearts of palm
   1 small head romaine lettuce
   2 medium tangerines.
STAPLES:
   Yellow onion
   Dried thyme
   Ground nutmeg
   Olive oil spray
   No-sugar-added oil and
      vinegar dressing
   Sugar substitute
   Salt
   Black peppercorns

deli salad with cucumber and cucumber

You can put this salad together in minutes with whatever you have in the refrigerator. Use the proportions in this recipe as a guideline for ordering similar dishes in restaurants or eating at salad bars.

deli salad

1/4 pound sliced smoked turkey breast

1/4 pound sliced lean roast beef

1/2 cup no-sugar-added deli coleslaw

1 medium cucumber, peeled and sliced

2 tablespoons mayonnaise made with olive or soybean oil

2 tablespoons horseradish

Arrange the meat slices with the coleslaw and cucumber on 2 plates. Mix the mayonnaise and horseradish together and spoon over the meat to serve.

Makes 2 servings.

One serving: 406 calories, 34g protein, 13g carbohydrate, 23g fat (5g saturated), 96mg cholesterol, 305mg sodium, 2g fiber

cantaloupe

1/2 cantaloupe, cubed

Divide the cantaloupe between 2 dessert bowls and serve.

Makes 2 servings.

One serving: 39 calories, 1g protein, 9g carbohydrate, 0g fat (0g saturated), 0mg cholesterol, 10mg sodium, 1g fiber

country bacon and egg salad with fresh berries

Egg salad is available on lunch menus, or it can be made from scratch at home. Wherever you eat it, use this recipe as a portion guideline.

egg salad

8 eggs (only 2 yolks are used)

1/2 pound sliced lean Canadian bacon

2 tablespoons mayonnaise made with olive or soybean oil

2 tablespoons Dijon mustard

2 tablespoons warm water

2 tablespoons diced red onion

1/4 cup fresh flat leaf parsley, chopped

2 celery stalks, diced (1 cup)

Salt and freshly ground black pepper to taste

Several romaine leaves, torn into bite-sized pieces

2 medium tomatoes, quartered

Preheat the toaster oven or broiler. Place the eggs in a medium saucepan and cover with cold water. Set over a medium-high heat and bring to a boil. Reduce the heat to low and gently simmer for 12 minutes. Drain the hot water and fill the pan with cold water. When the eggs are cool to the touch, peel, cut in half and discard 6 of the yolks. Mash the remaining 2 whole eggs and 6 egg whites with a fork.

Meanwhile, place the bacon in one layer on a foil-lined tray and toast in a toaster oven or under the broiler until brown. Combine the mayonnaise, mustard, water, onion, and parsley in a bowl. Stir in the eggs and celery, mixing well. Season with salt and pepper to taste. Place the lettuce and tomatoes on 2 plates. Spoon the egg salad on top of the lettuce. Cut the browned bacon into bite-sized pieces and sprinkle over the egg salad. Serve. *Makes 2 servings.*

One serving: 411 calories, 41g protein, 17g carbohydrate, 21g fat (4g saturated), 270mg cholesterol, 1743mg sodium, 1g fiber

fresh berries

2 cups fresh strawberries

Divide the strawberries between 2 dessert bowls and serve.
Makes 2 servings.

One serving: 45 calories, 1g protein, 11g carbohydrate, 1g fat (0g saturated), 0mg cholesterol, 2mg sodium, 3g fiber

helpful hints

● *You can make the egg salad in a food processor or mini chop. Be careful to pulse the blades and watch that it does not become too finely chopped or mushy.*

● *There are several brands of lean Canadian bacon available. Look for the one that has the lowest fat content.*

countdown

● *Preheat toaster oven or broiler.*

● *Make hard-boiled eggs.*

● *Make egg salad.*

shopping list

TO BUY:

1/2 pound lean Canadian bacon

1 bunch flat leaf parsley

1 head romaine lettuce

2 medium tomatoes

1 container fresh strawberries

STAPLES:

Celery

Eggs

Mayonnaise made with olive or soybean oil

Dijon mustard

Red onion

Salt

Black peppercorns

balsamic and dill salmon salad

Fresh salmon mixed with cucumber and dill makes a richly-flavored, yet light, salmon salad. If you have time, double the recipe and save half for another lunch.

balsamic and dill salmon salad

2 tablespoons mayonnaise made
    with olive or soybean oil
4 teaspoons balsamic vinegar
1/4 cup fresh dill or 2 teaspoons
    dried
1 medium cucumber, deseeded
    and diced (about 1 1/2 cups)
Olive oil spray
1/2 pound salmon fillet
Salt and freshly ground black
    pepper to taste
2 medium-sized green bell
    peppers, halved and deseeded

Combine the mayonnaise, balsamic vinegar, dill, and cucumber in a small bowl. Set a nonstick skillet over a medium-high heat and spray with olive oil. Add the salmon and sauté for 3 minutes. Turn and sauté for 2 more minutes. Flake the salmon into the mayonnaise mixture with a fork. Season with salt and pepper to taste and mix gently. Spoon the mixture into the pepper halves and serve.
Makes 2 servings.

One serving: 364 calories, 31g protein, 13g carbohydrate, 20g fat (4g saturated), 85mg cholesterol, 159mg sodium, 1g fiber

raspberries

2 cups fresh raspberries

Divide the raspberries between 2 dessert bowls and serve.
Makes 2 servings.

One serving: 61 calories, 1g protein, 14g carbohydrate, 1g fat (0g saturated), 0mg cholesterol, 0mg sodium, 6g fiber

hollywood cobb salad

Roasted chicken breast, avocado, and lettuce were key ingredients in Robert Cobb's first Cobb salad, which he served at the Brown Derby restaurant at Hollywood and Vine in the 1930s. It was so popular among the Hollywood moguls that it has become a favorite on restaurant menus throughout the States.

hollywood cobb salad

2 cups finely sliced iceberg lettuce

1 cup finely sliced chicory or curly endive

2 medium tomatoes, cut into large dice (2 cups)

1/2 pound sliced skinless deli chicken breast, cut into 1-inch cubes (2 cups)

1/2 small ripe avocado, pitted, peeled and cubed (1/2 cup)

2 tablespoons freeze dried chives

2 tablespoons no-sugar-added oil and vinegar dressing

Arrange the iceberg and chicory lettuce in 2 shallow bowls or on 2 plates. Arrange the tomatoes, chicken, and avocado in rows over the lettuce. Sprinkle with the chives, drizzle with dressing, and serve.

Makes 2 servings

One serving: 378 calories, 40g protein, 11g carbohydrate, 21g fat (4g saturated), 96mg cholesterol, 183mg sodium, 3g fiber

peaches

2 medium peaches

Divide the peaches between 2 plates and serve.

Makes 2 servings.

One serving: 37 calories, 1g protein, 10g carbohydrate, 0g fat (0g saturated), 0mg cholesterol, 0mg sodium, 1g fiber

helpful hints

- *Ask the deli to cut the chicken breast into 1-inch thick slices to make it easier to cut into cubes.*
- *A hard-boiled egg can be substituted for the avocado.*
- *To speed the ripening of an avocado, remove the stem and store it in a paper bag in a warm spot.*

countdown

- *Make dressing.*
- *Prepare ingredients.*
- *Assemble salad.*

shopping list

TO BUY:

1/2 pound sliced skinless deli chicken breast

1 jar dried chives

1 head iceberg lettuce

1 small head chicory lettuce

2 medium tomatoes

1 small avocado

2 medium peaches

STAPLES:

No-sugar-added oil and vinegar dressing

black bean and salsa wraps

helpful hints

- Look for romaine lettuce with large leaves.
- Black bean pâté is usually located with the dips and nachos in the snack section of the supermarket.

countdown

- Prepare ingredients.
- Assemble wraps.

shopping list

TO BUY:

1 carton light fruit-flavored yogurt

1 package grated, reduced-fat Monterey Jack cheese (2 ounces needed)

$1/2$ pound sliced turkey breast

1 jar no-sugar-added black bean pâté

1 jar no-sugar-added tomato salsa (4 ounces needed)

1 head romaine lettuce

With the help of prepared black bean pâté and deli turkey breast, you can assemble this lunch in 5 minutes. It can be made the night before and stored in the refrigerator until needed for lunch. You can use these wraps as hors d'oeuvres or eat them on a picnic.

black bean and salsa wraps

12 large romaine leaves, washed and patted dry

12 (11 x 4-inch) rectangles foil, parchment paper or greaseproof paper

$1/4$ cup prepared no-sugar-added black bean pâté

$1/2$ cup grated reduced-fat shredded Monterey Jack cheese (2 ounces)

$1/2$ pound sliced turkey breast

1 cup no-sugar-added tomato salsa

Remove 1 inch of the thick stem from each lettuce leaf and crush the remaining stem so that the leaf lies flat. Place the rectangles of foil on the work surface. Place one leaf on each square. Spread the pâté on each leaf and sprinkle with cheese. Top with a layer of turkey. Roll the lettuce up lengthwise like a cigar. Wrap the foil tightly around the lettuce to hold it in place. Cut in half crosswise and serve on 2 plates with the salsa on the side.

Makes 2 servings.

One serving: 349 calories, 15g protein, 17g carbohydrate, 5g fat (3g saturated), 10mg cholesterol, 1070mg sodium, 5g fiber

yogurt

1 cup light fruit-flavored yogurt

Divide the yogurt between 2 dessert bowls and serve.

Makes 2 servings.

One serving: 50 calories, 32g protein, 0g carbohydrate, 4g fat (1g saturated), 80mg cholesterol, 72mg sodium, 0g fiber

chili chicken

This chicken dish is full of hot, spicy South-western flavors, and it tastes delicious served over a cool bed of lettuce with the Green Onion Dressing.

chili chicken

1/2 cup red onion, chopped

2 medium-sized garlic cloves, crushed

1 tablespoon chili powder

1 teaspoon ground cumin

Pinch salt

Pinch freshly ground black pepper

1/2 pound boneless, skinless chicken breasts

1/4 cup freshly squeezed lemon juice (2 medium lemons)

2 tablespoons Dijon mustard

4 teaspoons olive oil

1 tablespoon water

4 scallions, sliced (1/2 cup)

1/2 small head cos lettuce, torn into bite-sized pieces

2 medium tomatoes, cut into wedges

Preheat the broiler. Combine the onion, garlic, chili powder, cumin, salt, and pepper in a small bowl. Remove any visible fat from the chicken and poke several holes in the meat with a knife or fork. Place in a bowl and spread the marinade evenly over the chicken. Let it marinate for 15 minutes, turning once. Cover a baking tray with foil. Place the chicken on the tray and broil it 4–5 inches from the heat for 5 minutes. Turn and broil for another 5 minutes. Remove from the broiler and let cool. When cool, slice into strips. Whisk the lemon juice and mustard together in a small bowl. Whisk in the oil, and then the water. Stir in the scallions. Place the lettuce on 2 plates. Top with the tomatoes and chicken strips. Drizzle the dressing over the salad or serve on the side.
Makes 2 servings.

> One serving: 367 calories, 41g protein, 18g carbohydrate, 16g fat (3g saturated), 96mg cholesterol, 603mg sodium, 1g fiber

helpful hints

● *Chop onion, garlic, and spices together in a food processor or mini chop to make a quick marinade.*

● *If pressed for time, use a bottled, no-sugar-added dressing and add scallions to it.*

countdown

● *Preheat broiler.*

● *While chicken marinates, prepare greens and make dressing.*

shopping list

TO BUY:

1/2 pound boneless, skinless chicken breast

1 small head romaine lettuce

2 medium tomatoes

2 lemons

1 small bunch scallions (4 needed)

STAPLES:

Red onion

Garlic

Olive oil

Ground cumin

Chili powder

Dijon mustard

Salt

Black peppercorns

which carbs
dinners

thai peanut-rub pork

This blend of spices and peanuts rubbed into the pork forms a well-seasoned crust. Rubs are a quick way to add flavor to meats and a great alternative to marinades, since you don't have to wait for the meat to absorb the marinade flavors. These Thai spices are fun, easy to use, and provide a different way to spice up pork tenderloin.

thai peanut-rub pork

Olive oil spray

20 dry-roasted, unsalted peanuts (2 tablespoons when ground)

1/4 cup fresh cilantro

1 1/2 teaspoons garlic powder

1 tablespoon ground coriander

2 (.035 ounce) envelopes sugar substitute (optional)

Pinch of cayenne pepper

10 ounces pork tenderloin

Preheat the broiler. Line a baking tray with foil, and spray with olive oil. Chop the peanuts and cilantro in a food processor. Add the garlic powder, ground coriander, sugar substitute, and cayenne, pulsing to incorporate. Alternatively, chop and mix by hand. Remove any visible fat from the pork. Rub the mixture on both sides of the pork, pressing the mixture onto the meat and making sure all the sides are coated. Place on a baking tray and broil 8 inches from the heat for 7 minutes, then turn and broil for another 8 minutes. The pork is done when a meat thermometer registers 160 degrees. Remove the pork to a plate and cover with foil to keep warm. Slice before serving.
Makes 2 servings.

> One serving: 333 calories, 45g protein, 6g carbohydrate, 15g fat (4g saturated), 133mg cholesterol, 137mg sodium, 1g fiber

stir-fry broccoli noodles

2 ounces (1/2 cup) whole wheat fettuccine

1/4 pound broccoli florets (2 cups)

2 tablespoons oyster sauce

2 tablespoons rice vinegar

Olive oil spray

4 medium-sized garlic cloves, crushed

1/4 cup chopped fresh cilantro

Bring a large saucepan of water to the boil, add the fettuccine, and boil for 8 minutes. Add the broccoli and boil for 2 minutes. Drain and set aside. Combine the oyster sauce and vinegar, then set aside. Spray a wok or skillet with olive oil and place over a high heat. Add the noodles, broccoli, and garlic. Stir-fry for 2 minutes, then push the ingredients to the sides of the pan. Add the oyster sauce mixture and toss well. Serve sprinkled with chopped cilantro.
Makes 2 servings.

> One serving: 208 calories, 10g protein, 37g carbohydrate, 3g fat (1g saturated), 0mg cholesterol, 491mg sodium, 6g fiber

helpful hints

- *If rice vinegar is unavailable, substitute 1 tablespoon water mixed with distilled white vinegar.*
- *Chop the cilantro for both recipes at one time and divide accordingly.*
- *To keep from looking back at the recipe as you stir-fry the ingredients, line them up on a chopping board or plate in the order of use.*
- *For crisp, not steamed, stir-fried vegetables, start with a very hot wok. Let the vegetables sit for a minute before tossing to allow the wok to regain its heat.*

countdown

- *Preheat broiler.*
- *Make pork dish.*
- *While pork cooks, make broccoli noodles.*

shopping list

TO BUY:

10 ounces pork tenderloin

1 small package dry roasted, unsalted peanuts (1 ounce needed)

1 box whole wheat fettuccine (2 ounces needed)

1 small bottle oyster sauce

1 small bottle rice vinegar

1 small bunch fresh cilantro

1 package broccoli florets (1/4 pound needed)

STAPLES:

Garlic

Olive oil spray

Garlic powder

Ground coriander

Sugar substitute

Cayenne pepper

pesto chicken

Pesto is a flavorful Italian sauce filled with garlic, basil, pine nuts, parsley, and olive oil. It's most widely used as a luscious dressing for pasta. Typically, pesto is not cooked. In this recipe, the sauce is added to the cooked chicken for a minute just before serving. The sauce is warmed by the chicken, while still preserving the fresh basil and parsley flavors.
● Steaming or boiling artichokes takes about 45 minutes. To cut the time in half, cut the artichokes in half and cook them in about 2 inches of water for 20 minutes. The artichokes can also be cooked in a microwave, as described in this recipe. ● Artichokes may be served hot or cold. To eat, pull off the outer petals one at a time. Dip the base of each petal into the sauce; pull the petal through your teeth to remove the soft, pulpy portion of petal, then discard. Always remove the fuzzy section near the base (called the choke) because it is inedible. The bottom, or heart, of the artichoke is entirely edible. Many think it's the best part. Cut it into small pieces and dip in the sauce.

helpful hints

● Pesto can be found in jars on the supermarket shelves.
● Artichokes are not available all year round. Asparagus or broccoli can be steamed or microwaved and served with this dressing instead.
● Fresh figs are not available all year round. Plums, apricots, or pears can be substituted.

countdown

● Start artichokes.
● Make pasta.
● Make chicken.

shopping list

TO BUY:
³/₄ pound boneless, skinless chicken breast
1 small container pesto
1 box whole wheat fettuccine (2 oucnes needed)
2 medium artichokes
4 medium figs
STAPLES:
No-sugar-added oil and vinegar dressing
Salt
Black peppercorns

pesto chicken

2 ounces (¹/₂ cup) whole wheat fettuccine
Salt and freshly ground black pepper to taste
³/₄ pound boneless, skinless chicken breast
¹/₄ cup store-bought pesto

Bring a large saucepan of water to a boil. Add the pasta and boil for 8 minutes, or according to the package instructions. Do not overcook. Drain, leaving about 3 tablespoons of pasta water on the pasta. Divide between 2 dinner plates and season with salt and pepper to taste.

Remove all visible fat from the chicken and pound the breast flat with the palm of your hand or a heavy pan to about ½ inch thick. Set a nonstick skillet over a medium-high heat and add the chicken. Brown for 2 minutes on each side, seasoning the cooked sides with salt and pepper. Lower the heat to medium and sauté for another minute. Spoon the pesto over the chicken. Remove the skillet from the heat. Cover and let sit for 1 minute. Divide the chicken and spoon over the pasta to serve.
Makes 2 servings.

One serving: 427 calories, 57g protein, 6g carbohydrate, 20g fat (5g saturated), 154mg cholesterol, 416mg sodium, 2g fiber

steamed artichokes

2 medium artichokes
2 tablespoons no-sugar-added oil and vinegar dressing

Cut the stem off the artichokes as close to the base as possible. Cut off the top quarter and prickly points of visible leaves. Slice the artichokes in half from top to stem. Scrape out the fuzzy chokes with a spoon. Remove the small inner leaves (they're usually purple) and discard. Fill a large nonstick skillet with 1 inch of water, place the artichokes cut-side down and bring to the boil. Cover and boil for 20 minutes. Check after the first 10 minutes, and add more water if needed.

Alternatively, to cook artichokes in the microwave, set the artichokes in a deep, microwave-safe bowl. Add 1/2 cup water, cover the bowl with plastic wrap and microwave for 7–8 minutes on high, giving the bowl a quarter turn halfway through the cooking time. Allow to stand for 5 minutes.

The artichokes are done when a petal pulls off easily. Remove the cooked artichokes from the pan and place on 2 plates. Place the dressing in 2 small bowls on the side and use as dipping sauce for the artichoke leaves and hearts.
Makes 2 servings.

One serving: 181 calories, 6g protein, 25g carbohydrate, 9g fat (1g saturated), 0mg cholesterol, 233mg sodium, 0g fiber

fresh figs

4 medium figs

Divide the figs between 2 plates and serve.
Makes 2 servings.

One serving: 74 calories, 1g protein, 19g carbohydrate, 0.5g fat (0g saturated), 0mg cholesterol, 0mg sodium, 3g fiber

grilled scallops parmigiana

helpful hints

● Buy good quality Parmesan cheese and grate it yourself. Freeze extra for quick use later—simply spoon out what you need and leave the rest frozen.

● Any type of berries can be used.

● To save cleaning an extra skillet, use the same one to cook the spinach and zucchini.

● The spinach and zucchini can be cooked in a microwave oven. Place in separate microwave-safe bowls and microwave the spinach on high for 2–3 minutes and the zucchini on high for 3–4 minutes. Toss the zucchini with olive oil and lemon juice; season with salt and pepper to taste.

countdown

● Preheat oven to 350 degrees.

● Start scallops.

● Make spinach.

● Make zucchini.

● Complete scallops.

Sweet, juicy scallops are easy to cook. The secret to this meal is buying fresh, good quality scallops. ● These baked Parmesan scallops take only 15 minutes to make, and the zucchini can be cooked while the scallops bake, so the entire meal can be prepared in 15–20 minutes. ● Scallops are readily available. You can use any type for this recipe. If you buy small scallops, then bake them for only 10 minutes.

grilled scallops parmigiana

³/₄ pound large scallops, rinsed

¹/₄ cup white wine

2 teaspoons olive oil

4 cups washed, ready-to-eat fresh spinach

³/₄ cup freshly grated Parmesan cheese

Salt and freshly ground black pepper to taste

Preheat the oven to 350 degrees. Place the scallops in a small baking dish just large enough to hold the scallops in one layer. Add the wine, tossing to coat the scallops. Bake for 15 minutes. While the scallops are baking, heat the oil in a medium-sized nonstick skillet over a medium-high heat. Add the spinach, and sauté for 2–3 minutes, or until wilted. Spoon onto 2 dinner plates. Remove the scallops from the oven and turn on the broiler. When the broiler is hot, sprinkle Parmesan cheese over the scallops and place under the broiler for 1 minute, or until golden. Watch them carefully, as they will brown very quickly. Season with salt and pepper to taste. Spoon over the spinach and serve.
Makes 2 servings.

One serving: 286 calories, 37g protein, 9g carbohydrate, 10g fat (3g saturated), 63mg cholesterol, 573mg sodium, 4g fiber

lemon-pepper zucchini

2 teaspoons olive oil

¹/₂ pound zucchini, sliced (about 2 cups)

2 tablespoons freshly squeezed lemon juice (1 lemon)

¹/₄ teaspoon freshly ground black pepper

Salt to taste

In the skillet used for the spinach, heat the oil over a medium-high heat. Add the zucchini and sauté for 5 minutes. Toss with the lemon juice and pepper. Season with salt to taste. Serve with the scallops.
Makes 2 servings.

One serving: 62 calories, 2g protein, 5g carbohydrate, 5g fat (1g saturated), 0mg cholesterol, 4mg sodium, 1g fiber

kiwi-berry jumble

2 kiwis, peeled and cubed
1 cup fresh raspberries

Combine the kiwi cubes and the raspberries.
Spoon into 2 dessert bowls and serve.
Makes 2 servings.

One serving: 77 calories, 1g protein,
18g carbohydrate, 1g fat (0g saturated),
0mg cholesterol, 4mg sodium, 3g fiber

shopping list

TO BUY:
  ¾ pound large scallops
  1 small bottle dry white wine
  *1 bag washed, ready-to-eat
    fresh spinach*
  ½ pound zucchini
  2 lemons
  2 kiwis
  1 container fresh raspberries
STAPLES:
  Olive oil
  Parmesan cheese
  Salt
  Black peppercorns

breaded veal cutlets

This meal takes only 15 minutes to make. ● *The breading adds flavor and keeps the veal moist.*

breaded veal cutlets

1/2 pound veal cutlets
Salt and freshly ground black pepper to taste
1 tablespoon fresh oregano or 2 teaspoons dried
1/4 cup plain bread crumbs, whole wheat if possible
2 egg whites, lightly beaten
2 teaspoons olive oil

Sprinkle both sides of the veal cutlets with a little salt and pepper. Combine the oregano with the bread crumbs on a plate. Roll the veal in the bread crumb mixture, coating well. Dip the veal into the egg whites. Roll the veal in the bread crumbs again. Heat the oil in a nonstick skillet over a medium-high heat. Sauté the veal for 1 minute, turn and sauté for 2 more minutes. Season with salt and pepper and serve with the spaghetti and spinach.
Makes 2 servings.

One serving: 314 calories, 34g protein, 3g carbohydrate, 17g fat (8g saturated), 100mg cholesterol, 155mg sodium, 0g fiber

spaghetti

2 ounces (1/2 cup) thin whole wheat spaghetti
1/2 cup no-sugar-added pasta sauce

Bring a large saucepan filled with water to a boil. Add the spaghetti and boil for 5 minutes, or according to the package instructions. Do not overcook. Drain, leaving about 3 tablespoons of water in the pan. Return the spaghetti to the pan, add the sauce and toss well.
Makes 2 servings.

One serving: 163 calories, 8g protein, 29g carbohydrate, 1g fat (1g saturated), 0mg cholesterol, 208mg sodium, 5g fiber

parmesan spinach

8 cups washed, ready-to-eat fresh spinach
2 tablespoons freshly grated Parmesan cheese
Salt and freshly ground black pepper to taste

Place the spinach in a microwave-safe bowl and microwave on high for 6 minutes. Or, place the spinach in a saucepan over a medium heat. Do not add water: the spinach will release enough of its own liquid. Cover and cook until the spinach is wilted, about 5 minutes, making sure it does not burn. Add the Parmesan cheese and season with salt and pepper.
Makes 2 servings.

One serving: 74 calories, 9g protein, 8g carbohydrate, 3g fat (1g saturated), 4mg cholesterol, 278mg sodium, 7g fiber

garlic shrimp stir-fry

Garlic, cashew nuts, and sesame oil flavor this quick shrimp dinner. ● *The cooking time for this dinner is about 8 minutes.* ● *Use the helpful hint suggestions for quick preparation of the ingredients to make this a complete 15-minute meal.*

garlic shrimp stir-fry

2 tablespoons low-salt soy sauce

2 tablespoons rice vinegar

2 tablespoons chopped fresh ginger

6 medium-sized garlic cloves, crushed

Several drops hot pepper sauce

4 teaspoons sesame oil

2 slices yellow onion

½ medium-sized red bell pepper, sliced (1 cup)

¾ pound medium shrimp, shelled and deveined

½ pound snow peas, trimmed (2 cups)

2 tablespoons cashews

Combine the soy sauce, rice vinegar, ginger, garlic, and hot sauce in a small bowl. Make sure all ingredients are prepared and ready for cooking.

Heat the sesame oil in a wok or skillet over a high heat. When the oil is smoking, add the onion and red bell pepper. Stir-fry for 3 minutes. Add the shrimp and snow peas and stir-fry for 2 minutes. Add the cashews and sauce and continue to stir-fry, tossing continuously for 2 minutes. Add salt to taste. Divide between 2 plates and serve.

Makes 2 servings.

One serving: 411 calories, 41g protein, 21g carbohydrate, 18g fat (3g saturated), 260mg cholesterol, 944mg sodium, 2g fiber

helpful hints

● *Buy shelled shrimp—it is well worth the time otherwise spent shelling them yourself.*

● *Washed and sliced cabbage can be used instead of the Chinese cabbage, but should be microwaved for 1 minute first.*

● *To chop fresh ginger quickly, cut it into small cubes and press through a garlic press with large holes. If using a press with small holes, just capture the juice that is squeezed out; it will give enough flavor for the recipe.*

● *If rice vinegar is unavailable, substitute 1 tablespoon water mixed with 1 tablespoon distilled white wine vinegar.*

● *To keep from having to look back at the recipe as you stir-fry the ingredients, line them up on a chopping board or plate in the order of use so you know which ingredient comes next.*

● *For crisp, not steamed, stir-fried vegetables, start with a very hot wok or skillet. Let the vegetables sit a minute before tossing to allow the wok to regain its heat.*

garlic shrimp stir-fry continued

chinese cabbage and bean sprouts

1 cup thinly sliced Chinese
   cabbage (Napa cabbage)
1 cup fresh bean sprouts
2 tablespoons low-carbohydrate
   miso dressing

Place the cabbage and bean sprouts in a
small bowl and toss with dressing. Serve with
the stir-fry.
Makes 2 servings.

One serving: 73 calories, 5g protein,
8g carbohydrate, 3g fat (0.5g saturated),
0mg cholesterol, 321mg sodium, 1g fiber

countdown

● *Prepare ingredients.*
● *Make cabbage and*
bean sprouts.
● *Make shrimp stir-fry.*

shopping list

TO BUY:
   ³/4 pound medium shrimp,
      shelled and deveined
   1 small package cashew nuts
      (1 ounce needed)
   1 small bottle sesame oil
   1 small bottle low-
      carbohydrate miso dressing
   1 small bottle rice vinegar
   1 medium-sized red bell
      pepper
   1 small piece fresh ginger
   ¹/2 pound fresh snow peas
   1 small head Chinese cabbage
      (Chinese leaves)
   1 small package fresh bean
      sprouts
STAPLES:
   Yellow onion
   Garlic
   Hot pepper sauce
   Low-salt soy sauce

sole amandine

Sole Amandine, a French classic, appears on menus at French restaurants, from the most elegant to simple brasseries. Dressed up or down, lemon juice and almonds are all the fillet of sole needs to give it a wonderful flavor. ● This quick dinner takes only 10 minutes to make. It's a perfect mid-week meal when you're on the run.

sole amandine

³/₄ pound sole fillet

4 teaspoons olive oil

Salt and freshly ground black pepper to taste

2 tablespoons slivered almonds

2 tablespoons freshly squeezed lemon juice (1 lemon)

2 tablespoons freshly chopped parsley (optional)

Rinse the sole and pat dry with paper towel. Heat the oil in a medium-sized nonstick skillet over a medium-high heat. Sauté the fish for 2 minutes on each side. Remove to 2 plates, season with salt and pepper to taste, and cover with foil to keep warm. Add the almonds to the same skillet and sauté until slightly golden, about 1 minute. Sprinkle the fish with lemon juice, almonds, and parsley and serve. *Makes 2 servings.*

One serving: 264 calories, 28g protein, 4g carbohydrate. 17g fat (2g saturated), 60mg cholesterol, 98mg sodium, 1g fiber

quick lima beans

2 cups frozen baby lima beans

2 teaspoons olive oil

Salt and freshly ground black pepper to taste

Defrost the lima beans. Bring a small pot of water to a boil. Add the beans, cook for 1 minute, and drain. Alternatively place in a microwave-safe dish and heat on high for 2 minutes. Add the oil to the same skillet used for the fish and sauté for 1 minute. Season with salt and pepper and serve. *Makes 2 servings.*

One serving: 154 calories, 7g protein, 21g carbohydrate, 5g fat (1g saturated), 0mg cholesterol, 3mg sodium, 4g fiber

grilled tomatoes

2 medium tomatoes, halved

Salt and freshly ground black pepper to taste

Preheat the broiler. Season the tomato halves with salt and pepper. Broil for 4 minutes and serve with the fish and beans. *Makes 2 servings.*

One serving: 25 calories, 2g protein, 5g carbohydrate, 0g fat (0g saturated), 0mg cholesterol, 10mg sodium, 0g fiber

helpful hints

● *Any type of non-oily fish fillet can be used.*

● *To save washing another skillet, use the same skillet for the fish and lima beans.*

countdown

● *Preheat broiler or toaster oven.*

● *Make fish.*

● *Make lima beans.*

● *Make salad.*

shopping list

TO BUY:

³/₄ pound sole fillet

1 small package slivered almonds (1 ounce needed)

1 small package frozen baby lima beans

1 lemon

1 small bunch parsley (optional)

2 medium tomatoes

STAPLES:

Olive oil

Salt

Black peppercorns

smothered steak with caramelized onions

helpful hints

- Beef fillet, sirloin, round, skirt, or flank steak can also be used.
- Fresh pineapple cubes are available in the produce sections of most supermarkets.
- Any type of lettuce can be used.

countdown

- Preheat broiler.
- Make steak.
- Make salad.
- Assemble pineapple.

Caramelized onions, mushrooms, and garlic are perfect toppings for steak. There's no reason to shy away from enjoying a steak if you pick a lean cut. ● Here it is served with succulent artichoke hearts and followed by a simple pineapple dessert.

smothered steak with caramelized onions

10 ounces strip steak, visible fat removed
Olive oil spray
1 cup red onion, sliced
$1/2$ cup fat-free, low-salt chicken broth
4 medium-sized garlic cloves, crushed
$1/2$ pound portobello mushrooms, sliced
Salt and freshly ground black pepper to taste

Line a baking tray with foil and place under the broiler. Spray the steak with oil on both sides and set aside. Heat a small nonstick skillet over a medium-high heat and add the onion. Sauté for 1 minute. Add the chicken broth, cover with a lid, and cook over a high heat for 3 minutes. Uncover and cook for another minute, or until all of the liquid has evaporated. Add the garlic and mushrooms and sauté for 2 minutes. Season with salt and pepper to taste. Remove the hot baking tray from the broiler and place the steak on tray. Grill for 4 minutes for a 1-inch thick steak, another 4 minutes for thicker steak and 2 minutes for a thinner one. Turn the steak and season the cooked side. Transfer the steak to 2 plates, smother with the onion and mushrooms, and serve.
Makes 2 servings.

One serving: 365 calories, 53g protein, 10g carbohydrate, 14g fat (6g saturated), 127mg cholesterol, 237mg sodium, 0g fiber

hearts of palm salad

Several red lettuce leaves, washed and torn into bite-sized pieces

1/2 cup canned or jarred hearts of palm, drained and sliced thinly

2 tablespoons no-sugar-added oil and vinegar dressing

Place the lettuce on 2 plates and top with the hearts of palm. Drizzle with salad dressing and serve.

Makes 2 servings.

One serving: 90 calories, 1g protein, 3g carbohydrate, 9g fat (1g saturated), 0mg cholesterol, 234mg sodium, 1g fibre

pineapple kabobs

1 tablespoon ground cinnamon

2 (.035-ounce) envelopes sugar substitute

2 cups pineapple cubes

2 skewers

Line a baking tray with foil. Mix the cinnamon and sugar substitute together in a medium-sized bowl. Toss the pineapple cubes in the mixture, making sure all sides are coated. Thread the cubes onto 2 skewers and place on the baking tray. Broil 6–7 inches from the heat for 5 minutes. Turn the skewers over and broil for an additional 3 minutes. Serve warm.

Makes 2 servings.

One serving: 86 calories, 1g protein, 23g carbohydrate, 1g fat (0g saturated), 0mg cholesterol, 3mg sodium, 2g fiber

shopping list

TO BUY:

10 ounces strip steak

1 can or jar hearts of palm

1/2 pound portobello mushrooms

1 small head red lettuce leaves

1 package fresh pineapple cubes

STAPLES:

Garlic

Red onion

Olive oil spray

No-sugar-added oil and vinegar dressing

Fat-free, low-salt chicken broth

Ground cinnamon

Sugar substitute

Salt

Black peppercorns

whisky pork chops

Whisky lends an intriguing flavor to this simple French pork dish. This is a hearty meal and takes about 30–40 minutes to make from start to finish. ● *Enjoy it with full-flavored rosemary lentils and beetroot salad, followed by a refreshing cinnamon grapefruit.*

whisky pork chops

2 teaspoons olive oil
2 (5-ounce) boneless, centre loin
    pork chops, visible fat removed
1/2 cup whisky
1/2 cup fat-free, low-salt chicken
    broth
2 tablespoons Dijon mustard
Salt and freshly ground black
    pepper to taste

Heat the oil in a medium-sized nonstick skillet over a medium-high heat. Add the pork chops and brown for 2 minutes on both sides. Pour off excess fat. Add the whisky and flambé: if cooking over gas, warm the whisky in the pan for a few seconds and then tip the pan to let the flame ignite the liquid. Immediately remove from the heat and let the flame burn down. If you cook with electric heat, then throw a lighted match into the warmed whisky. Be sure to remove the match before serving.

Stir in the broth, cover, and lower the heat. Cook over a low heat for 3 minutes, or until the chops are cooked through and a meat thermometer registers 160 degrees. Remove the chops to a plate and cover with foil to keep warm. Add the mustard and blend in with the sauce. Cook for 1–2 minutes to reduce and slightly thicken. Season with salt and pepper to taste. Remove the chops to 2 plates, spoon the sauce over them and serve.
Makes 2 servings.

One serving: 448 calories, 42g protein,
1g carbohydrate, 12g fat (3g saturated),
133mg cholesterol, 596mg sodium, 0g fiber

helpful hints

● *Lentils don't need to be soaked and will cook in about 20 minutes. Start them first so that they will be ready by the time the pork is finished.*

● *For safety's sake, when flambéing, keep the pan lid nearby to snuff out the flame if necessary.*

● *You can buy whisky in small splits at liquor stores.*

countdown

● *Start lentils.*
● *Preheat broiler.*
● *Make pork chops.*
● *Assemble salad.*
● *Make cinnamon grapefruit.*

rosemary lentils

1 cup fat-free, low-salt chicken
    broth
1 cup water
1/2 cup dried lentils
1/2 cup yellow onion, diced
2 teaspoons fresh rosemary or
    1 teaspoon dried
2 medium-sized garlic cloves,
    crushed
Salt and freshly ground black
    pepper to taste
1/4 cup chopped fresh parsley

Bring the broth and water to a rolling boil in a medium-sized pot. Add the lentils, onion, rosemary, and garlic slowly, so that the water does not stop boiling. Reduce the heat to medium, cover with a lid and simmer for 20 minutes. Remove the lid and continue to cook over a high heat, until any remaining liquid has been absorbed. Season, sprinkle with fresh parsley, and serve with the pork.
Makes 2 servings.

One serving: 85 calories, 7g protein, 15g carbohydrate, 0.5g fat (0g saturated), 0mg cholesterol, 285mg sodium, 2g fiber

beet salad

2 cups canned beets, sliced
2 tablespoons distilled white
    vinegar
2 (.035-ounce) envelopes sugar
    substitute

Place the sliced beets on 2 salad plates. Combine the vinegar and sugar substitute, spoon over the beets and serve.
Makes 2 servings.

One serving: 58 calories. 2g protein, 15g carbohydrate, 0g fat (0g saturated), 0mg cholesterol, 285mg sodium, 0g fiber

cinnamon grapefruit

1 grapefruit
1/2 teaspoon cinnamon
2 (0.035-ounce) envelopes sugar
    substitute

Preheat the broiler. Line a baking tray with foil or use a small oven-to-table dish. Peel the grapefruit over a bowl to catch the juice. With a serrated knife, cut the grapefruit into 1/2-inch slices (as you would slice a tomato). Place in a single layer in the dish. Sprinkle with the cinnamon and broil for 3 minutes. Mix the sugar substitute into the grapefruit juice, and spoon over the broiled grapefruit before serving.
Makes 2 servings.

One serving: 40 calories, 1g protein, 11g carbohydrate, 0g fat (0g saturated), 0mg cholesterol, 0mg sodium, 1g fiber

shopping list

TO BUY:
  2 (5-ounce) boneless, center
      loin pork chops
  1 small bottle whisky
  1 package cooked beetroots
  1 small package red lentils
  1 small bunch fresh parsley
  1 small bunch fresh rosemary
      or 1 jar dried
  1 grapefruit
STAPLES:
  Yellow onion
  Garlic
  Olive oil
  Distilled white vinegar
  Fat free, low-salt chicken
      broth
  Dijon mustard
  Ground cinnamon
  Sugar substitute
  Salt
  Black peppercorns

seared sesame tuna

helpful hints

● *To chop fresh ginger quickly, cut it into small cubes and press through a garlic press with large holes. If using a press with small holes, just capture the juice that is squeezed out; it will give enough flavor for the recipe.*

● *To save clean-up time, cook the tuna first, then remove and stir-fry the bok choy and pasta in the same wok.*

● *To keep from having to look back at the recipe as you stir-fry the ingredients, line them up on a chopping board or plate in the order of use so you know which ingredient comes next.*

● *For crisp, not steamed, stir-fried vegetables, start with a very hot wok or skillet. Let the vegetables sit a minute before tossing to allow the wok to regain its heat.*

Seared tuna coated with black and white sesame seeds is served in many restaurants, but you can make it at home in minutes. ● *Taste can vary considerably among the species of tuna. The yellowfin and blackfin tuna are more delicately flavored and particularly worth looking for.* ● *Black sesame seeds are available in some supermarkets. You can use either all white sesame seeds or a combination of both.* ● *A side dish of bok choy and shiitake noodles completes this Oriental-style meal.*

seared sesame tuna

10 ounces fresh tuna steak
3 tablespoons sesame seeds
4 teaspoons olive oil
Salt and freshly ground black
   pepper to taste

Rinse the tuna and pat dry with paper towel. Spoon the sesame seeds over both sides of the tuna, pressing the seeds into the fish with the back of a spoon. Heat the oil in a wok or nonstick skillet over a high heat. When the oil begins to smoke, add the tuna. Brown for 1 minute, then turn. Brown for another minute, then lower the heat to medium-high. Cook for another 3–4 minutes. Season with salt and pepper to taste. The tuna should be seared outside and just barely warm inside. Immediately remove from the pan to slow the cooking process. Cut the tuna in half, divide between 2 plates and serve.
Makes 2 servings.

One serving: 353 calories, 36g protein, 1g carbohydrate, 23g fat (4g saturated), 53mg cholesterol, 60mg sodium, 0g fiber

stir-fry bok choy with shiitake noodles

2 ounces (¹/₂ cup) whole wheat
   thin spaghetti

2 tablespoons low-salt soy sauce

2 tablespoons dry sherry

2 tablespoons water

4 medium-sized garlic cloves,
   crushed

2-in piece fresh ginger, peeled and
   chopped (2 tablespoons)

2 teaspoons olive oil

¹/₄ pound bok choy, sliced
   (2 cups)

¹/₄ pound shiitake mushrooms,
   sliced (2 cups)

4 scallions, sliced (¹/₂ cup)

Salt and freshly ground black
   pepper to taste

Bring a large saucepan filled with water to a boil.
Add the spaghetti and boil for 5 minutes, or
according to the package instructions. Do not
overcook. Drain.

Combine the soy sauce, sherry, water, garlic,
and ginger in a small bowl. Make sure all
ingredients are prepared and ready for the wok.

Heat the oil until smoking in the same wok or
skillet used for tuna. Add the spaghetti, bok
choy, and mushrooms. Stir-fry for 2 minutes.
Draw to the sides of the wok, leaving a well in
the middle. Add the sauce and toss with the
vegetables for 2 minutes. Add the scallions, and
season with salt and pepper to taste. Toss well.
Spoon onto plates with the tuna.
Makes 2 servings.

One serving: 273 calories, 10g protein,
38g carbohydrate, 6g fat (1g saturated),
0mg cholesterol, 629mg sodium, 6g fiber

countdown

- *Prepare all ingredients.*
- *Boil pasta.*
- *Make tuna in wok and
  remove.*
- *Stir-fry bok choy and
  pasta.*

shopping list

TO BUY:

   10 ounces fresh tuna steak

   1 small jar sesame seeds
      (white, black, or
      combination)

   1 box whole wheat thin
      spaghetti (2 ounces
      needed)

   1 small bottle dry sherry

   1 small bok choy (¹/₄ pound
      needed)

   1 container shiitake
      mushrooms (¹/₄ pound
      needed)

   1 small bunch scallions
      (4 needed)

   2-inch piece fresh ginger

STAPLES:

   Garlic

   Olive oil

   Low-salt soy sauce

   Salt

   Black peppercorns

chicken provençal

The mild, warm climate and bright sun of the South of France nurture the colorful array of Provençal ingredients. Ripe tomatoes, garlic, olives, and fresh herbs delicately spice the cuisine of this region. Memories of meals we had in Provence inspired this dinner.
● Anchovies are used as a base for the chicken sauce. They practically melt to nothing when sautéed, yet give the sauce a rich flavor. Be sure to rinse them well before cooking to remove most of the salt. ● Serve with brown rice and a salad of endive and watercress.

helpful hints

- *Fresh thyme gives the dish a sweet flavor, though dried can be used.*
- *If using dried spices, make sure they are less than 6 months old.*
- *Any type of tomatoes can be substituted for plum tomatoes.*
- *The quickest way to wash watercress is to place it head first into a bowl of water. Leave for a minute, then lift out and shake dry, leaving dirt and grit behind.*
- *To give chicken a crisp texture, make sure the skillet is very hot before browning.*
- *I call for regular brown rice instead of quick-cooking brown rice because it contains more nutrients. If you're really pressed for time, the quick-cooking brown rice works fine.*
- *I like to cook my rice like pasta, using a pan of boiling water that's large enough for the rice to roll freely. Use the method given here or follow the directions on the package.*

chicken provençal

³/₄ pound boneless, skinless chicken breast
¹/₂ medium-sized red onion, diced (1 cup)
4 anchovy fillets packed in olive oil, rinsed
4 medium plum tomatoes, diced (1¹/₂ cups)
2 medium-sized garlic cloves, crushed
2 tablespoons fresh thyme leaves or 2 teaspoons dried
1 teaspoon balsamic vinegar
2 teaspoons olive oil
8 pitted black olives, halved
Freshly ground black pepper to taste

Remove any visible fat from the chicken. Set a nonstick skillet over a medium-high heat. Add the chicken and onion. Brown the chicken for 2 minutes on each side. While the chicken browns, add the anchovies and mash them with the back of your cooking spoon. Lower the heat and add the tomatoes, garlic, and thyme. Cover and simmer for 5 minutes. Divide the chicken between 2 plates. Stir the sauce and add the vinegar, oil, and black olives. Season with pepper. Spoon the sauce over the chicken.
Makes 2 servings.

> One serving: 416 calories, 62g protein, 31g carbohydrate, 16g fat (3g saturated), 144mg cholesterol, 585mg sodium, 2g fiber

brown rice

¹/₂ cup brown rice
Salt and freshly ground black pepper to taste

Rinse the rice and place in a large saucepan. Fill with water and bring to a boil. Boil for 30 minutes. Drain and season to taste. Divide between 2 plates and place the chicken and sauce on top.
Makes 2 servings.

> One serving: 85 calories, 3g protein, 18g carbohydrate, 1g fat (0g saturated), 0mg cholesterol, 0mg sodium, 1g fiber

endive and watercress salad

2 small heads Belgian endive

1 small bunch fresh watercress, stemmed and washed

2 tablespoons no-sugar-added oil and vinegar dressing

Salt and freshly ground black pepper to taste

Wipe the endives with a damp paper towel. Remove 1 inch from the bases. Cut the leaves crosswise into 1-inch slices. Place in a small bowl. Break the watercress into smaller pieces and add to the bowl. Drizzle dressing over the top and season with salt and pepper to taste. Serve.

Makes 2 servings.

One serving: 87 calories, 1g protein, 2g carbohydrate, 9g fat (2g saturated), 0mg cholesterol, 101mg sodium, 0g fiber

countdown

- Make rice.
- Make chicken.
- Make salad.

shopping list

TO BUY:

3/4 pound boneless, skinless chicken breast

1 container pitted black olives

1 small package brown rice

1 tin anchovy fillets packed in olive oil

4 medium plum tomatoes

1 bunch fresh thyme or 1 jar dried

2 small heads Belgian endive

1 small bunch watercress

STAPLES:

Red onion

Garlic

Olive oil

Balsamic vinegar

No-sugar-added oil and vinegar dressing

Salt

Black peppercorns

mussels marinière

Imagine eating on the quay in Deauville, France, watching the fishing boats come in, breathing the fresh sea air, and drinking a glass of chilled white wine. What a treat! Moules à la Marinière, or Mussels in White Wine, is a French dish normally enjoyed in these quaint surroundings. If you can't go to France, prepare this dish for an experience almost as satisfying! It takes less than 15 minutes to prepare, never mind the fabulous taste. ● *Store mussels in the refrigerator. When ready for use, carefully scrub them with a vegetable brush under cold water. Scrape off the beard or thin hairs along the shell. Their shells should be tightly closed or snap shut when tapped. Discard any that do not close.* ● *Serve the mussels in large soup bowls with the reduced broth.*

helpful hint

- *The onion, celery, and carrots can be sautéed ahead of time. Cook the mussels in wine just before serving.*

countdown

- *Prepare ingredients.*
- *Cook vegetables.*
- *Add mussels.*

shopping list

TO BUY:

  2 pounds mussels

  1 small bottle dry white wine

  1 small bunch fresh parsley

  1 bag washed, ready-to-eat young salad leaves

STAPLES:

  Celery

  Yellow onion

  Carrots

  Olive oil

  No-sugar-added oil and vinegar dressing

  Multigrain bread

  Black peppercorns

mussels marinière

2 teaspoons olive oil

1/2 cup sliced yellow onion

2 celery stalks, sliced (1 cup)

2 medium carrots, sliced (1 cup)

1/2 cup dry white wine

Freshly ground black pepper to taste

2 pounds mussels

1/2 cup fresh parsley, chopped

2 slices multigrain bread

Heat the oil in a large saucepan over a medium-high heat. Sauté the onion, celery, and carrots until they start to cook but not color, about 5 minutes. Add the wine and freshly ground pepper to taste. Add the mussels and cover tightly with a lid. Bring to a boil and let boil for about 3 more minutes. The wine will boil up over the mussels causing them to open. As soon as they open, remove the pan from the heat. Do not over cook.

    Lift the mussels out of the pan with a slotted spoon and divide between 2 large soup bowls. Discard any closed mussels—do not try to force them open. Sprinkle with parsley and serve. Meanwhile, bring the liquid to the boil and reduce rapidly by half. Ladle out the reduced broth to serve, leaving ¼ inch of the broth in the pan—it may have some sand from the mussels in it. Serve with bread to dip in the broth.

Makes 2 servings.

> One serving: 374 calories, 33g protein, 31g carbohydrate, 11g fat (1g saturated), 64mg cholesterol, 861mg sodium, 5g fiber

mesclun salad

4 cups washed, ready-to-eat mesclun salad or field greens

2 tablespoons no-sugar-added oil and vinegar dressing

Toss the salad leaves with the dressing.

Makes 2 servings.

> 8g fat (1g saturated), 0mg cholesterol, 81mg sodium, 0g fiber

spicy crab and vegetable stir-fry

Oriental spices give this crab a zesty tang. In Vietnam this dish is normally made with whole crab claws in the shell. I have simplified the shopping and cooking by using canned or frozen crab. ● This entire meal is made in a wok. A nonstick skillet can also be used and you will still achieve a good result. ● Lemongrass has long, thin, green-gray leaves with a scallion-like base. Slice the end off the bulb and cut slices up to the woody part of the stem. Grated lemon rind can be substituted. ● Follow with an indulgent-tasting parfait for dessert.

spicy crab and vegetable stir-fry

2 (6½-ounce) cans backfin lump crabmeat, drained

¼ cup tomato paste

½ teaspoon hot pepper sauce

½ cup water

2 (.035-ounce) envelopes sugar substitute

4 teaspoons canola oil

¼ cup chopped shallots

2 medium-sized garlic cloves, crushed

2 tablespoons chopped fresh ginger or 2 teaspoons ground ginger

4 stalks lemongrass, sliced, or grated rind from 2 lemons

½ pound fresh bean sprouts (3 cups)

½ pound snow peas, trimmed (2 cups)

2 tablespoons unsalted, roasted peanuts, chopped

Flake the crabmeat with a fork into a medium-sized bowl, looking carefully for any shell or cartilage that might remain. Combine the tomato paste, hot pepper sauce, water, and sugar substitute in a small bowl and set aside. Make sure all ingredients are prepared and ready for stir-frying. Heat the oil in a wok or skillet over a high heat until smoking. Add the shallots, garlic, ginger, and lemongrass and stir-fry for 2 minutes. Add the bean sprouts and snow peas. Stir-fry for another 2 minutes. Add the crab and stir-fry for 3 more minutes.

Push the ingredients to the sides of the pan leaving a well in the centre. Add the sauce and toss with the ingredients for an additional minute. Remove to 2 plates, sprinkle with peanuts and serve.

Makes 2 servings.

One serving: 493 calories, 52g protein, 25g carbohydrate, 23g fat (3g saturated), 144mg cholesterol, 694mg sodium, 4g fiber

helpful hints

● Use a food processor to chop the shallots and peanuts.

● To chop fresh ginger quickly, cut it into small cubes and press through a garlic press with large holes. If using a press with small holes, just capture the juice that is squeezed out; it will give enough flavor for the recipe.

● If using ground ginger instead of fresh, add it to the sauce.

● To keep from having to look back at the recipe as you stir-fry the ingredients, line them up on a chopping board or plate in the order of use so you know which ingredient comes next.

● For crisp, not steamed, stir-fried vegetables, start with a very hot wok or skillet. Let the vegetables sit a minute before tossing to allow the wok to regain its heat.

● Any type of berries can be used.

● Any flavor of light yogurt can be used.

● Be careful toasting the pecans, as they burn easily.

spicy crab and vegetable stir-fry continued

continued

countdown

- *Prepare all ingredients*
- *Stir-fry crab dish.*
- *Prepare parfait.*

shopping list

TO BUY:

1 pot light white chocolate–strawberry flavored yogurt

2 (6¹/₂-ounce) tinned or frozen sweet crabmeat

1 tube tomato paste

1 small package roasted peanuts (1 ounce needed)

1 small package pecans (¹/₂ ounce needed)

2 large shallots

1 small piece fresh ginger or 1 jar ground

1 small bunch lemongrass (4 stalks needed)

¹/₂ pound fresh bean sprouts

¹/₂ pound snow peas

1 container fresh raspberries

STAPLES:

Garlic

Canola oil

Hot pepper sauce

Sugar substitute

raspberry parfait

¹/₄ pound fresh raspberries

2 (0.035-ounce) envelopes sugar substitute

1 cup light, white chocolate–strawberry yogurt

6 pecan pieces, toasted (1 tablespoon)

Purée the raspberries in a food processor and blend in the sugar substitute. Scoop half the yogurt into 2 bowls or parfait glasses. Pour in half the sauce and top with the remaining yogurt. Pour the remaining sauce over the yogurt and top with the toasted pecans.

Refrigerate until ready to serve.

Makes 2 servings.

> One serving: 110 calories, 5g protein, 15g carbohydrate, 4g fat (0.5g saturated), 3mg cholesterol, 58mg sodium, 2g fiber

neapolitan steak

The Italian city of Naples claims pizza as its symbol. The same earthy flavors they use in their popular topping go with steak. Here is a quick version of the zesty, tomato-based sauce that can be made in 20 minutes for a great, quick, mid-week supper. ● *Continue the Italian theme with side dishes of Parmesan linguine and Italian greens.*

neapolitan steak

1/2 pound flank or skirt steak, visible fat removed

1 cup no-sugar-added canned, peeled plum tomatoes

1/4 cup yellow onion, diced

2 medium-sized garlic cloves, crushed

2 teaspoons dried oregano

1 teaspoon balsamic vinegar

2 teaspoons olive oil

8 pitted black olives, halved

2 (.035-ounce) envelopes sugar substitute

Salt and freshly ground black pepper to taste

Set a medium-sized nonstick skillet over a medium-high heat. Brown the steak for 2 minutes on each side. Lower the heat and continue to cook for 3–4 minutes. Remove the steak to a plate and cover with foil or another plate to keep warm. Lower the heat and add the tomatoes, onion, garlic, and oregano. Cover and simmer for 5 minutes. Stir in the vinegar, oil, black olives and sugar substitute. Season with salt and pepper to taste. Remove from the heat, slice the steak and serve with the sauce on top. *Makes 2 servings.*

One serving: 336 calories, 42g protein, 10g carbohydrate, 16g fat (6g saturated), 101mg cholesterol, 240mg sodium, 4g fiber

parmesan linguine

2 ounces (1/2 cup) whole wheat linguine or spaghetti

2 teaspoons olive oil

Salt and freshly ground black pepper to taste

2 tablespoons freshly grated Parmesan cheese

Bring a large saucepan filled with water to the boil. Add the pasta and cook for 8 minutes, or according to the package instructions. Do not overcook. Drain, leaving 3 tablespoons of water on the pasta, and toss with oil. Season with salt and pepper to taste and sprinkle with Parmesan cheese. Serve with the steak. *Makes 2 servings.*

One serving: 208 calories, 9g protein, 26g carbohydrate, 6g fat (2g saturated), 4mg cholesterol, 113mg sodium, 5g fiber

helpful hints

● *Make sure the dried oregano is less than 6 months old.*

● *Any type of washed, ready-to-eat salad leaves can be used.*

● *Buy good quality Parmesan cheese and grate it yourself. Freeze extra for quick use later—simply spoon out what you need and leave the rest frozen.*

countdown

● *Begin boiling water for pasta.*

● *Make salad.*

● *Make steak.*

● *Make pasta.*

neapolitan steak continued

italian greens

4 cups washed, ready-to-eat, Italian-style salad leaves

4 teaspoons balsamic vinegar

Salt and freshly ground black pepper to taste

Place the salad leaves in a bowl and sprinkle with balsamic vinegar. Add salt and pepper to taste and toss before serving.

Makes 2 servings.

One serving: 10 calories, 1g protein, 2g carbohydrate, 0g fat (0g saturated), 0mg cholesterol, 6mg sodium, 0g fiber

spicy chicken legs

Aromatic flavors of Chinese 5-spice powder make this dish a winner. It takes a little longer to cook this dish—about 30 minutes—but the flavor is worth it.
● Boneless, skinless chicken legs and thighs are now available. With the skin removed, the fat content is greatly reduced. Their richer-flavored meat make a nice alternative to boneless, skinless chicken breasts. ● This dish tastes great the second day. Make extra for another quick meal. ● Serve with a simple Chinese side dish, or garlic bean sprouts and rice.

spicy chicken legs

½ cup fat-free, low-salt chicken broth

¼ cup rice vinegar

1 teaspoon Chinese 5-spice powder

6 large garlic cloves, peeled

2 tablespoons low-salt soy sauce

½ cup water

2 teaspoons sesame oil

10 ounces boneless, skinless chicken legs or thighs, visible fat removed

¼ pound (2 cups) broccoli florets

½ pound sliced button mushrooms (3 cups)

Combine the chicken broth, vinegar, Chinese 5-spice, whole garlic cloves, soy sauce, and water in a small bowl. Make sure all ingredients are prepped and ready for stir-frying. Heat the oil in a wok or skillet over a high heat until smoking. Brown the chicken on all sides, about 2 minutes. Add the chicken broth mixture and reduce the heat to medium-low. Simmer gently for 15 minutes, turning the chicken several times. The liquid should be just at the bubbling stage. Add the broccoli and mushrooms and continue cooking for 5 minutes. The sauce will boil down to a glaze as the chicken cooks. Remove the garlic cloves. Spoon the completed dish into a bowl and cover with foil to keep warm.
Makes 2 servings.

One serving: 419 calories, 45g protein, 13g carbohydrate, 20g fat (4g saturated), 130mg cholesterol, 897mg sodium, 1g fiber

helpful hints

● *To save clean-up time, use the same wok or skillet for the chicken and the rice with bean sprouts.*

● *If Chinese 5-spice powder is unavailable you can make it at home by mixing equal measures of ground cinnamon, cloves, fennel seeds, star anise, and peppercorns.*

● *Distilled white vinegar diluted with a little water can be used instead of rice vinegar.*

● *To keep from having to look back at the recipe as you stir-fry the ingredients, line them up on a chopping board or plate in the order of use so you know which ingredient comes next.*

● *For crisp, not steamed, stir-fried vegetables, start with a very hot wok or skillet. Let the vegetables sit for a minute before tossing to allow the wok to regain its heat.*

countdown

● *Start rice.*
● *Place chicken on to cook.*
● *Complete bean sprouts and rice.*

spicy chicken legs continued

garlic bean sprouts and rice

1/2 cup brown rice

Salt and freshly ground black
pepper to taste

2 teaspoons sesame oil

2 cups fresh bean sprouts

2 medium-sized garlic cloves,
crushed

Rinse the rice and place in a large saucepan
filled with water. Bring to a boil and cook for 30
minutes. Drain and season with salt and pepper
to taste.

Again, make sure all ingredients are prepared
and ready for stir-frying. Place the wok over a
high heat and add the oil. Add the rice, bean
sprouts, and garlic, and sauté for 2–3 minutes.
Season with salt and pepper to taste. Place on 2
plates and spoon the stir-fried chicken and
vegetables on top.

Makes 2 servings.

One serving: 207 calories, 11g protein,
25g carbohydrate, 9g fat (1g saturated),
0mg cholesterol, 10mg sodium, 1g fiber

right carbs

introduction

You're now entering the third and permanent phase of the good-carb lifestyle: great food that's good for you, too. This balanced approach to eating incorporates high-fiber carbohydrates into breakfast, lunch, and dinner menus.

As with the other sections, I have organised the menus into a meal-at-a-glance chart with some easy and quick meals mid-week, alongside more elaborate ones for the weekends. They are arranged to give variety throughout the day and over the course of the week. The meals appear in the same order within the chapter. Just follow the meals in the order given for an easy two-week plan.

breakfast

The French Toast with Ham and the Ranchero Burrito are 2 of the 14 savory breakfasts you can choose from. Try them all to add variety to your morning repertoire.

lunch

Choose from the wide selection to fit any appetite. When you're in a hurry, grab a Baby Spinach, Mushroom, and Canadian Bacon Salad. Most restaurant menus will have a shrimp or tuna salad, or a pasta salad with turkey (or chicken). Make the recipe provided here and use it as a guide for proportions when eating out. When you have more time, enjoy Tomatoes Stuffed with Anchovies and Capers or Ham and Mushroom Pita Pizza.

dinner

Enjoy these meals in the proportions given, and you won't have to count calories and carbs or question what you eat. Dishes like Beef Stir-Fry with Oyster Sauce, Roasted Pork and Peach Salsa, or Country Minestrone with Meatballs will entice you to stick to this good-carbohydrate, balanced style of eating.

Following the Right Carb 14-day plan, you will consume an average of 125–135 grams of carbohydrates per day. Carbohydrate percentage is based on carbohydrates less fiber consumed—the standard way to calculate carbohydrate consumption. The balance of these meals is 38 percent of calories from carbohydrates, 30 percent of calories from lean protein, 22 percent of calories from monounsaturated fat, and 7 percent of calories from saturated fat.[1]

---

[1] The Right Carb phase approximates a 40-30-30 dietary profile. While there are differences of opinion, it is generally agreed that fat levels (primarily mono-unsaturated) should make up to 30 per cent of one's diet. Carbohydrate intake should be restricted to 30 per cent more than protein intake. So if the calories from protein are 30 per cent of diet, the correct carbohydrate level should be 40%.

right carbs 14-day menu plan

week 1	breakfast	lunch	dinner
sunday	Smoked Salmon Omelette 143	Layered Crab Salad 158–159	Japanese Beef Sukiyaki 175
monday	Grilled Ham and Cheese Sandwich 144	Tomatoes with Green sauce .160–161	Fish in a Pouch 176
tuesday	Spinach and Parmesan Omelette 145	Shrimp Caesar Wrap 162	Chicken with Parmesan and tomato sauce . . .177–178
wednesday	Ranchero Burrito 146	Turkey - avocado Pitta 163	Cioppino (Seafood Stew) 179–180
thursday	Western Omelette . . .147	Salmon Burgers 164	Pork Souvlaki 181
friday	Mediterranean Platter 148	Chicken Tostada 165	Mediterranean Veal and Olives 182
saturday	Vietnamese Pancakes 149	Caribbean Shrimp Salad 166	Herbed Meatball Minestrone 183–184

week 2	breakfast	lunch	dinner
sunday	French Toast with Ham 150	Ham and Mushroom Pita Pizza 167	Curried Shrimp and Lentil Salad 185–186
monday	Shiitake and Swiss Scramble 151	Fresh Tuna Salad 168	Chicken Fajitas 187-188
tuesday	Goat Cheese and Hearts of Palm Omelette 152	Spinach, Mushroom, and Canadian Bacon Salad 169	Roast Beef and Shiitake Hash 189–190
wednesday	Cottage Cheese and Cucumber Sandwich 153	Turkey and Asparagus Pasta Salad 170	Bahamian Fish Boil 191–192
thursday	Toasted Turkey Sandwich 154	Waldorf Salad with Roast Beef Sandwich 171	Summer and Winter Chicken Casserole 193
friday	Egg-in-the-Hole 155	Grouper Sandwich and Tomato Tapenade Salad 172	Beef Stir-fry with Oyster Sauce 194–195
saturday	Frittata Primavera 156	Chicken Sandwich with Sun dried Tomato Sauce 173	Pork and Peach Salsa 196

right carbs
breakfasts

smoked salmon omelettes

This is perfect for a weekend breakfast or parties.

smoked salmon omelettes

2 whole eggs

4 egg whites

½ cup snipped fresh dill or
  3 tablespoons dried

Salt and freshly ground black
  pepper to taste

Olive oil spray

¼ pound sliced smoked salmon

1 medium tomato, sliced

2 tablespoons reduced-fat sour
  cream

Several sprigs fresh dill for garnish
  (optional)

Preheat the broiler. Whisk the eggs, egg whites, and dill in a medium-sized bowl. Season with salt and pepper to taste. Set an 8- to 9-inch nonstick skillet over a medium-high heat. Spray with olive oil. Add half the egg mixture and swirl in the skillet to form a thin layer. Cook for 1 minute and place under the broiler for 1 minute, or until the omelette is cooked on top. Remove from broiler. Slide the omelette onto a plate and repeat for the second one. Place the smoked salmon and tomato slices on one half of each omelette, letting some of the salmon peek out from the edge. Spoon sour cream over the salmon and add sprigs of dill, again letting them peek out from the omelettes. Fold the omelettes in half once, and then in half again to form a triangle. Serve hot.

Makes 2 servings.

bran cereal

1 cup high-fiber, no-sugar-added
  bran cereal

1 cup skim milk

1 sliced banana (1½ cups)

Divide the cereal between 2 bowls and add the milk and banana to each.

Makes 2 servings.

Total breakfast one serving: 428 calories,
33g protein, 61g carbohydrate, 15g fat (4g saturated),
237mg cholesterol, 832mg sodium, 15g fiber

helpful hint

- *If using dried dill, make sure the bottle is less than 6 months old. The leaves should be green, not gray.*

countdown

- *Preheat broiler.*
- *Make omelettes and fill.*
- *Assemble cereal.*

shopping list

TO BUY:

1 small carton reduced-fat
  sour cream

¼ pound sliced smoked
  salmon

1 medium tomato

1 small bunch fresh dill or
  1 jar dried

1 banana

STAPLES:

Eggs

Olive oil spray

High-fiber, no-sugar-added
  bran cereal

Skim milk

Salt

Black peppercorns

helpful hints

- The sandwich toaster can be made in a toaster oven.
- Any type of whole grain bread can be used.

countdown

- Preheat broiler.
- Make sandwich.
- Assemble cereal.

shopping list

TO BUY:

1 small package shredded, reduced-fat sharp Cheddar cheese

½ pound sliced lean ham

2 small tomatoes

STAPLES:

Oatmeal

Skim milk

Whole wheat bread

Olive oil spray

Sugar substitute

grilled ham and cheese sandwich

This is a simple ham and cheese melted sandwich. It's a quick-grab breakfast that can be made in 5 minutes and taken with you for a breakfast-on-the-run.

grilled ham and cheddar sandwich

4 slices whole wheat bread

Olive oil spray

½ pound sliced lean ham (about 4 slices)

¼ cup shredded, reduced-fat sharp Cheddar cheese

2 small tomatoes, sliced

Preheat the broiler. Line a baking tray with foil. Place the bread on the tray and spray with olive oil. Place under the broiler for 1 minute. Remove and place the ham on the bread and sprinkle with cheese. Return to the broiler for 2 minutes, or until the cheese melts. Serve as an open-faced sandwich with a sliced tomato on the side. Or, if taking it with you, place the tomato slices on one slice and cover with another slice to make a closed sandwich.

Makes 2 servings.

oatmeal

1 cup oatmeal

2 cups water

1 cup skim milk

2 (0.35 ounce) envelopes sugar substitute (optional)

To prepare in the microwave, combine the oatmeal and water in a microwave-safe bowl. Microwave on high for 4 minutes. Stir in the milk and sugar substitute, divide between 2 bowls and serve warm.

Alternatively, to prepare on the stovetop, combine the oatmeal and water in a small saucepan over medium-high heat, and bring to a boil. Reduce the heat to medium, and cook for about 5 more minutes, stirring occasionally. Stir in the milk and sugar substitute, divide between 2 bowls, and serve warm.

Makes 2 servings.

Total breakfast one serving: 488 calories, 39g protein, 60g carbohydrate, 14g fat (5g saturated), 52mg cholesterol, 116mg sodium, 10g fiber

whisky pork chops **p126**

frittata primavera **p156**

spinach and parmesan omelette

My husband made this breakfast one very hurried morning before going to work. His comment? 'I can't believe it took me only 15 minutes—start to finish!'

spinach and parmesan omelette

2 whole eggs

4 egg whites

Salt and freshly ground black pepper to taste

4 cups washed, ready-to-eat fresh spinach (5 ounces)

2 teaspoons olive oil

2 tablespoons freshly grated Parmesan cheese

Preheat the oven to 400 degrees. Lightly beat the whole eggs and egg whites together in a medium-sized bowl. Season with salt and pepper to taste. Set a medium-sized nonstick skillet over medium heat. Add the spinach and sauté for 3 minutes, or until wilted. Stir the cooked spinach into the egg mixture. In the same skillet, heat the oil over a medium heat. Pour the egg mixture into the skillet, and let set for 1 minute. Sprinkle with Parmesan, and place in the oven for 3 minutes, or until eggs are set to desired consistency. Serve immediately. *Makes 2 servings.*

bran-yogurt parfait

1 ½ cups blueberries

2 (.035-ounce) envelopes sugar substitute

1 cup light blueberry-flavored yogurt

1 cup high-fiber, no-sugar-added bran cereal

Purée the blueberries in a food processor or press through a strainer. Stir in the sugar substitute. Divide half the cup of the yogurt between 2 bowls or parfait glasses, and sprinkle each with bran. Pour some blueberry purée over the bran in each bowl. Spoon the remaining yogurt over the purée and drizzle with the remaining blueberry purée before serving. *Makes 2 servings.*

Total breakfast one serving: 366 calories, 26g protein, 53g carbohydrate, 14g fat (3g saturated), 220mg cholesterol, 564mg sodium, 20g fiber

helpful hints

● *Buy good quality Parmesan cheese and ask the grocer to grate it for you or chop it in the food processor yourself. Freeze extra for quick use later—simply spoon out what you need and leave the rest frozen.*

● *Washed, ready-to-eat fresh spinach is available in most supermarkets. It makes using fresh spinach a dream.*

countdown

● *Preheat oven to 400 degrees.*

● *Prepare all ingredients.*

● *Make omelette.*

● *Assemble cereal.*

shopping list

TO BUY:

1 carton light blueberry-flavored yoghurt

1 bag washed, ready-to-eat fresh spinach

1 small carton blueberries

STAPLES:

Eggs

Olive oil

Parmesan cheese

Sugar substitute

High-fiber, no-sugar-added bran cereal

Salt

Black peppercorns

ranchero burrito

helpful hints

● If you like your food hot and spicy, buy a hot black bean pâté and a hot pepper jack cheese.

countdown

● *Preheat broiler or toaster oven.*
● *Make burrito.*
● *Slice tomato.*
● *Prepare bran cereal and juice.*

shopping list

TO BUY:

1 small package shredded, reduced-fat Monterey Jack cheese
1/4 pound sliced smoked turkey breast
1 package whole wheat tortillas
1 jar black bean pâté
1 medium tomato

STAPLES:

Low-sodium tomato juice
High-fiber, no-sugar-added bran cereal
Skim milk

This burrito is quick to make and easy to eat. Black bean pâté, shredded Monterey jack, and smoked turkey breast—all supermarket products designed to make our life easier—make this a 5-minute meal. Black bean pâté is usually found in the snack section near the chips in the supermarket. You can choose hot, medium, or mild. Look for one that does not have added sugar.

ranchero burrito

2 (6-inch) whole wheat tortillas
1/4 cup black bean pâté
1/4 pound sliced smoked turkey breast
1/2 cup shredded, reduced-fat Monterey jack cheese
1 medium tomato, sliced

Warm the tortillas in a microwave oven for 10 seconds, or place in a toaster oven for 15–20 seconds, to make them easier to roll. Spread the warmed tortillas with the black bean pâté, top with turkey, and sprinkle with Monterey jack cheese. Roll up and microwave for 45 seconds on high, or until the cheese melts. Or, place in a toaster oven for 2 minutes. Cut in half crosswise and serve with tomato slices on the side. *Makes 2 servings.*

bran cereal

1 cup high-fiber, no-sugar-added bran cereal
1 cup skim milk

Divide the cereal and milk between 2 bowls. *Makes 2 servings.*

tomato juice

1 cup low-sodium tomato juice

Divide between 2 glasses. *Makes 2 servings.*

Total breakfast one serving: 353 calories, 34g protein, 51g carbohydrate, 9g fat (4g saturated), 52mg cholesterol, 939mg sodium, 14g fiber

western omelette

Also known as a Denver omelette, this dish was said to be part of the chuck wagon legends in the Old West. Apparently they used plenty of onions to disguise old eggs. This is a modern version that takes about 10 minutes to make.

western omelette

1 cup egg substitute

1/4 teaspoon cayenne pepper

Salt to taste

2 teaspoons olive oil

1/2 cup frozen, diced onion

2 cups frozen, diced green bell pepper

1 cup canned roasted red bell pepper, drained and diced

1/4 pound diced, lean ham (1 cup)

Preheat the broiler. Season the egg substitute with cayenne and salt to taste. Heat the oil in a medium-sized nonstick skillet over a medium-high heat. Add the onion and green bell pepper and sauté for 2 minutes. Add the roasted red bell pepper and ham, and sauté for another minute. Add the egg mixture and let set for 2 minutes. Place under the broiler for 5 minutes, or until set to the desired consistency. Slide out of the skillet and serve.

Makes 2 servings.

oatmeal

1 cup oatmeal

2 cups water

1 cup skim milk

2 (.035-ounces) envelopes sugar substitute (optional)

To prepare in the microwave, combine the oatmeal and water in a microwave-safe bowl. Microwave on high for 4 minutes. Stir in the milk and sugar substitute, divide between 2 bowls and serve warm.

Alternatively, to prepare on the stovetop, combine the oatmeal and water in a small saucepan over a medium-high heat and bring to a boil. Reduce the heat to medium and cook for about 5 more minutes, stirring occasionally. Stir in the milk and sugar substitute, divide between 2 bowls, and serve warm.

Makes 2 servings.

Total breakfast one serving: 385 calories, 31g protein, 54g carbohydrate, 12g fat (4g saturated), 93mg cholesterol, 782mg sodium, 16g fiber

helpful hints

● *Use a skillet with an ovenproof handle.*

● *Frozen onion and green bell peppers are used to cut down on preparaton time. Use fresh instead if you have a few extra minutes.*

countdown

● *Preheat broiler.*

● *Make oatmeal.*

● *Make omelette.*

shopping list

TO BUY:

1/4 pound sliced lean ham

1 small jar or can roasted red bell pepper

STAPLES:

Olive oil

Egg substitute

Frozen, diced onion

Frozen, diced green bell pepper

Cayenne pepper

Sugar Substitute

Oatmeal

Skim milk

Salt

mediterranean platter

Sun-dried tomatoes, oranges, and strawberries bring thoughts of a sunny Mediterranean morning. Better yet, it takes only a few minutes to assemble this breakfast.

mediterranean platter

½ cup low-fat ricotta cheese

¼ cup sun-dried tomatoes, drained and sliced

1 medium cucumber, peeled and sliced

2 medium oranges, peeled and sliced

¼ pound sliced roasted boneless chicken breast

2 slices low-carbohydrate whole wheat bread

Combine the ricotta cheese with the sun-dried tomatoes. Place on 2 plates. Arrange the cucumber, oranges, and chicken slices around the ricotta mixture. Toast the bread and serve on the side.

Makes 2 servings.

bran cereal and fresh berries

1 cup high-fiber, no-sugar-added bran cereal

1 cup skim milk

1 cup sliced strawberries

Divide the cereal between 2 bowls and add milk to each. Sprinkle with the strawberries.

Makes 2 servings.

Total breakfast one serving: 428 calories, 40g protein, 69g carbohydrate, 13g fat (5g saturated), 80mg cholesterol, 443mg sodium, 22g fiber

vietnamese pancakes

This paper-thin crêpe is topped with mushrooms, onion, roasted pork shoulder, and bean sprouts. When you are looking for a delicious variation from more traditional omelettes and frittatas, this version will fit the bill. It takes about 10 minutes to make and is worth every minute.

vietnamese pancakes

2 eggs

4 egg whites

2 tablespoons whole wheat flour

2 tablespoons low-sodium soy sauce

4 scallions, thinly sliced (½ cup)

2 teaspoons canola oil

¼ pound lean roasted pork shoulder, cut into thin strips (about ½ cup)

½ pound portobello mushrooms, sliced (3 cups)

½ cup diced yellow onion,

2 cups bean sprouts

With a wire whisk, mix the eggs, egg whites, whole wheat flour, and soy sauce together in a small bowl until smooth. Add the scallions and set aside. Heat the oil in a 9- to 10-inch nonstick skillet over a medium heat. Add the pork, mushrooms, onion, and bean sprouts. Sauté until the onion turns golden—about 4 minutes. Remove to a bowl and add half the egg mixture to the hot pan. Swirl the mixture around the pan to form a thin crêpe. Cook for 3 minutes, or until the center is cooked and the sides of the pancake start to curl up. Slide onto a plate. Repeat with the second half of the mixture. Divide the pork and vegetable mixture between both crêpes, and serve.
Makes 2 servings.

bran cereal

1 cup high-fiber, no-sugar-added bran cereal

1 cup skim milk

Divide cereal between 2 bowls and add milk to each.
Makes 2 servings.

> Total breakfast one serving: 349 calories, 29g protein, 50g carbohydrate, 9g fat (2g saturated), 55mg cholesterol, 851mg sodium, 15g fiber

helpful hints

● If pressed for time, use presliced mushrooms and frozen, diced onion.

● Lean ham can be substituted if pork shoulder is unavailable.

countdown

● Prepare ingredients.

● Make pancakes.

● Assemble cereal.

shopping list

TO BUY:

¼ pound lean roasted pork shoulder

½ pound portobello mushrooms

1 package bean sprouts

1 bunch scallions (4 needed)

STAPLES:

Eggs

Yellow onion

Skim milk

Whole wheat flour

High-fiber, no-sugar-added bran cereal

Canola oil

Low-salt soy sauce

french toast with ham

helpful hint

- Look for low-sodium V-8 juice

countdown

- Pour juice.
- Make French toast.
- Assemble cereal.

shopping list

TO BUY:

1 small package sliced lean ham (1/4 pound needed)

1 bottle low-salt, no-sugar-added V-8 or tomato juice

STAPLES:

Egg substitute

Olive oil

Low-carbohydrate whole wheat bread

High-fiber, no-sugar-added bran cereal

Skim milk

Salt

Black peppercorns

For a change from scrambled eggs or omelettes, try this delicious French Toast. You can cook it with cheese or meat to vary the flavor, and it takes only minutes to make.

french toast with ham

1/2 cup egg substitute

Salt and freshly ground black pepper to taste

2 slices low-carbohydrate whole wheat bread

2 teaspoons olive oil

1/4 pound sliced lean ham, cubed (1 cup)

Pour the egg substitute into a small bowl, and season with salt and pepper to taste. Add the bread and let it soak.

Heat the olive oil in a small skillet over a medium heat. Remove the bread from the egg substitute and add to the skillet. Cook for 1 minute, then turn. Add the ham to the cooked sides, cover with a lid and cook for 2 more minutes before serving.

Makes 2 servings.

bran cereal

1 cup high-fiber, no-sugar-added bran cereal

1 cup skim milk

Divide the cereal and milk between 2 bowls.

Makes 2 servings.

vegetable juice

1 1/2 cups low-salt, no-sugar-added V-8 or tomato juice

Divide between 2 glasses.

Makes 2 servings.

Total breakfast one serving: 340 calories, 28g protein, 49g carbohydrate, 10g fat (2g saturated), 29mg cholesterol, 1019mg sodium, 17g fiber

shiitake and swiss scramble

Shiitake mushrooms and sautéed onions form the base for these scrambled eggs. Although originally from Japan and Korea, shiitakes are now grown in the United States and are available in most supermarkets.

● To speed preparation, use frozen, diced onion to save chopping time.

shiitake and swiss scramble

2 teaspoons olive oil
½ cup onion, diced
½ cup shiitake mushrooms, sliced
2 eggs
4 egg whites
Salt and freshly ground black
  pepper to taste
¼ shredded, reduced-fat Swiss or
  Gruyère cheese
2 slices low-carbohydrate whole
  wheat bread

Heat the oil in a medium-sized nonstick skillet over a medium heat. Add the onion and mushrooms and sauté for 3 minutes. Whisk the eggs and egg whites together lightly and season with salt and pepper to taste. Add the eggs to the skillet and scramble with the vegetables, for about 1 minute. Sprinkle with the cheese, cover and allow to sit until the cheese melts, about 30 seconds. Toast the bread and place on 2 plates. Top each piece of toast with the scrambled eggs and serve immediately.
Makes 2 servings.

spiced oatmeal

1 cup oatmeal
2 cups water
2 (.035-ounce) envelopes sugar
  substitute (optional)
½ teaspoon ground ginger
1 cup skim or 1% milk

To prepare in the microwave, combine the oatmeal and water in a microwave-safe bowl. Microwave on high for 4 minutes. Stir in the sugar substitute and ginger. Stir in the milk, divide between 2 bowls and serve warm.

Alternatively, to prepare on the stovetop, combine the oatmeal and water in a small saucepan over a medium-high heat and bring to a boil. Reduce the heat to medium and cook for about 5 more minutes, stirring occasionally. Stir in the sugar substitute and ginger. Stir in the milk, divide between 2 bowls, and serve warm.
Makes 2 servings.

Total breakfast one serving: 446 calories, 33g protein, 49g carbohydrate, 17g fat (4g saturated), 223mg cholesterol, 377mg sodium, 7g fiber

helpful hint

● Any type of mushroom can be substituted.

countdown

● Make oatmeal.
● Make eggs.

shopping list

TO BUY:
  1 small package shredded, reduced fat Swiss cheese
  1 small package shiitake mushrooms (1ounce needed)
STAPLES:
  Frozen, diced onion
  Eggs
  Olive oil
  Oatmeal
  Skim milk
  Low-carbohydrate whole wheat bread
  Ground ginger
  Sugar substitute
  Salt
  Black peppercorns

goat cheese and hearts of palm omelette

Hearts of palm are the tender heart of the Sabal palm tree. If you can find fresh hearts of palm, they're really a treat. Otherwise, they are sold in cans or jars in the supermarket.

goat cheese and palm hearts omelette

Olive oil spray

2 cups sliced hearts of palm

1 cup egg substitute

2 ounces herbed goat cheese,
   broken into small pieces

Salt and freshly ground black
   pepper to taste

2 slices whole grain bread

Set a medium-sized nonstick skillet over a medium-high heat and spray with olive oil. Add the hearts of palm. Combine the egg substitute with the goat cheese. Pour into the skillet, cover with a lid, and cook for 3–4 minutes. Sprinkle with salt and pepper to taste. Cut the omelette in half and slide onto 2 plates with a spatula. Serve with toasted whole grain bread.

Makes 2 servings.

oatmeal

1 cup oatmeal

2 cups water

1 cup skim milk

2 (.035-ounce) envelopes
   sugar substitute, (optional)

To prepare in the microwave, combine the oatmeal and water in a microwave-safe bowl. Microwave on high for 4 minutes. Stir in the milk and sugar substitute, divide between 2 bowls and serve warm.

Alternatively, to prepare on the stovetop, combine the oatmeal and water in a small saucepan over a medium-high heat, and bring to a boil. Reduce the heat to medium and cook for about 5 more minutes, stirring occasionally. Stir in the milk and sugar substitute, divide between 2 bowls, and serve warm.

Makes 2 servings.

Total breakfast one serving: 461 calories, 35g protein, 53g carbohydrate, 15g fat (7g saturated), 24mg cholesterol, 1166mg sodium, 11g fiber

cottage cheese and cucumber sandwich

This is a quick and simple breakfast to make. Be sure to read the label on the cottage cheese, making sure it is low-fat with no sugar added.

cottage cheese and cucumber sandwich

2 slices rye bread
Olive oil spray
1 cup low-fat cottage cheese
1 medium cucumber, sliced

Toast the bread. Spray with olive oil. Place the toast on 2 plates, spread each toast with cottage cheese, and top with cucumber slices. Serve the remaining cucumber slices on the side.
Makes 2 servings.

yogurt crunch

1 cup light fruit-flavored yogurt
1 cup high-fiber, no-sugar-added bran cereal

Divide the yogurt between 2 bowls. Sprinkle with the bran cereal and stir together.
Makes 2 servings.

Total breakfast one serving: 285 calories, 24g protein, 51g carbohydrate, 6g fat (2g saturated), 13mg cholesterol, 651mg sodium, 17g fiber

helpful hint

● *Any type of whole grain bread can be used.*

countdown

● *Make sandwich.*
● *Assemble cereal.*

shopping list

TO BUY:
   1 small carton light fruit-flavored yogurt
   1 small carton low-fat cottage cheese
   1 medium cucumber
STAPLES:
   Olive oil spray
   High-fiber, no-sugar-added bran cereal
   Rye bread

countdown

- Preheat broiler.
- Prepare grapefruit.
- Make sandwich.
- Assemble cereal.

shopping list

TO BUY:

1 small package reduced-fat
    cream cheese
¼ pound sliced lean smoked
    turkey breast
1 medium tomato
1 medium grapefruit

STAPLES:

Olive oil spray
Low-carbohydrate whole
    wheat bread
High-fiber, no-sugar-added
    bran cereal
Skim milk
Salt
Black peppercorns

toasted turkey sandwich

Sliced smoked turkey, tomato, and cream cheese on toast make a quick, 10-minute breakfast.

toasted turkey sandwich

2 slices low-carbohydrate whole
    wheat bread
Olive oil spray
2 tablespoons reduced-fat cream
    cheese
¼ pound sliced lean smoked
    turkey breast (1½ cups)
1 medium tomato, sliced
Salt and freshly ground black
    pepper to taste

Preheat the broiler. Spray the bread with olive oil and toast until golden brown. Spread the toast with cream cheese and top with the turkey and tomato slices. Season with salt and pepper to taste. Serve on 2 plates.
Makes 2 servings.

grapefruit

1 medium grapefruit, halved

With a serrated knife, cut around the edge of the grapefruit to separate the flesh from the skin. Cut between the segments and serve on 2 plates.
Makes 2 servings.

bran cereal

1 cup high-fiber, no-sugar-added
    bran cereal
1 cup skim milk

Divide the cereal between 2 bowls and add milk to each.
Makes 2 servings.

Total breakfast one serving: 338 calories,
29g protein, 53g carbohydrate, 9g fat (3g saturated),
53mg cholesterol, 411mg sodium, 17g fiber

egg-in-the-hole

We used to call it Hole-in-the-Middle. Some call it Egg-in-the-Hole and others call it Toad-in-the-Hole. Regardless, it's an old American favorite. I remember my father making this for breakfast; my job was to tear the hole out of the bread. Somehow I never got the hole to be the same size as the egg, but it was still very delicious. Whether the egg neatly fits the hole or runs over the bread, this is a quick and easy, and fun breakfast.

egg-in-the-hole

*2 slices low-carbohydrate whole
   wheat bread*
Olive oil spray
2 eggs
*2 slices reduced-fat Swiss
   cheese (1½ ounces)*
*Salt and freshly ground black
   pepper to taste*

Tear a hole in each slice of bread about 2 inches in diameter. Heat a nonstick skillet over a low heat and spray with olive oil. Add the bread and the cutout pieces to the skillet. Cook until golden, about 2 minutes. Turn the bread and cutouts over, and break one egg into each hole. Cook for 1 minute, turn over, and place the cheese slices over the eggs. Season with salt and pepper to taste. Cover with a lid and cook for 2–3 minutes, or until the eggs have set to the desired consistency. Serve with the cutouts.
Makes 2 servings.

bran cereal

*1 cup high-fiber, no-sugar-added
   bran cereal*
1 cup skim milk

Divide the cereal and milk between 2 bowls.
Makes 2 servings.

grapefruit

1 medium grapefruit, halved

With a serrated knife, cut around the edge of the grapefruit to separate the flesh from the skin. Cut between the segments and serve on 2 plates.
Makes 2 servings.

Total breakfast one serving: 340 calories,
   25g protein, 51g carbohydrate, 13g fat (4g saturated),
   226mg cholesterol, 414mg sodium, 17g fiber

helpful hints

● *It doesn't matter if the egg spills over onto the bread or pan.*

● *To determine the weight of each slice of cheese, divide the package weight by the number of slices.*

● *If you like your egg yolk firm, gently flip the bread and egg over before adding the cheese. Place the cheese on the top side.*

countdown

Prepare grapefruit.
Make egg.
Assemble cereal.

shopping list

TO BUY:
   *1 small package sliced,
      reduced-fat Swiss cheese
      (1½ ounces, needed)*
   1 grapefruit
STAPLES:
   Olive oil spray
   Eggs
   *High-fiber, no-sugar-added
      bran cereal*
   Skim milk
   *Low-carbohydrate whole
      wheat bread*
   Salt
   Black peppercorns

helpful hints

- Zucchini can be substituted for the yellow squash
- Regular green basil can be substituted for purple.

countdown

- Start frittata.
- While frittata cooks, assemble cereal.

shopping list

TO BUY:

1 small package shredded, reduced-fat mature cheddar cheese

1 small yellow squash

½ pound whole portobello mushrooms

1 small bunch asparagus

1 package purple basil

STAPLES:

Egg substitute

Red onion

Olive oil

High-fiber, no-sugar-added bran cereal

Skim milk

Salt

Black peppercorns

frittata primavera

A frittata is an Italian omelette that is cooked slowly so that it becomes thick, more like a quiche than an omelette.

frittata primavera

1 cup egg substitute

2 cups fresh purple basil leaves

Salt and freshly ground black pepper to taste

8 large spears asparagus or 16 thin (2 ounces)

4 teaspoons olive oil

1 cup yellow squash, sliced

½ cup sliced red onion

½ pound whole portobello mushrooms, sliced thinly (2 cups)

¼ cup shredded, reduced-fat, aged Cheddar cheese

Combine the egg substitute and basil in a medium-sized bowl. Season with salt and pepper to taste. Cut or snap off the 1-inch fibrous stems on the asparagus and discard. Slice the remaining asparagus into 1-inch pieces. Heat the oil in a medium-sized nonstick skillet over a medium-high heat and add the squash, onion, mushrooms, and asparagus. Sauté for 5 minutes. Pour the egg mixture into the skillet, and swirl around the vegetables. Sprinkle the frittata with cheese. Cover, reduce the heat to low, and cook for 10 minutes more before serving.

Makes 2 servings.

bran cereal

1 cup high-fibre, no-sugar-added bran cereal

1 cup skim milk

Divide the cereal and milk between 2 bowls.

Makes 2 servings.

Total breakfast one serving: 359 calories, 25g protein, 45g carbohydrate, 14g fat (3g saturated), 12mg cholesterol, 542mg sodium, 15g fibre

right carbs
lunches

layered crab salad

Layering sweet crabmeat with fresh vegetables and light vinaigrette dressing makes a delicious and colorful salad. It's perfect for a weekend lunch or entertaining. There is no cooking required, so this meal can be assembled in mere minutes. Cooked crabmeat is sold frozen or in cans. The meat should be white with a little pink coloring. There are many brands and qualities available. Try different ones to find one that suits your palate. This salad is also great for any type of leftover cooked seafood. ● Sherry wine vinegar has a very subtle flavor that perfectly complements the crab. ● The Italians like to cover sliced bread with leftover cheese or vegetables and heat it in a wood fire. The resulting crostini or "little crusts" are used to garnish salads and appetizers. My version uses freshly grated Parmesan cheese.

helpful hints

● Bottled, no-sugar-added oil and vinegar dressing can be used instead of the recipe provided. Add tarragon and onion to the bottled dressing.

● Buy good quality Parmesan cheese and ask the grocer to grate it for you, or chop it in the food processor yourself. Freeze extra for quick use later—simply spoon out what you need and leave the rest frozen.

● Any type of salad greens can be used.

● If using dried tarragon, make sure the bottle is less than 6 months old.

● Red wine or balsamic vinegar can be used.

countdown

● Preheat broiler or toaster oven.

● Make dressing.

● Make crab salad.

● Make crostini.

layered crab salad

2 tablespoons sherry vinegar

4 teaspoons Dijon mustard

4 teaspoons olive oil

2 tablespoons water

½ cup chopped red onion

2 tablespoons fresh tarragon or 2 teaspoons dried tarragon

Salt and freshly ground black pepper to taste

¼ pound jumbo lump cooked crabmeat

1 bag ready-to-eat mixed young salad greens (about 5 cups)

1 medium cucumber, peeled and sliced

2 medium tomatoes, sliced

Whisk the sherry wine vinegar and mustard together in a medium-sized bowl. Whisk in the olive oil and water until smooth. Add the onion and tarragon, and season with salt and pepper to taste. Mix half the dressing with the crabmeat. Arrange the salad greens in the bottom of a glass salad bowl. Layer the cucumber slices on top. Drizzle the remaining dressing over the salad. Spoon the crabmeat over the cucumber. Arrange the sliced tomatoes around the edge of the bowl, sprinkle with salt and pepper to taste and serve.

Makes 2 servings.

One serving: 259 calories, 25g protein, 15g carbohydrate, 11g fat (1g saturated), 88mg cholesterol, 592mg sodium, 1g fiber

parmesan crostini

Olive oil spray
2 slices multigrain bread
2 tablespoons freshly grated
  Parmesan cheese

Preheat the broiler or toaster oven. Spray olive oil over the bread. Sprinkle with Parmesan cheese. Place under the broiler about 6 inches from the heat for 2–3 minutes, or until the cheese starts to melt. Serve with the salad. *Makes 2 servings.*

One serving: 83 calories, 6g protein, 10g carbohydrate, 4g fat (1g saturated), 4mg cholesterol, 221mg sodium, 3g fiber

grapes and yogurt

1 cup light fruit-flavored yogurt
30 grapes (2/3 cup)

Spoon the yogurt into 2 dessert bowls and sprinkle with grapes. *Makes 2 servings.*

One serving: 79 calories, 4g protein, 16g carbohydrate, 0g fat (0g saturated), 3mg cholesterol, 59mg sodium, 0g fiber

shopping list

TO BUY:
  1 carton light fruit-flavored
    yogurt
  1/4 pound jumbo lump
    cooked crabmeat (fresh,
    canned or frozen)
  1 small bottle sherry wine
    vinegar
  1 small bunch fresh tarragon
    or 1 jar dried
  1 medium cucumber
  2 medium tomatoes
  1 bag ready-to-eat, mixed
    baby greens
  1 small bunch grapes
    (30 needed)
STAPLES:
  Olive oil
  Olive oil spray
  Red onion
  Multigrain bread
  Parmesan cheese
  Dijon mustard
  Salt
  Black peppercorns

tomatoes with green sauce

This recipe was given to me by a friend from Tuscany. It always reminds me of sitting on her porch looking out on the rolling green hills and heavily laden olive trees. This light lunch can be made in minutes and enjoyed in your own backyard. ● Serve this lunch on the weekend or when you're having friends for lunch. ● Bruschetta is a Roman garlic bread. When testing the season's first pressing of olive oil, the Romans would taste it on a slice of bread that was sometimes rubbed with fresh garlic. If you like a lot of garlic, crush the garlic clove onto the bread instead of rubbing. ● A fresh strawberry smoothie completes this summery meal.

tomatoes with green sauce

6 eggs (only the whites are used)

2 ripe tomatoes, stemmed and halved crosswise

2 anchovy fillets, drained and rinsed

4 teaspoons capers, drained

2 tablespoons bread crumbs (whole wheat if possible)

2 tablespoons balsamic vinegar

1/2 cup chopped fresh parsley, divided into 2 piles

4 teaspoons olive oil

Salt and freshly ground black pepper to taste

Place the eggs in a small saucepan and cover with cold water. Bring to a boil, then reduce the heat to a very gentle simmer. Cook for 12 minutes. Drain and rinse eggs under cold water. When cool enough to handle, peel the eggs, cut in half; remove and discard the yolks.

Hollow out the tomatoes with a spoon, reserving the pulp. Mash the anchovy fillets with a fork and place in the bowl of a food processor. Add the capers, tomato pulp (about 1 cup), and egg whites, then coarsely chop. If you don't have a food processor, chop by hand. In a small bowl, soak the bread crumbs in the vinegar. Set aside half of the parsley for garnish. Add the remaining parsley and egg white mixture to the bread crumbs. Stir in the olive oil and season with salt and pepper to taste. Combine well. Fill the tomatoes with the mixture, sprinkle with the reserved parsley and serve.

Makes 2 servings.

One serving: 173 calories, 16g protein, 8g carbohydrate, 10g fat (1g saturated), 0mg cholesterol, 489mg sodium, 0g fiber

garlic bruschetta

Olive oil spray
1 small garlic clove, halved
2 slices crusty country multigrain bread

Spray the bread with olive oil and rub the cut side of the garlic on the bread. Toast the bread and serve with the tomatoes.
Makes 2 servings.

One serving: 61 calories, 4g protein, 11g carbohydrate, 2g fat (0g saturated), 0mg cholesterol, 115mg sodium, 3g fiber

strawberry smoothie

1½ cups strawberries
1 cup light strawberry-flavored yogurt
2 teaspoons vanilla extract
2 (0.35-ounce) envelopes sugar substitute
4 cups ice cubes

Place the strawberries, yogurt, vanilla extract, and sugar substitute in a blender. Blend until smooth. Add the ice cubes and blend until thick. Pour into 2 glasses.
Makes 2 servings.

One serving: 96 calories, 5g protein, 18g carbohydrate, 0.5g fat (0g saturated), 3mg cholesterol, 59mg sodium, 2g fiber

shopping list

TO BUY:
- 1 carton light strawberry-flavored yogurt
- 1 small tin anchovies packed in olive oil
- 1 small jar capers
- 1 small container bread crumbs
- 2 ripe tomatoes
- 1 small bunch fresh parsley
- 1 container fresh strawberries

STAPLES:
- Eggs
- Garlic
- Olive oil
- Olive oil spray
- Balsamic vinegar
- Multigrain bread
- Vanilla extract
- Sugar substitute
- Salt
- Black peppercorns

shrimp caesar wrap

Caesar Salad, one of America's most popular salads, is said to have been created in 1924 in Tijuana, Mexico, by a restaurateur named Caesar Cardini. I don't think he ever dreamed that 70 years later, his combination of anchovies, garlic, lemon juice, croûtons, and lettuce would be on nearly every restaurant menu in the United States.

helpful hints

- 1 tablespoon low-sugar (less than .5 grams per 2 tablespoons) Caesar salad dressing can be substituted for this homemade one.
- Buy peeled shrimp.
- Any type of lettuce can be used.
- Buy good quality Parmesan cheese and grate it yourself. Freeze extra for quick use later—simply spoon out what you need and leave the rest frozen.

countdown

- Make dressing.
- Make wrap.
- Assemble yogurt and pear.

shopping list

TO BUY:
1 carton light fruit-flavored yogurt
½ pound large shrimp
1 small tin anchovies packed in olive oil
1 package 12-inch whole wheat flour tortillas
1 small head romaine lettuce
1 lemon
2 medium pears
STAPLES:
Garlic
Olive oil
Worcestershire sauce
Parmesan cheese
Black peppercorns

shrimp caesar wrap

8 anchovies, rinsed
2 small garlic cloves, crushed
2 tablespoons freshly squeezed lemon juice (1 lemon)
4 teaspoons olive oil, divided
4 teaspoons Worcestershire sauce
½ pound large shrimp, peeled and deveined
2 (12-inch) whole wheat flour tortillas
6 large romaine lettuce leaves, torn into bite-size pieces
2 tablespoons freshly grated Parmesan cheese
Freshly ground black pepper to taste

To make the dressing, put the anchovies, garlic, lemon juice, 2 teaspoons of the olive oil, and the Worcestershire sauce in a food processor and blend thoroughly, or mix and mash together well by hand. Heat the remaining 2 teaspoons of olive oil in a small nonstick skillet over a medium-high heat. Add the shrimp and sauté for 2 minutes. Remove the skillet from the heat, leaving the shrimp in the skillet to finish cooking.

Wrap the tortillas in paper towels and microwave on high for 20 seconds to soften. Remove from the microwave, discard the paper towel, and place the tortillas on a countertop. Spread the dressing over each tortilla. Place lettuce evenly over the dressing and sprinkle with Parmesan cheese. Cut the shrimp in half and place on the lettuce, making sure to add any juices from the skillet. Season with black pepper to taste. Fold up the top and bottom edges of the tortilla, then roll up tightly to make a neat package. Slice in half and serve.
Makes 2 servings.

One serving: 333 calories, 33g protein, 18g carbohydrate, 15g fat (3g saturated), 178mg cholesterol, 1076mg sodium, 5g fiber

pears and yogurt

1 cup light fruit-flavored yogurt
2 medium pears, cored and sliced

Spoon the yogurt into 2 dessert bowls and top with the pear slices.
Makes 2 servings

One serving: 148 calories, 5g protein, 34g carbohydrate, 1g fat (0g saturated), 3mg cholesterol, 59mg sodium, 4g fiber

turkey-avocado pita

Turkey, crunchy alfalfa sprouts, and nutty avocado blend together for a fresh taste in this pita pocket sandwich. It's sometimes hard to find a ripe avocado, but you can ripen one quickly by removing the small stem and storing in a paper bag in a warm spot until soft to the touch.

turkey-avocado pita

1 whole wheat pita bread, halved

¼ pound sliced smoked turkey breast, cut into ½-inch strips

½ small ripe avocado, pitted, peeled and sliced

1 cup alfalfa sprouts, tops only

1 small tomato, sliced

1 tablespoon no-sugar-added oil and vinegar dressing

Broil or toast the pita halves for 1 minute, or until the bread is warm. Place the turkey, avocado slices, alfalfa sprouts, and tomato slices in the pockets of the pita bread. Spoon the dressing over the turkey and vegetables before serving. Makes 2 servings.

One serving: 339 calories, 25g protein, 29g carbohydrate, 15g fat (3g saturated), 40mg cholesterol, 154mg sodium, 6g fiber

fresh berries yogurt

1 cup light mixed berry-flavored yogurt

1½ cups fresh raspberries

Place the yogurt in 2 small dessert dishes and sprinkle with the berries. Makes 2 servings.

One serving: 81 calories, 5g protein, 16g carbohydrate, 0.5g fat (0g saturated), 3mg cholesterol, 58mg sodium, 3g fiber

helpful hints

- *Any type of sprouts can be used.*
- *Any flavor of light yogurt can be used.*

countdown

- *Preheat broiler or toaster oven.*
- *Peel avocado.*
- *Make sandwich.*
- *Assemble yogurt.*

shopping list

TO BUY:

1 carton light mixed berry-flavored yogurt

¼ pound sliced smoked turkey breast

1 small package whole wheat pita bread

1 small ripe avocado

1 carton alfalfa sprouts

1 small tomato

1 small carton fresh raspberries

STAPLES:

No-sugar-added oil and vinegar dressing

salmon burgers

My sons have given me a strong warning, "Don't mess with my burgers". The fact is that this all-American dish is changing. I've recently noticed salmon burgers on several menus and decided to create this quick lunch. The flavorful salmon meat requires very little fish for a rich-tasting burger. ● *The salmon can be chopped in a food processor. However, it is very soft and takes only a few minutes to chop by hand if you don't have a food processor.*

helpful hints

● *Buy no-salt-added tomato purée in a can. You can keep the unused portion in a plastic container or self-seal bag in the refrigerator or freezer.*

countdown

● *Make salmon burgers.*
● *Assemble cantaloupe and yogurt cup.*

shopping list

TO BUY:

1 carton light fruit-flavored yogurt
6 ounces salmon fillet
1 small container wholemeal bread crumbs
1 small can no-salt-added tomato purée
1 small bunch scallions (8 needed)
1 small tomato
1 small cantaloupe

STAPLES:

Eggs
Multigrain bread
Mayonnaise made with olive or soybean oil
Salt
Black peppercorns

salmon burgers

6 ounces salmon fillet
8 scallions, sliced (divided) (1 cup)
¼ whole wheat bread crumbs
1 tablespoon no-salt-added tomato purée
2 egg whites
Salt and freshly ground black pepper to taste
2 tablespoons mayonnaise made with olive or soybean oil
2 slices multigrain bread
1 small tomato, sliced

Remove any fat or dark meat from the salmon. Cut the pink meat into 2-inch cubes and chop in a food processor, or by hand. Add half the scallions to the salmon along with the bread crumbs, tomato purée, and egg whites. Season with salt and pepper to taste. Form into 2 burgers about 4 inches in diameter and ½ inch thick. Set a nonstick skillet over a medium-high heat and brown the burgers on one side, about 1 minute. Reduce the heat to medium and cook for 3 minutes. Turn over, raise the heat to medium-high, and cook for another 2 minutes. Meanwhile, mix the mayonnaise and remaining scallions together in a small bowl. Season with salt and pepper to taste. Toast the bread. To serve, place the salmon burgers on the toasted bread and top with mayonnaise. Serve tomato slices alongside the salmon burger.
Makes 2 servings.

One serving: 350 calories, 31g protein, 19g carbohydrate, 17g fat (3g saturated), 65mg cholesterol, 1341mg sodium, 3g fiber

cantaloupe yogurt

1 cup light fruit-flavored yogurt
1 cantaloupe, cubed (4 cups)

Spoon the yogurt into 2 dessert bowls and top with the cantaloupe.
Makes 2 servings.

One serving: 127 calories, 6g protein, 27g carbohydrate, 1g fat (0g saturated), 3mg cholesterol, 77mg sodium, 3g fiber

chicken tostadas

Crisp tortillas, smooth beans, hot flavors, and cool tomatoes make this recipe a favorite quick meal. A tostada is simply a crisp tortilla. Here it is topped with chicken and vegetables, but the variations are endless. ● To save washing the processor bowl during preparation, chop all of the vegetables first and then mash the beans. If you don't have a food processor, simply chop the vegetables by hand, and mash the beans with a fork.

chicken tostadas

2 (8-inch) whole wheat tortillas

Olive oil spray

2 tablespoons no-sugar-added oil and vinegar dressing

2 teaspoons ground cumin

2 medium-sized jalapeño peppers, seeded and sliced

¼ pound sliced roasted chicken breast, skinned, cut into ½-inch strips

½ cup chopped red onion

2 medium-sized garlic cloves, crushed

½ cup canned dark red kidney beans, rinsed and drained

4 tablespoons water

Salt and freshly ground black pepper to taste

2 cups washed, ready-to-eat lettuce, shredded

Preheat the oven to 400 degrees. Line a baking tray with foil. Place the tortillas on the tray and spray both sides of the tortillas with olive oil. Bake for 5 minutes in the oven. Remove from the oven, turn and bake for 5 more minutes.

Combine the dressing with 1 teaspoon cumin, and 1 tablespoon chopped jalapeño and toss with the chicken.

If using a food processor, chop the onion and reserve 2 tablespoons for the garnish. Add the garlic and remaining jalapeños to the onion in the processor bowl. Add the beans, remaining teaspoon of ground cumin, and water. Purée to a smooth paste. Season with salt and pepper to taste.

Spread the tortillas with the bean paste. Place the chicken on top of the beans and top with the lettuce. Sprinkle with the remaining chopped red onion and serve.

Makes 2 servings.

> One serving: 332 calories, 25g protein, 33g carbohydrate, 14g fat (2g saturated), 48mg cholesterol, 402mg sodium, 1g fiber

cilantro tomatoes

2 medium tomatoes, diced (about 2 cups)

4 tablespoons chopped fresh cilantro

Salt and freshly ground black pepper to taste

Combine the tomatoes and cilantro and season with salt and pepper to taste. Serve with the tostadas.

Makes 2 servings.

> One serving: 31 calories, 2g protein, 6g carbohydrate, 0g fat (0g saturated), 0mg cholesterol, 13mg sodium, 0g fiber

helpful hints

● The tortilla can be baked in a toaster oven.

● Red onion is used for the beans and as a garnish. Chop it all at one time and divide accordingly.

● For optimum flavor, make sure the ground cumin is less than 6 months old.

countdown

● Preheat oven to 400 degrees.

● Bake tortilla.

● Prepare tomatoes.

shopping list

TO BUY:

¼ sliced roasted chicken breast

1 package (8-inch) whole wheat tortillas

1 small can dark red kidney beans (4 ounces needed)

2 medium tomatoes

1 small bunch cilantro

2 medium jalapeño peppers

1 bag washed, ready-to-eat shredded lettuce

STAPLES:

Red onion

Garlic

Olive oil spray

No-sugar-added oil and vinegar dressing

Ground cumin

Salt

Black peppercorns

caribbean shrimp salad

Emerald waters and crystal-clear blue skies create the backdrop for this tropical lunch. Shrimp, hot pepper sauce, and black beans are staples throughout the Caribbean. ● Based on total worldwide consumption, mangoes are second in popularity only to bananas. They can be found in many supermarkets. They can be messy to cube, but I offer an easy method below.

helpful hint

● *Any type of bean, such as red or white kidney beans can be used.*

countdown

● *Make yogurt cup.*
● *Make shrimp salad.*

shopping list

TO BUY:

1 carton light tropical fruit-flavored yogurt
½ pound cooked shrimp
1 small can black beans (8 ounces needed)
1 medium-sized green bell pepper
1 small tomato
1 small head lettuce
1 mango
2 limes

STAPLES:

Red onion
Celery
Mayonnaise made with olive or soybean oil
Hot pepper sauce
Salt
Black peppercorns

caribbean shrimp salad

2 tablespoons mayonnaise made with olive or soybean oil
2 tablespoons warm water
Several drops hot pepper sauce
2 tablespoons freshly squeezed lime juice
½ cup canned black beans, rinsed and drained
1 medium-sized green bell pepper, diced (1 cup)
2 celery stalks, diced (1 cup)
½ cup red onion, diced
1 small tomato, diced
½ pound cooked shrimp, cubed
Salt and freshly ground black pepper to taste
Several lettuce leaves, washed and torn into bite-size pieces

Combine the mayonnaise, water, hot pepper sauce, and lime juice in a medium-sized bowl. Add the black beans, green pepper, celery, onion, tomato, and shrimp. Toss well. Season with salt and pepper to taste. Place the lettuce leaves on a plate and spoon the shrimp salad on top of the lettuce to serve.

Makes 2 servings.

> One serving: 346 calories, 31g protein, 27g carbohydrate, 14g fat (2g saturated), 178mg cholesterol, 341mg sodium, 3g fiber

mango yogurt

1 mango
½ cup light tropical fruit-flavored yogurt

Slice off each side of the mango as close to the seed as possible. Take the mango half in your hand, skin- side down. Score the fruit in a cross-hatch pattern through to the skin. Bend the skin backwards so that the cubes pop up like a porcupine. Slice the cubes off the skin. Score and slice any fruit left on the pit.

Divide the yogurt between 2 cups and top with the mango cubes.

Makes 2 servings.

> One serving: 117 calories, 5g protein, 26g carbohydrate, 0.3g fat (0g saturated), 3mg cholesterol, 60mg sodium, 1g fiber

ham and mushroom pita pizza

This dish is covered with onion, mushrooms, peppers, and ham—and it can be made faster than ordering out for pizza. ● A secret to cooking the pizza fast is to preheat the baking tray.

ham and mushroom pitta pizza

Olive oil spray
1 medium-sized green bell
    pepper, sliced (about 1 cup)
4 slices red onion (½ cup)
2 small portobello mushrooms,
    sliced (about 1 cup)
1 whole-wheat pita bread
1 medium tomato sliced
¼ pound sliced lean ham,
    torn into bite size pieces
1 cup shredded, reduced-fat
    mozzarella cheese (4 ounces)

Preheat the broiler. Line a baking tray with foil and place under the broiler. Set a nonstick skillet over a medium-high heat and spray with olive oil. Add the pepper, onion, and mushrooms and sauté for 5 minutes. Slice open the pita bread so that you have 2 round pizza bases. Remove the baking tray from the broiler and place the pita halves on the foil, cut-side up. Spray the pita bread with olive oil and place the tomato slices on top. Spoon the pepper mixture over the tomatoes and top with the ham and cheese. Broil for 3 minutes, or until the cheese is bubbly. Serve hot. Makes 2 servings.

One serving: 354 calories, 36g protein, 35g carbohydrate, 8g fat (3g saturated), 35mg cholesterol, 1009mg sodium, 5g fiber

fennel salad

1 small fennel bulb, sliced
    (2 cups)
1 tablespoon no-sugar-added oil
    and vinegar dressing
Salt and freshly ground black
    pepper to taste

Remove the stem and fern-like leaves from the fennel. Wash and reserve the leaves. Thinly slice the fennel. Toss the fennel with the dressing. Snip small pieces from the fennel leaves with scissors (about ¼ cup) and sprinkle on top as a garnish. Season with salt and pepper to taste. Serve with the pizza. Makes 2 servings.

One serving: 53 calories, 0g protein, 0g carbohydrate, 4g fat (1g saturated), 0mg cholesterol, 38mg sodium, 0g fiber

banana

1 medium banana

Slice the banana in half and serve.
Makes 2 servings.

One serving: 70 calories, 1g protein, 18g carbohydrate, 0.5g fat (0g saturated), 0mg cholesterol, 1mg sodium, 1g fiber

helpful hints

● Any type of ready-to-eat salad can be substituted for the fennel salad.
● The fennel bulb can be sliced with a mandolin or in a food processor fitted with a thin-slicing blade.

countdown

● Preheat broiler.
● Prepare all ingredients.
● Make pizza.
● While pizza bakes, make salad.

shopping list

TO BUY:
    1 small package shredded
        reduced-fat mozzarella
        cheese (4 ounces needed)
    ¼ pound lean ham
    1 small package whole
        wheat pita bread
    1 medium-sized bell green
        pepper
    2 portobello mushrooms
        (2 ounces needed)
    1 medium tomato
    1 small fennel bulb
    1 medium banana
STAPLES:
    Olive oil spray
    Red onion
    No-sugar-added oil and
        vinegar dressing
    Salt
    Black peppercorns

fresh tuna salad

A salad made from fresh tuna rather than canned is a treat. In fact, if you have any leftover cooked fish, it can be used in this salad. ● Crab boil, also called shrimp boil, is a mixture of herbs and spices that is added to water to flavor fish. It usually includes bay leaves, peppercorns, mustard seeds, allspice, cloves, and dried ginger (see hints).

helpful hints

● *Do not overcook the tuna, or it will become very dry. Note that it will continue to cook in its own heat when removed from the saucepan.*
● *Make double if you have time, and store in the refrigerator for another lunch.*
● *If crab boil is unavailable, make your own from 1 bay leaf, 10 peppercorns, ½ teaspoon mustard seed and ¼ teaspoon each of allspice, cloves, and ginger.*

countdown

● *Cook tuna.*
● *Make salad.*
● *Toast bread.*

shopping list

TO BUY:
   1 carton light fruit-flavored yogurt
   6 ounces fresh yellow or black fin tuna
   1 packet crab boil
   2 medium tomatoes
   1 bunch fresh parsley
   1 bag washed, ready-to-eat mesclun salad
   2 medium peaches
STAPLES:
   Celery
   Olive oil spray
   Yellow onion
   Mayonnaise made with olive or soybean oil
   Rye bread
   Salt
   Black peppercorns

fresh tuna salad

6 ounces fresh yellow or black fin tuna
2 teaspoons crab boil seasoning (optional)
2 celery stalks, diced (1 cup)
2 medium tomatoes, chopped
½ cup chopped yellow onion
¼ cup chopped fresh parsley
2 tablespoons mayonnaise made with olive or soybean oil
Salt and freshly ground black pepper to taste
2 cups washed, ready-to-eat mesclun salad
2 slices rye bread
Olive oil spray

Place the tuna in a medium saucepan and cover with cold water. Add the crab boil seasoning. Bring to a simmer and gently cook until the tuna turns opaque or white, about 3–5 minutes. Reserve 2 tablespoons of the poaching liquid. Drain the fish and pat dry with a paper towel. Gently combine the celery, tomatoes, onion, parsley, mayonnaise, and poaching liquid in a medium-sized bowl. Flake in the tuna. Season with salt and pepper to taste and stir to incorporate the tuna and seasoning. Place the mesclun salad on 2 plates and top with the tuna salad. Spray the bread with olive oil and toast. Serve with the salad.
Makes 2 servings.

One serving: 339 calories, 28g protein, 23g carbohydrate, 18g fat (3g saturated), 37mg cholesterol, 318mg sodium, 4g fiber

fresh peach yogurt

1 cup light fruit-flavored yogurt
2 medium peaches, pitted and sliced

Divide the yogurt between 2 dessert bowls and top with the peach slices.
Makes 2 servings.

One serving: 87 calories, 5g protein, 18g carbohydrate, 0g fat (0g saturated), 3mg cholesterol, 58mg sodium, 1g fiber

spinach, mushroom, and canadian bacon salad

Baby spinach leaves and mushrooms topped with warm bacon is a flavorful lunchtime salad. This version uses lean Canadian bacon and takes only minutes to make. ● There are several brands of lean Canadian bacon available, and they vary considerably in fat content, so look for the one with lowest fat content. ● A warm dessert of pineapple and pine nuts rounds off this delightfully crunchy meal.

spinach, mushroom and canadian bacon salad

6 ounces sliced lean Canadian bacon, cut into thin strips

1 cup cooked chickpeas

2 tablespoons no-sugar-added oil and vinegar dressing

8 scallions, sliced (1 cup)

Salt and freshly ground black pepper to taste

¼ pound button mushrooms, sliced (about 1 ½ cups)

4 cups washed, ready-to-eat fresh spinach, torn into bite-size pieces

1 cup fresh bean sprouts, rinsed and drained

Place the Canadian bacon and chickpeas on a foil-lined baking tray and broil for 10 minutes, or until crisp. (Alternatively, brown the bacon and chickpeas in a toaster oven.) Combine the dressing and scallions together in a medium-sized bowl. Season with salt and pepper to taste. Add mushrooms, spinach, and sprouts. Toss well. Sprinkle with the Canadian bacon strips and chickpeas, and serve.

Makes 2 servings.

One serving: 387 calories, 29g protein, 35g carbohydrate, 15g fat (3g saturated), 40mg cholesterol, 911mg sodium, 9g fiber

pineapple and toasted pine nuts

2 tablespoons pine nuts

1 cup fresh pineapple cubes

Place the pine nuts on a foil-lined tray under the broiler or in the toaster oven for 1 minute. Toss the pineapple and pine nuts together and divide between 2 dessert bowls.

Makes 2 servings.

One serving: 72 calories, 0.5g protein, 10g carbohydrate, 0.5g fat (0g saturated), 0mg cholesterol, 1mg sodium, 1g fiber

helpful hints

● *The pine nuts can be toasted at the same time as the bacon and chickpeas. Watch them carefully, as they burn easily.*

● *To clean whole mushrooms, wipe them gently with damp paper towel.*

● *Buy fresh pineapple cubes in the produce section of the supermarket.*

countdown

● *Preheat broiler.*

● *Broil Canadian bacon.*

● *Toast pine nuts.*

● *Make salad.*

● *Toss pineapple and pine nuts together.*

shopping list

TO BUY:

6 ounces sliced lean Canadian bacon

1 small can chickpeas

1 small container pine nuts

1 small bunch scallions (8 needed)

1 small package button mushrooms (4 ounces needed)

1 bag washed, ready-to-eat fresh spinach

1 package fresh bean sprouts (1 cup needed)

1 small container fresh pineapple cubes

STAPLES:

No-sugar-added oil and vinegar dressing

Salt

Black peppercorns

helpful hints

- *Whole wheat pasta can be found in the pasta section of most supermarkets.*
- *A quick way to chop basil is to cut it with scissors.*
- *To save time and saucepans, add the carrots and asparagus to pasta while cooking.*

countdown

- *Cook pasta.*
- *Prepare turkey salad.*
- *Prepare yogurt.*

shopping list

TO BUY:

1 carton light orange-flavored yogurt

¼ pound smoked turkey breast

1 box whole wheat short-cut pasta (penne or macaroni)

¼ pound asparagus

1 medium tomato

1 small bunch fresh basil

2 medium tangerines

STAPLES:

Carrots

No-sugar-added oil and vinegar dressing

Salt

Black peppercorns

turkey and asparagus pasta salad

This turkey, asparagus, tomato and basil pasta salad can be assembled in the time it takes to boil water and cook the pasta. My first experience with whole wheat pasta was a surprise. It has a nutty flavor, very good texture, and can be used like regular pasta.

turkey and asparagus pasta salad

½ cup whole wheat penne or other short-cut pasta (2 ounces)

¼ pound asparagus

½ cup sliced carrots

1 medium tomato, cut into 1-inch cubes (1 cup)

¼ pound sliced smoked turkey breast

½ cup fresh basil, snipped with scissors

3 tablespoons no-sugar-added oil and vinegar dressing

Salt and freshly ground black pepper to taste

Bring a large saucepan filled with water to the boil. Add the pasta and cook for 10 minutes, or according to the package instructions. Do not overcook. While the pasta is cooking, cut or snap off the 1-inch fibrous stems on the asparagus and discard. Slice the remaining asparagus into 1-inch pieces (you should have about 1 cup). Add the asparagus and carrots for the last 2 minutes of cooking time. Drain. Place the pasta, asparagus, carrots, tomato, turkey, and basil in a bowl. Add the dressing and toss well. Season with salt and pepper if needed and serve warm.

Makes 2 servings.

One serving: 334 calories, 23g protein, 26g carbohydrate, 15g fat (3g saturated), 40mg cholesterol, 170mg sodium, 5g fiber

tangerine and orange yogurt

1 cup light orange-flavored yogurt

2 medium tangerines, peeled and segmented

Divide the yogurt into 2 dessert bowls and top with tangerine slices.

Makes 2 servings.

One serving: 87 calories, 5g protein, 18g carbohydrate, 0.2g fat (0g saturated), 3mg cholesterol, 59mg sodium, 0g fiber

waldorf salad with roast beef sandwich

Salad greens with crisp apples and nuts were first served at the Waldorf Astoria Hotel in Manhattan in 1893 and, has been a standard on menus ever since. Add an open-faced roast beef sandwich to the spread and enjoy an all-American lunch.

waldorf salad

1 tablespoon mayonnaise made
    with olive or soybean oil
1 tablespoon freshly squeezed
    lemon juice (about 1/2 lemon)
Salt and freshly ground black
    pepper to taste
4 pecan halves, broken into pieces
    (1 tablespoon)
2 celery stalks, sliced (1 cup)
1 small red apple, cored and cut
    into 1/2-inch cubes
    (about 1 1/2 cups)
Several romaine lettuce leaves,
    washed and dried

Combine the mayonnaise and lemon juice in a medium-sized bowl. Season with salt and pepper to taste. Toast the pecans in the toaster oven for 1 minute, or until brown, to bring out their flavor (optional). Be careful: they burn easily. Toss the celery, apple, and pecans in the mayonnaise mixture. Place the lettuce leaves on 2 plates and spoon the salad onto the leaves to serve.
Makes 2 servings.

One serving: 151 calories, 2g protein,
16g carbohydrate, 10g fat (1g saturated),
3mg cholesterol, 116mg sodium, 4g fiber

roast beef sandwich

2 slices rye bread
1 tablespoon Dijon mustard
1/4 pound sliced lean roast beef,
1 small tomato, sliced

Spread the bread with mustard. Divide the roast beef between each slice of bread. Top with the tomato slices. Serve any extra tomato slices on the side.
Makes 2 servings.

One serving: 179 calories, 22g protein,
13g carbohydrate, 6g fat (2g saturated),
46mg cholesterol, 337mg sodium, 3g fiber

yogurt

1 cup light fruit-flavored yogurt

Divide the yogurt between 2 dessert bowls.
Makes 2 servings.

One serving: 50 calories, 4g protein,
9g carbohydrate, 0g fat (0g saturated),
51mg cholesterol, 511mg sodium, 6g fiber

helpful hints

● *Any type of lettuce can be used.*
● *Toasting pecans can be tricky, as they burn quickly. Watch them carefully.*

countdown

● *Make salad.*
● *Make sandwich.*
● *Assemble yogurt.*

shopping list

TO BUY:
1 carton light fruit-flavored
    yogurt
1/4 pound sliced lean roast
    beef
1 small package pecan halves
    (1/2 ounce needed)
1 small tomato
1 small head romaine lettuce
1 lemon
1 small red apple
STAPLES:
Celery
Mayonnaise made with olive
    or soybean oil
Dijon mustard
Rye bread
Salt
Black peppercorns

grouper sandwich and tomato tapenade salad

This dish of fresh fish sautéed with onions, and served on melted cheese toast, reminds me of the lunches we have while sitting on the docks and watching the boats come in with their fresh catch. ● A tapenade is a thick paste usually made from capers, olives, oil, and vinegar. It is a great hors d'oeuvre or topping, in this case, to dress fresh sliced tomatoes.

grouper sandwich

6 ounces grouper fillet

2 teaspoons olive oil

Salt and freshly ground black pepper to taste

½ cup diced red onion

2 slices whole wheat bread

2 slices reduced-fat cheddar cheese (1½ ounces)

Rinse the fillet and pat dry with paper towel. Heat the oil in a small nonstick skillet over a medium-high heat. Add the fillet and sauté for 5 minutes. Turn and season the cooked side. Add the onion to the skillet and sauté for 3 more minutes. Toast the bread on one side, turn, cover with cheese, and return to the toaster oven until the cheese melts. Divide the grouper in half, place on top of the melted cheese and spoon the onion over the fillet to serve.
Makes 2 servings.

One serving: 249 calories, 26g protein, 13g carbohydrate, 11g fat (4g saturated), 46mg cholesterol, 341mg sodium, 3g fibre

tomato tapenade salad

2 medium-sized garlic cloves, crushed

2 tablespoons drained capers

4 pitted green olives

2 teaspoons balsamic vinegar

1 medium tomato, sliced

Salt and freshly ground black pepper to taste

Place the garlic, capers, olives, and balsamic vinegar in a food processor and purée. Alternatively, finely chop by hand. Divide the tomato slices between 2 plates. Sprinkle with salt and pepper to taste and spoon the tapenade on top. Serve at room temperature.
Makes 2 servings.

One serving: 27 calories, 1g protein, 4g carbohydrate, 1g fat (0g saturated), 0mg cholesterol, 410mg sodium, 0g fibre

orange-vanilla yogurt

2 medium-sized oranges

1 cup light vanilla-flavored yogurt

Peel and segment the oranges. Divide the yogurt between 2 dessert bowls and top with the orange segments.

One serving: 174 calories, 6g protein, 39g carbohydrate, 0.5g fat (0g saturated), 3mg cholesterol, 0mg sodium, 6g fibre

chicken sandwich with sun-dried tomato sauce

Sun-dried tomatoes and capers make a great sauce for chicken breasts. The chicken can be sautéed in minutes in garlic and lemon juice, or buy roasted chicken to save time. ● People often ask me what a caper is. Capers are small, unopened flowers from a bush that grows in the Mediterranean region. Capers are picked, dried, and pickled in a vinegar brine. There are many types of capers in the supermarket. They vary from the small, nonpareil type from southern France to larger versions. The flavor depends largely on the brining and pickling process. Buy a good-quality, well-known brand for the best results.

chicken sandwich with sun-dried tomato sauce

2 (3-ounce) boneless, skinless chicken breasts

2 teaspoons freshly squeezed lemon juice (½ small lemon)

4 medium-sized garlic cloves, crushed

¼ teaspoon freshly ground black pepper

2 slices 8-grain bread

2 tablespoons sun-dried tomatoes, drained and diced

3 tablespoons capers, drained

2 tablespoons mayonnaise made with olive or soybean oil

Several leaves red-leaf lettuce

Remove any visible fat from the chicken and pound it flat to about ¼ inch with a meat mallet or the bottom of a sturdy frying pan. Combine the lemon juice, garlic, and black pepper in a small bowl. Set a medium-sized nonstick skillet over a medium-high heat. Add the lemon mixture and chicken. Cook for 3 minutes. Turn and cook for 3 more minutes. Toast the bread. Combine the sun-dried tomatoes and capers with the mayonnaise. (Use the same bowl as for the lemon mixture.) Place the bread on 2 plates, cover with lettuce, top with chicken, and spread, with sauce to serve.

Makes 2 servings.

One serving: 327 calories, 32g protein, 16g carbohydrate, 17g fat (2g saturated), 77mg cholesterol, 596mg sodium, 4g fibre

apple yogurt

1 cup light fruit-flavored yogurt

2 apples, cored and sliced

Divide the yogurt between 2 bowls and top with the apple slices.

One serving: 131 calories, 4g protein, 30g carbohydrate, 0.5g fat (0g saturated), 3mg cholesterol, 58mg sodium, 4g fibre

helpful hint

● The sauce can be made several days ahead and refrigerated.

countdown

● Make chicken.
● Assemble dessert.

shopping list

TO BUY:

1 carton light fruit-flavored yogurt

2 (3-ounce) boneless, skinless chicken breasts

1 bottle diced sun-dried tomatoes in olive oil

1 small jar capers

1 small loaf 8-grain bread

1 small head red-leaf lettuce

1 lemon

2 apples

STAPLES:

Garlic

Mayonnaise made with olive or soybean oil

Salt

Black peppercorns

right carbs
dinners

japanese beef sukiyaki

This is a fun beef dish that's cooked at the table with an electric frying pan or wok. Alternatively, you can cook the entire meal in the kitchen and bring it to the table. The recipe for beef sukiyaki is for two servings, but can easily be doubled or tripled.

japanese beef sukiyaki

1 cup angel hair or thin whole wheat spaghetti (1 ounce)

¼ cup fat-free, low-salt chicken broth

¼ cup low-salt soy sauce

½ cup dry sherry

2 (.035 ounce) envelope sugar substitute

4 teaspoons sesame oil

1 cup sliced yellow onion,

4 celery stalks, sliced (2 cups)

6 ounces beef sirloin, cut into strips about 4 inches long and 1inch wide

¼ pound mushrooms, sliced (¾ cup)

5 ounces washed, ready-to-eat fresh spinach (4 cups)

1 cup sliced water chestnuts drained

8 scallions, sliced (about 1 cup)

Freshly ground black pepper to taste

Bring a large saucepan filled with water to a boil. When the water boils, add the noodles and boil for 5 minutes, or according to the package instructions. Do not overcook. Drain and divide between 2 plates.

Combine the chicken broth, soy sauce, sherry, and sugar substitute in a small bowl. Make sure all ingredients are prepared and ready for stir-frying. Heat the sesame oil in nonstick skillet or wok. Add the onion and celery, and cook for 3 minutes. Add the beef and cook for 1 minute, tossing constantly. Add half of the sauce and stir. Add the mushrooms and cook for 30 seconds. Add the spinach, water chestnuts, and scallions and cook for 1 minute. Add the remaining sauce and cook for 30 seconds more, continuing to stir. Season with black pepper to taste. Remove immediately from the pan and serve over the noodles. Spoon the sauce on top.
Makes 2 servings.

One serving: 666 calories, 46g protein, 68g carbohydrate, 18g fat (6g saturated), 76mg cholesterol, 1604mg sodium, 14g fiber

fresh peaches in kirsch

2 medium peaches, pitted and sliced

2 tablespoons kirsch

Divide the peach slices between 2 dessert bowls and sprinkle with kirsch.
Makes 2 servings.

One serving: 69 calories, 1g protein, 10g carbohydrate, 0g fat (0g saturated), 0mg cholesterol, 0mg sodium, 1g fiber

helpful hints

● Any type of liqueur or brandy can be substituted for the kirsch.
● To keep from having to look back at the recipe as you stir-fry the ingredients, line them up on a cutting board or plate in the order of use so you know which ingredient comes next.

countdown

● Cook spaghetti.
● Prepare remaining ingredients.
● Bring to table and cook.

shopping list

TO BUY:
6 ounces beef sirloin
1 can sliced water chestnuts
1 bottle sesame oil
1 box angel hair or thin whole wheat spaghetti (2 ounces needed)
1 small bottle dry sherry
1 small bottle kirsch
1 container sliced mushrooms (4 ounces needed)
1 bunch scallions (8 needed)
1 bag washed, ready-to-eat fresh spinach (5 ounces needed)
2 medium peaches
STAPLES:
Celery
Yellow onion
Fat-free, low-salt chicken broth
Low-salt soy sauce
Sugar substitute
Black peppercorns

fish in a pouch

helpful hints

- If possible, buy diced sun-dried tomatoes to save the time spent dicing whole ones.
- Olive oil with a small crushed garlic clove works fine as a substitute for garlic-infused oil.
- For optimum flavor, make sure the dried thyme is less than 6 months old.
- Fat-free, low-salt chicken broth can be substituted for the dry white wine.

countdown

- Preheat broiler.
- Make fish.
- While fish cooks, make couscous.

shopping list

TO BUY:
10 ounces thin fish fillet (snapper or sole)
1 jar diced sun-dried tomatoes
1 small bottle dry white wine or 1 can fat-free, low-salt chicken broth
1 small box couscous
1 bottle garlic-infused olive oil
1 small package sliced mushrooms, (3 ounces needed)
½ pound zucchini
1 small bunch grapes
STAPLES:
Dried thyme
Foil
Salt
Black peppercorns

The ingredients are folded in a piece of foil. The natural juices are sealed in as the fish steams, and a burst of aroma escapes when you open the foil parcel. You can assemble the parcel about an hour in advance and then place it in the oven when needed. ● There's a large variety of flavored or infused olive oils available. Using them is an easy way to add flavor to a dish.

fish in a pouch

10 ounces thin fish fillets (snapper, sole)
2 (10-inch) squares foil
Salt and freshly ground black pepper to taste
1 cup sliced mushrooms (3 ounces)
½ cup diced and drained sun-dried tomatoes
½ teaspoon dried thyme
¼ cup dry white wine or fat-free, low salt chicken broth

Preheat the broiler. Line a baking tray with foil and place in the oven about 5 inches from the broiler to the heat. Centre the fish on the foil squares. Season with salt and pepper. Spread the mushrooms and sun-dried tomatoes over the fish. Sprinkle with the thyme and pour the wine or chicken broth on top. Fold the edges of foil together, sealing tightly to prevent them from leaking. Place the packets on the baking tray and broil for 15 minutes. Serve the fish in the pouch or remove to plates and spoon the sauce and vegetables on top.
Makes 2 servings.

One serving: 213 calories, 31g protein, 6g carbohydrate, 6g fat (0g saturated), 52mg cholesterol, 169mg sodium, 2g fiber

garlic zucchini couscous

1 cup water
2 cups zucchini, sliced (½ pound)
⅔ cup couscous
4 teaspoons garlic-infused olive oil
Salt and freshly ground black pepper to taste

Combine the water and zucchini in a medium saucepan, and bring to the boil over a high heat. Remove from the heat, add the couscous, cover and set aside for 5 minutes. Add the infused oil and toss with a fork. Season to taste and serve.
Makes 2 servings.

One serving: 263 calories, 8g protein, 38g carbohydrate, 10g fat (1g saturated), 0mg cholesterol, 8mg sodium, 2g fiber

grapes

30 grapes (2 cups)

Divide the grapes between 2 dessert plates.
Makes 2 servings.

One serving: 58 calories, 1g protein, 16g carbohydrate, 0g fat (0g saturated), 0mg cholesterol, 2mg sodium, 0g fiber

ham and mushroom pita pizza **p167**

chicken sandwich with sun-dried tomato sauce   **p173**

chicken with parmesan and tomato sauce

This quick dinner takes only 20 minutes to make. The pasta and broccoli are cooked in the same saucepan to save washing an extra pan.

chicken with parmesan and tomato sauce

Olive oil spray

1/2 pound boneless, skinless chicken breast, visible fat removed

Salt and freshly ground pepper to taste

1/2 cup low-sugar, low-fat tomato sauce for pasta

2 tablespoons freshly grated Parmesan cheese

Set a medium-sized nonstick skillet over a medium-high heat. Spray with olive oil and brown the chicken for 2 minutes on each side. Season each cooked side with salt and pepper to taste. Add the pasta sauce and simmer for 4 minutes. Sprinkle with Parmesan cheese, cover with a lid, and set aside for 1 minute. Divide between 2 plates and serve with the pasta and broccoli.

Makes 2 servings.

One serving: 248 calories, 39g protein, 4g carbohydrate, 9g fat (3g saturated), 100mg cholesterol, 390mg sodium, 1g fiber

pasta and broccoli

2 ounces whole wheat spaghetti (1/2 cup uncooked)

2 cups broccoli florets (4 ounces)

2 teaspoons olive oil

Salt and freshly ground black pepper to taste

Bring a large pot of water to the boil and add the pasta. Cook for 5 minutes, add the broccoli, and continue to cook for 4 minutes. Drain and toss with the olive oil. Season with salt and pepper to taste.

Makes 2 servings.

One serving: 206 calories, 9g protein, 30g carbohydrate, 6g fat (1g saturated), 0mg cholesterol, 28mg sodium, 6g fiber

helpful hints

● Buy good quality Parmesan cheese and grate it yourself. Freeze extra for quick use later—simply spoon out what you need and leave the rest frozen.

● When draining pasta, leave a little water on the pasta for added sauce.

● If pressed for time, omit the poached spiced pears and serve 1 medium pear per person.

countdown

● Place water for pasta on to boil.

● Make poached spiced pears.

● Make pasta and broccoli.

● Make chicken.

chicken with parmesan and tomato sauce continued

italian-style salad

4 cups washed, ready-to-eat, Italian-style salad

1 cup frozen corn kernals

2 tablespoons no-sugar-added salad dressing

Toss the salad and corn with the dressing.

Makes 2 servings.

One serving: 151 calories, 3g protein, 19g carbohydrate, 9g fat (1g saturated), 0mg cholesterol, 85mg sodium, 2g fiber

poached spiced pears

2 cups water

2 (.035-ounce) envelopes sugar substitute

8 whole cloves

8 strips lemon peel from 1 lemon

2 ripe pears

2 sprigs fresh mint

Place the water, sugar substitute, cloves, and lemon peel in a medium-sized saucepan. Peel the pears over the pan to catch the juice. Core and slice the pears. Add the pear slices to the saucepan. Bring to a simmer and poach gently for 10 minutes. Remove the pear slices and arrange in a circle on 2 dessert plates. Place a sprig of mint in the centre of each plate.

Makes 2 servings.

One serving: 98 calories, 1g protein, 26g carbohydrate, 1g fat (0g saturated), 0mg cholesterol, 1mg sodium, 4g fiber

cioppino (seafood stew)

Cioppino is a 20-minute, one-pot meal that is great in winter or summer. Italian immigrants are credited with bringing this soup—a hearty combination of seafood and vegetables—to San Francisco.

cioppino

½ pound fresh sea scallops

6 ounces grouper fillet

3 teaspoons olive oil

Salt and freshly ground black pepper to taste

1 cup red onion, sliced

2 medium-sized green bell peppers, sliced (2 cups)

5 medium-sized garlic cloves, crushed

¼ pound unpeeled red potatoes, washed, halved and sliced (1 cup)

2 cups low-salt, no-sugar-added canned whole tomatoes (including juice)

2 cups bottled clam juice

¼ teaspoon red pepper flakes

2 tablespoons balsamic vinegar

½ cup chopped fresh basil

2 slices multigrain bread

Olive oil spray

Wash the scallops and grouper and pat dry with a paper towel. Cut the grouper into 1-inch pieces about the same size as the scallops. Heat the olive oil in a medium-sized nonstick skillet over a high heat. Add the fish and scallops and sauté for 2 minutes. Remove to a large soup bowl and season with salt and pepper to taste. In the same skillet, sauté the onion, pepper, and 4 garlic cloves over a high heat for 3 minutes. Add the potatoes, tomatoes, clam juice, and red pepper flakes, breaking up the whole tomatoes with a spoon. Bring to a simmer, cover, and simmer for 15 minutes. Add the balsamic vinegar and season with salt and pepper to taste. Spoon the mixture over the fish and sprinkle with the basil.

Spray the bread with olive oil. Cut the remaining garlic clove in half and rub the bread with the cut sides of the garlic. Place in the toaster oven or under the broiler to toast. Serve with the cioppino.

Makes 2 servings.

One serving: 502 calories, 46g protein, 50g carbohydrate, 14g fat (2g saturated), 67mg cholesterol, 966mg sodium, 8g fiber

helpful hints

- *Any type of firm, non-oily white fish can be used, for example turbot, halibut or monkfish.*
- *Several drops hot pepper sauce can be substituted for red pepper flakes.*
- *Look for watermelon cut into cubes in the produce section of the supermarket or at a salad bar.*
- *If pressed for time, omit the Watermelon Spritzer and serve 1 cup of watermelon cubes per person.*

countdown

- *Make stew.*
- *While stew simmers, make salad.*
- *Make watermelon spritzer.*

shopping list

TO BUY:

½ pound fresh sea scallops

6 ounces grouper fillet

1 bottle no-sugar-added
lemon-lime or citrus-flavored
seltzer (16 ounces needed)

1 small bottle red pepper
flakes

1 can no-sugar-added whole
tomatoes

2 bottles clam juice
(18 ounces needed)

1 can or jar sliced beets

2 medium-sized green bell
peppers

¼ pound red potatoes

1 small bunch fresh basil

1 container watermelon
cubes or ¼ whole
watermelon (10 ounces
needed)

2 limes

STAPLES:

Red onion

Garlic

Olive oil

Olive oil spray

Balsamic vinegar

No-sugar-added oil and
vinegar dressing

Multigrain bread

Sugar substitute

Salt

Black peppercorns

cioppino (seafood stew) continued

beet and onion salad

2 cups canned sliced beets,
drained

½ cup sliced red onion

2 tablespoons no-sugar-added oil
and vinegar dressing

Salt and freshly ground black
pepper to taste

Divide the sliced beets between 2 plates. Sprinkle with the onion and drizzle with the dressing. Season with salt and pepper to taste and serve with the cioppino.

Makes 2 servings.

One serving: 129 calories, 2g protein,
13g carbohydrate, 9g fat (1g saturated),
0mg cholesterol, 159mg sodium, 0g fiber

watermelon spritzer

2 cups no-sugar-added lemon-
lime or citrus-flavored seltzer,
chilled

2 tablespoons freshly squeezed
lime juice

2 (.035-ounce) envelopes
sugar substitute

2 cups watermelon cubes

Place the sparkling water, lime juice, sugar substitute, and watermelon cubes in a blender. Blend until smooth. Pour into 2 glasses and serve immediately.

Makes 2 servings.

One serving: 53 calories, 1g protein,
13g carbohydrate, 0.6g fat (0g saturated),
0mg cholesterol, 3mg sodium, 1g fiber

pork souvlaki

Barbecued, skewered meats called souvlaki are sold as a quick meal on many street corners in Athens. A simple Greek marinade of lemon juice, olive oil, oregano, and garlic flavors the meat. ● Bulghur is wheat kernels that have been steamed, dried, and crushed. It has a chewy texture and tastes delicious in salads.

pork souvlaki

¼ cup freshly squeezed lemon juice (2 lemons)

2 teaspoons olive oil

2 teaspoons dried oregano

2 medium-sized garlic cloves, crushed

½ pound pork tenderloin, visible fat removed and meat cut into 1½-inch cubes

2 small green bell peppers, cut into 2-inch square pieces

½ small yellow onion, cut into pieces ½-inch wide and 2 inches long

2 kabob skewers

Preheat the broiler. Combine the lemon juice, oil, oregano, and garlic in a medium-sized bowl or large ziplock bag. Add the pork and marinate for 15 minutes. Remove the pork from the marinade and thread onto skewers, alternating with the green bell pepper and onion pieces. If using the broiler, line a baking tray with foil and place the souvlaki on the tray. Or, place on a preheated stove-top grill for 5 minutes. Broil or grill for 5 minutes. Turn and cook for 5 more minutes. Serve over the bulghur wheat

Makes 2 servings.

One serving: 299 calories, 36g protein, 16g carbohydrate, 10g fat (3g saturated), 106mg cholesterol, 82mg sodium, 1g fiber

bulghur wheat salad

1 cup fat-free, low-salt chicken broth

½ cup coarse bulghur or cracked wheat

Salt and freshly ground black pepper to taste

¼ cup raisins

¼ cup pine nuts

2 teaspoons olive oil

Pour the broth into a small saucepan and bring to the boil over a high heat. Add the bulghur wheat and a pinch of salt and pepper. Lower the heat, stir, and cover with a lid. Gently simmer for 10 minutes, or until the liquid is absorbed. Stir the raisins, pine nuts, and olive oil into the cooked bulghur. Season with additional salt and pepper to taste.

Makes 2 servings.

One serving: 245 calories, 5g protein, 32g carbohydrate, 5g fat (1g saturated), 0mg cholesterol, 553mg sodium, 4g fiber

apricots

8 medium-size fresh apricots

Divide between 2 plates.

Makes 2 servings.

One serving: 67 calories, 2g protein, 16g carbohydrate, 0.5g fat (0g saturated), 0mg cholesterol, 1mg sodium, 3g fiber

helpful hints

● *If using wooden skewers, soak in water before using.*

● *To make marinating the pork easier, place it in self-seal bags. You only need to flip the bag over to turn the meat in the marinade— and there's no bowl to wash.*

countdown

● *Preheat broiler or stove top grill*

● *Marinate pork.*

● *Make salad.*

● *Cook souvlaki.*

shopping list

TO BUY:

½ pound pork tenderloin

½ cup corse bulghur or cracked wheat

1 small container pine nuts

1 small box raisins

2 small green peppers

2 lemons

8 medium-sized fresh apricots

STAPLES:

Yellow onion

Garlic

Olive oil

Dried oregano

Fat free, low-salt chicken broth

Salt

Black peppercorns

mediterranean veal and olives

helpful hint

● *Most supermarkets sell veal stew meat that is already cut into small pieces. Buy lean veal, or remove as much fat from the meat as possible before you cook it.*

countdown

● *Prepare veal.*
● *While veal cooks, make barley.*

shopping list

TO BUY:

½ pound veal stewing meat
1 can low-salt, no-sugar-added crushed tomatoes (8 ounces needed)
1 small jar pitted black olives
1 small package pine nuts
1 small box quick-cooking pearl barley
1 small bottle dry white wine
1 small container orange juice
½ pound broccoli florets
1 small bunch fresh basil
1 orange

STAPLES:

Yellow onion
Garlic
Olive oil
Olive oil spray
Fat free, low-salt chicken broth
Salt
Black peppercorns

Olives and pine nuts give this 20-minute veal stew a rich Mediterranean flavor. ● Warm, bright sunshine, rolling hills touched with varying shades of green from the rows of olive trees, good food, thoughts of Italy and Greece... these memories inspired this quick, veal dinner and accompanying dish of orange barley.

mediterranean veal and olives

Olive oil spray
½ pound veal stewing meat, visible fat trimmed, and meat cut into 1-inch cubes
1 cup diced yellow onion
2 medium-sized garlic cloves, crushed
½ cup dry white wine 1 cup low-salt, no-sugar-added canned crushed tomatoes
3 to 4 broccoli florets (½ pound)
8 black olives, pitted and halved
2 tablespoons pine nuts
½ cup fresh basil, torn into bite-size pieces
Salt and freshly ground black pepper to taste

Set a nonstick skillet over a medium-high heat and spray with olive oil. Brown the veal on all sides for 3 minutes. Remove the veal, add the onion and garlic to the skillet, and cook for 2 minutes. Add the wine and cook for another minute. Add the tomatoes and broccoli. Reduce the heat to medium-low and return the veal to the pan. Cover and simmer for 15 minutes. Add the olives and pine nuts. Cook for 5 more minutes. Add the basil, season with salt and pepper to taste, and serve.
Makes 2 servings.

One serving: 409 calories, 38g protein, 22g carbohydrate, 13g fat (4g saturated), 100mg cholesterol, 497mg sodium, 5g fiber

orange barley

½ cup fat-free, low-salt chicken broth
½ cup quick-cooking pearl barley
2 teaspoons olive oil
1 tablespoon orange juice
1 orange, peeled and split into segments
Salt and freshly ground black pepper to taste

Bring the broth to the boil in a medium saucepan and add the barley. Boil for 10 minutes, uncovered. Drain and add the oil, orange juice, and orange segments. Season with salt and pepper to taste and serve with the veal.
Makes 2 servings.

One serving: 222 calories, 5g protein, 41g carbohydrate, 5g fat (1g saturated), 0mg cholesterol, 142mg sodium, 0g fiber

herbed meatball minestrone

'Minestra' is Italian for soup, and minestrone is a hearty vegetable soup. This meatball minestrone is a complete meal in one pot. The recipe can be doubled easily so, if you have time, make extra to use another time. ● Spices can add exciting flavors with very little effort. Fennel seeds are oval, green-brown seeds that come from the common fennel plant. They have an anise taste and are used in many liqueurs. They can be found in the spice section of your market, and they will keep for 6 months. Here, combined with oregano, they give the meatballs a unique flavor. ● Follow this comforting main course with a second helping of soul food—ginger-spiced apple sauce.

herbed meatball minestrone

2 teaspoons fennel seeds
1 teaspoon dried oregano
1/4 pound lean ground beef sirloin
Salt and freshly ground black pepper to taste
2 teaspoons olive oil
1/2 cup sliced yellow onion
2 celery stalks, sliced (about 1 cup)
4 medium-sized garlic cloves, crushed
1 cup canned low-salt, no-sugar-added diced tomatoes
2 cups fat-free, low-salt chicken broth
2 cups water
1/2 cup whole wheat spaghetti or linguine, broken into small pieces (2 ounces)
8 cups washed, ready-to-eat fresh spinach (10 ounces)
1/2 cup canned small navy beans, rinsed and drained
2 tablespoons freshly grated Parmesan cheese

Mix the fennel seeds and oregano into the ground beef. Add a little salt and pepper to taste. Form into meatballs about 1½ to 2 inches in diameter. Heat the oil in a medium-sized nonstick saucepan over a medium-high heat. Brown the meatballs on all sides, about 5 minutes, or until cooked through. Remove to a plate. Add the onion and celery to the saucepan. Sauté for 3 minutes without letting them brown. Add the garlic, tomatoes, chicken broth, and water. Bring to a boil. Add the pasta and cook gently for 8–9 minutes, stirring once or twice to make sure the pasta rolls freely in the liquid. Add the spinach and beans to the cooking pasta. Return the meatballs to the soup and cook until heated through, about 2 minutes. Season to taste and serve in 2 large soup bowls with Parmesan cheese sprinkled on top.
Makes 2 servings.

One serving: 510 calories, 45g protein, 62g carbohydrate, 14g fat (5g saturated), 55mg cholesterol, 965mg sodium, 21g fiber

helpful hints

● If you are not serving the soup immediately or are making some to freeze later, cook the pasta in a separate pot of water for 10 minutes. Drain, reserving 3 tablespoons of the cooking liquid. Add 1/2 teaspoon olive oil to the liquid and toss with the pasta to keep it from sticking. Add the pasta to the soup a few minutes before serving to warm through. The pasta will absorb the soup liquid if left to sit for any length of time.
● Cannellini beans or chickpeas can be substituted for navy beans.
● Frozen spinach can be used instead of fresh. Defrost and squeeze dry before using.
● Buy good quality Parmesan cheese and grate it yourself. Freeze extra for quick use later—simply spoon out what you need and leave the rest frozen.
● If pressed for time, omit the Ginger-spiced Apple Sauce and serve 1 medium apple per person.

countdown

● Make minestrone.
● Core, peel and cook apples.
● Assemble salad.
● Complete apple sauce.

herbed meatball minestrone

continued

shopping list

TO BUY:

*¼ pound lean ground beef
sirloin*

*1 can low-salt, no-sugar-
added diced tomatoes
(16 ounces needed)*

*1 small can navy beans
(4 ounces needed)*

1 jar fennel seeds

*1 box whole wheat spaghetti
or linguine (2 ounces
needed)*

*1 bag washed, ready-to-eat
fresh spinach (10 ounces
needed)*

*1 bag washed, ready-to-eat,
Italian-style salad*

1-inch piece fresh ginger

2 Granny Smith apples

1 lemon

STAPLES:

Celery

Yellow onion

Garlic

Parmesan cheese

Olive oil

*No-sugar-added oil and
vinegar dressing*

Dried oregano

*Fat-free, low-salt chicken
broth*

Ground cinnamon

Sugar substitute

Salt

Black peppercorns

italian salad

*2 cups washed, ready-to-eat,
Italian-style salad*

*2 tablespoons no-sugar-added oil
and vinegar dressing*

Toss the salad with the dressing and serve.
Makes 2 servings.

> One serving: 79 calories, 0g protein,
> 1g carbohydrate, 8g fat (1g saturated),
> 0mg cholesterol, 78mg sodium, 0g fiber

ginger-spiced apple sauce

*2 Granny Smith apples, cored and
cut into eighths*

½ cup water

*2 tablespoons freshly squeezed
lemon juice (1 lemon)*

*2 (.035-ounce) envelopes
sugar substitute*

2 tablespoons grated fresh ginger

½ teaspoon ground cinnamon

Place the apples and water in a medium
saucepan. Cover with a lid and bring to a boil.
Cook for 10 minutes. Alternatively, place the
apples and water in a microwave-safe bowl.
Cover and microwave on high for 5 minutes. Let
stand for 2 to 3 minutes.

Place the cooked apples and water in the bowl
of a food processor, and add the lemon juice and
sugar substitute. Grate the ginger over the bowl,
making sure to catch any ginger juice. Process
until thoroghly mixed. Spoon into 2 dessert
bowls. Sprinkle the apple sauce with a little
cinnamon and serve.
Makes 2 servings.

> One serving: 90 calories, 0.5g protein,
> 24g carbohydrate, 0.5g fat (0g saturated),
> 0mg cholesterol, 1mg sodium, 4g fiber

curried shrimp and lentil salad

This meal takes a little more time, about 30 minutes, but is very much worth the effort. Juicy shrimp cooked in a light curry sauce produce a flavor-packed, ethnic meal—try it when you want something with a zing. ● Authentic curries are made with a blend of about 15 spices. I have used store-bought curry powder to shorten the preparation time for this meal. This type of powder loses its flavor quickly and should be not used if more than 3–4 months old.

curried shrimp

1 tablespoon olive oil

2 medium-sized garlic cloves, crushed

1-inch piece fresh ginger, chopped (2 tablespoons)

2 tablespoons whole wheat flour

2 teaspoons ground cumin

1½ tablespoons curry powder

1 cup fat-free, low-salt chicken broth

½ pound broccoli florets (about 2 cups)

½ cup sliced red onion

¼ cup raisins

¾ pound large shrimp, shelled and deveined

Salt and freshly ground black pepper to taste

2 tablespoons heavy whipping cream

Heat the olive oil in a nonstick skillet over a medium heat. Add the garlic, ginger, whole wheat flour, cumin, and curry powder, stirring to blend well. Add the chicken broth. Cook until the sauce begins to thicken, about 1 minute. Add the broccoli florets, onion, and raisins. Cover and simmer for 5 minutes. Add the shrimp and cook uncovered for 2 minutes, or until the shrimp are cooked. Season with salt and pepper to taste. Remove from the heat and blend in the cream. Divide between 2 plates and serve.

Makes 2 servings.

One serving: 451 calories, 42g protein, 36g carbohydrate, 17g fat (5g saturated), 281mg cholesterol, 564mg sodium, 1g fiber

helpful hints

● *Buy shelled shrimp—it is well worth the time otherwise spent shelling them yourself.*

● *To chop fresh ginger quickly, cut it into small cubes and press through a garlic press with large holes. If using a press with small holes, just capture the juice that is squeezed out; it will give enough flavor for the recipe.*

● *Lentil salad can be made a day ahead and served warm or at room temperature. Make extra if you have time for a great lunch or snack*

● *To shorten preparation time for this meal, omit the lentil salad and serve a quick-cooking brown rice instead.*

countdown

● *Start lentil salad.*

● *Prepare ingredients for curried shrimp.*

● *Cook curried shrimp.*

● *Finish lentil salad.*

shopping list

TO BUY:

1 small carton heavy
*   whipping cream*
¾ pound large shrimp,
*   peeled*
1 can litchis
1 jar curry powder
1 small package dried lentils
1 small box raisins
*   (¼ cup needed)*
½ pound broccoli florets
1 small bunch scallions
*   (4 needed)*
1-inch piece fresh ginger

STAPLES:

Olive oil
No-sugar-added oil and
*   vinegar dressing*
Red onion
Garlic
Whole wheat flour
Fat-free, low-salt chicken
*   broth*
Ground cumin
Salt
Black peppercorns

curried shrimp and lentil salad continued

lentil salad

1 cup fat-free, low-salt
*   chicken broth*
1 cup water
½ cup lentils
2 whole garlic cloves
4 scallions, thinly sliced (½ cup)
2 tablespoons no-sugar-added oil
*   and vinegar dressing*
Salt and freshly ground black
*   pepper to taste*

Bring the stock and water to the boil in a medium saucepan. Rinse the lentils and slowly pour into the boiling broth, so that the broth continues to boil. Add the garlic and reduce the heat to medium-low. Simmer for 20 minutes, or until lentils are cooked through but still firm. Meanwhile, mix the scallions with the dressing. Add salt and pepper to taste. Drain the lentils and remove the garlic cloves. Mix the dressing with the lentils while still warm.
Makes 2 servings.

One serving: 147 calories, 6g protein, 13g carbohydrate, 9g fat (1g saturated), 0mg cholesterol, 357mg sodium, 2g fiber

litchis

1 cup drained, canned litchis

Divide the litchis between 2 dessert bowls and serve.
Makes 2 servings.

One serving: 63 calories, 1g protein, 16g carbohydrate, 0.5g fat (0g saturated), 0mg cholesterol, 1mg sodium, 1g fiber

chicken fajitas

Fajitas make deliciously light meals. Served with an array of colorful vegetables and wrapped in warm tortillas, these little Mexican sandwiches are an entire meal in themselves. ● *Enjoy grapefruit with a kick for dessert.*

chicken fajitas

1 cup freshly squeezed lemon juice (2 lemons)

3 teaspoons canola oil, divided

1 teaspoon ground cumin

Pinch ground cayenne

½ pound boneless, skinless chicken breast, very thinly sliced

4 (8-inch) whole wheat tortillas

1 cup sliced red onion

2 medium-size red bell peppers, sliced (2 cups)

2 medium-size green bell peppers, sliced (2 cups)

4 garlic cloves, crushed

2 medium tomatoes, diced

½ cup shredded, reduced-fat Monterey Jack cheese

½ cup chopped fresh cilantro

Preheat the oven to 350 degrees. Mix the lemon juice, 1 teaspoon of the oil, the cumin, and cayenne together in a microwave-safe bowl. Microwave for 30 seconds on high. Alternatively, place in a small saucepan, bring to the boil and then immediately remove from the heat. Place the chicken in the warm marinade for 15 minutes, stirring to make sure all of the chicken is covered. Tightly wrap the tortillas in 2 foil packages and place in the preheated oven for 10 minutes. Remove and leave wrapped in foil.

Heat the remaining 2 teaspoons of oil in a medium-sized nonstick skillet until the oil begins to smoke. Remove the chicken from the marinade, saving any marinade that remains (most will be absorbed by the chicken), and sauté the chicken for about 1 minute. Add the onion, peppers, and garlic. Sauté for 2 minutes. Add the marinade and toss with the chicken and vegetables for another minute, or until the sauce reduces and just coats the chicken.

To serve, arrange the diced tomatoes, shredded cheese, and chopped cilantro in small bowls. Spoon the chicken and vegetables onto a warm serving dish along with the wrapped tortillas. Fill the tortillas with the chicken and vegetables, sprinkle with the tomatoes, grated cheese, and cilantro ,and fold to eat.
Makes 2 servings.

One serving: 650 calories, 65g protein, 56g carbohydrate, 23g fat (8g saturated), 116mg cholesterol, 614mg sodium, 2g fiber

helpful hints

● *Red, yellow, and green bell peppers make this a colorful dish, but you can use one or any combination of bell peppers you like.*

● *Heating dried spices releases their oils, increasing their flavor.*

● *Triple Sec and other orange liqueurs can be bought in small splits of about 2 ounces at most liquor stores.*

countdown

● *Preheat oven to 350 degrees*

● *Make fajitas.*

● *Make grapefruit.*

chicken fajitas continued

shopping list

TO BUY:

1 small package shredded,
   reduced-fat Montrerey Jack
   cheese

½ pound boneless, skinless,
   chicken breast

1 small package whole
   wheat tortillas

1 small bottle Triple Sec

2 medium-size red bell
   peppers

2 medium-size green bell
   peppers

2 medium tomatoes

1 small bunch fresh cilantro

2 lemons

1 small grapefruit

STAPLES:

Red onion

Garlic

Canola oil

Ground cumin

Cayenne pepper

tipsy grapefruit

1 grapefruit
1 tablespoon Triple Sec or other
   orange liqueur

Separate the grapefruit segments with a serrated knife and scoop out onto 2 dessert plates. Sprinkle with the Triple Sec and serve.
Makes 2 servings.

One serving: 101 calories, 1g protein,
17g carbohydrate, 0g fat (0g saturated),
0mg cholesterol, 1mg sodium, 1g fibre

roast beef and shiitake hash

Roast beef, shiitake mushrooms, and fresh thyme transform a 1950s-style American "hash" to a modern version that takes only 20 minutes to make. I've shortened the cooking time by using lean roast beef from the deli and making a light gravy with chicken broth. The gravy just coats the hash. I've updated the flavor using shiitake mushrooms, pine nuts, and fresh thyme. This hash keeps well, so make double if you have time.

roast beef and shiitake hash

2 teaspoons olive oil

¼ pound unpeeled red potatoes, washed and cut into 1-inch cubes (about 1 cup)

½ cup diced red onion

2 medium-size red bell peppers, diced (2 cups)

¼ pound shiitake mushrooms, diced (1½ cups)

½ pound sliced lean roast beef, diced (2 cups)

2 tablespoons whole wheat flour

1 cup fat-free, low-salt chicken broth

Salt and freshly ground black pepper to taste

Heat the oil in a nonstick skillet over a medium-high heat. Add the potatoes and sauté for 5 minutes, tossing to turn halfway through. Add the onion, bell peppers, and mushrooms. Sauté for 10 minutes, again tossing to turn halfway through. Add the roast beef and toss for 1 minute. Push the ingredients to the side of the skillet, leaving a hole in the center. Add the flour, then the broth, and stir until the sauce thickens. Toss with the ingredients to lightly bind the hash. Season with salt and pepper to taste. Divide between 2 plates and serve.
Makes 2 servings.

One serving: 409 calories, 39g protein, 29g carbohydrate, 14g fat (4g saturated), 93mg cholesterol, 364mg sodium, 1g fibre

green salad

4 cups washed, ready-to-eat mixed salad

½ cup cannellini beans

2 tablespoons no-sugar-added oil and vinegar salad dressing

Salt and freshly ground black pepper to taste

Place the salad leaves and beans in a bowl and drizzle with the dressing. Season with salt and pepper to taste and toss. Serve with the hash.
Makes 2 servings.

One serving: 136 calories, 4g protein, 14g carbohydrate, 9g fat (1g saturated), 0mg cholesterol, 82mg sodium, 3g fibre

helpful hints

- Ask the deli to cut the roast beef in a single slice to make it easier to cube.
- Pecans or almonds can be substituted for the walnuts.
- If pressed for time, substitute 1 medium apple per person for the Cinnamon Walnut Baked Apples

countdown

- Make hash.
- While hash cooks, make salad.
- Make baked apples.

shopping list

TO BUY:

½ pound sliced lean roast beef

1 can cannellini beans (4 ounces needed)

1 small package broken walnuts (about 1 ounce needed)

¼ pound red potatoes

2 medium-sized red bell peppers

1 container shiitake mushrooms (4 ounces needed)

1 bag washed, ready-to-eat lettuce

2 Red Delicious apples

roast beef and shiitake hash continued

cinnamon-walnut baked apples

STAPLES:
  Olive oil
  Red onion
  Whole wheat flour
  Fat-free, low-salt chicken
    broth
  Ground cinnamon
  Sugar substitute
  No-sugar-added oil and
    vinegar salad dressing
  Salt
  Black peppercorns

2 tablespoons broken walnuts
1 teaspoon ground cinnamon
2 (.035-ounce) envelope
  sugar substitute
2 Red Delicious apples, cored

Chop the walnuts with the cinnamon and sugar substitute in a food processor. Place the apples in 2 small dessert bowls, and fill the core of each apple with the cinnamon-walnut mixture. (Some of the mixture may spill over the top. This is fine.) Cover each bowl with another bowl or microwave-safe plastic wrap. Microwave on high for 4 minutes. Remove and let stand, covered for 2 minutes. Serve in the dessert bowls.

Makes 2 servings.

One serving: 159 calories, 2g protein, 24g carbohydrate, 8g fat (0.8g saturated), 0mg cholesterol, 1mg sodium, 4g fiber

bahamian fish boil

With excellent fresh fish available all year round, the natives of the Bahamas are masters at cooking fish. ● This 20-minute meal is made in one pot. The fish should be cooked just long enough so that it is tender and juicy. Also, be sure to season the fish well before it cooks. ● For an interesting change, try this chayote salad. Chayote , also called "mirliton" or "christophene", looks like a gnarled pear. It has a flavor similar to zucchini, but retains its crisp texture when cooked.

bahamian fish boil

¼ pound sweet potatoes or yams, peeled and cut into ½ -inch pieces (½ cup)

4 celery stalks, sliced (2 cups)

½ cup sliced yellow onion

8 sprigs fresh thyme or 2 teaspoons dried

3 cups cold water

¾ pound mahi mahi fillet cut into 1-inch pieces

2 tablespoons freshly squeezed lemon juice (1 lemon)

Salt and freshly ground black pepper to taste

Several drops hot pepper sauce

1 tablespoon olive oil

2 slices country style, multigrain bread

Place the potatoes, celery, onion, thyme, and water in a saucepan. Cover and cook over a medium-high heat for 15 minutes. Meanwhile, season both sides of the fish with the lemon juice, salt, and pepper, pressing the seasoning into the fillet. Lower the heat and add the fish to the saucepan. Cover and gently simmer for 5 minutes. Add the pepper sauce and olive oil, then season with additional salt and pepper to taste. Meanwhile, toast the bread. Serve the soup in large soup bowls with the toasted bread. *Makes 2 servings.*

One serving: 353 calories, 38g protein, 34g carbohydrate, 10g fat (1g saturated), 126mg cholesterol, 418mg sodium, 6g fiber

helpful hints

● Fresh thyme works best in this dish. If using dried, make sure the bottle is less than 6 months old.

● Any type of white fish can be used. A delicate, flaky fish such as sole will need only 2 minutes to cook.

● Any type of hot pepper sauce can be used.

● Any type of washed, ready-to-eat lettuce can be used instead of the chayote salad.

countdown

● Start vegetables boiling in the broth.

● Season fish and add to broth.

● While fish cooks, make salad.

shopping list

TO BUY:

¾ pound mahi mahi fillet

¼ pound sweet potatoes or yams

1 bunch fresh thyme or 1 jar dried

2 small chayotes

1 bag washed, ready-to-eat lettuce

1 medium mango

1 lemon

bahamian fish boil continued

continued

STAPLES:
Celery
Yellow onion
Garlic
Hot pepper sauce
Olive oil
No-sugar-added oil and
    vinegar dressing
Multigrain bread
Salt
Black peppercorns

chayote salad

2 tablespoons no-sugar-added oil
    and vinegar dressing
2 medium-sized garlic cloves,
    crushed
2 small chayotes, peeled and
    sliced (about 2 cups)
Salt and freshly ground black
    pepper to taste
Several lettuce leaves, washed and
    dried

Heat the dressing in a medium-sized nonstick skillet over a medium-high heat and add the garlic and chayote slices. Toss for 3–4 minutes. Season with salt and pepper to taste. Place the lettuce leaves on a plate and spoon the chayote on top before serving.

Makes 2 servings.

One serving: 126 calories, 2g protein, 11g carbohydrate, 9g fat (1g saturated), 0mg cholesterol, 83mg sodium, 0g fiber

mango

1 medium mango

Slice off each side of the mango as close to the seed as possible. Take the mango half in your hand, skin-side down. Score the fruit in a cross-hatch pattern. Bend the skin backwards so that the cubes pop up like a porcupine. Slice the cubes off the skin. Score and slice any fruit left on the pit.

Divide the mango cubes between 2 dessert bowls.

Makes 2 servings.

One serving: 67 calories, 1g protein, 18g carbohydrate, 0g fat (0g saturated), 0mg cholesterol, 2mg sodium, 1g fiber

aromatic poached sole **p176**

mediterranean veal and olives   **p182**

summer-and-winter chicken casserole

This flavorful casserole takes only 30 minutes to make and is a meal in a bowl, but light enough to enjoy year-round.

summer-and-winter chicken casserole

3 cups fat-free, low-salt chicken broth

2 cups low-salt, no-sugar-added, canned diced tomatoes (including juice)

1 cup sliced red onion

2 celery stalks, sliced (1 cup)

1 cup sliced white cabbage

½ cup whole wheat fusilli pasta (2 ounces)

1 tablespoon horseradish

1 tablespoon balsamic vinegar

8 cups washed, ready-to-eat fresh spinach

2 slices whole wheat bread

2 ounces shredded, reduced-fat Swiss cheese

Salt and freshly ground black pepper to taste

Bring the chicken broth and tomatoes to a boil in a large saucepan over a medium-high heat. Add the onion and celery. Cover, lower the heat to medium, and cook on a slow boil for 10 minutes. Add the cabbage and fusilli. Boil uncovered for 10 minutes. Combine the horseradish and vinegar. Add to the pan and stir in the spinach. Simmer for 2 minutes, until the spinach is just wilted. Toast the bread. Add the cheese to the casserole. Season with salt and pepper to taste. Serve with the toasted bread.

Makes 2 servings.

One serving: 434 calories, 36g protein, 66g carbohydrate, 7g fat (3g saturated), 15mg cholesterol, 1289mg sodium, 22g fiber

grilled cinnamon oranges

2 medium oranges

½ teaspoon ground cinnamon

2 tablespoons slivered almonds

2 (.035-ounce) envelopes sugar substitute

Preheat the broiler. Line a baking tray with foil or use a small oven-to-table dish. Peel the oranges over a bowl to catch the juice. With a serrated knife, cut the oranges into circular ½-inch slices over the bowl. Place the orange slices in a single layer in the baking dish. Sprinkle with the cinnamon and almonds and broil for 3 minutes. Combine the sugar substitute with the reserved orange juice. Pour the juice over the grilled oranges and serve.

Makes 2 servings.

One serving: 129 calories, 4g protein, 19g carbohydrate, 6g fat (0.5g saturated), 0mg cholesterol, 0mg sodium, 4g fiber

helpful hints

● Any type of short-cut whole wheat pasta can be used.

● If pressed for time, omit the grilled cinnamon oranges and serve 1 orange per person.

countdown

● Preheat broiler.
● Prepare all ingredients.
● Make casserole.
● While casserole cooks, toast bread.
● Make grilled oranges.

shopping list

TO BUY:

1 small package shredded, reduced-fat Swiss cheese (2 ounces needed)

1 can low-salt, no-sugar-added, canned diced tomatoes (16 ounces needed)

1 small jar horseradish

1 package slivered almonds

1 box whole wheat fusilli pasta (2 ounces needed)

¼ head white cabbage

1 bag washed, ready-to-eat fresh spinach

2 medium oranges

STAPLES:

Celery

Red onion

Fat-free, low-salt chicken broth

Balsamic vinegar

Whole wheat bread

Ground cinnamon

Sugar substitute

Salt

Black peppercorns

beef stir-fry with oyster sauce

You can make a beef, broccoli, and water chestnut stir-fry in less time than it takes to send out for Chinese food. The popularity of Chinese food in America has made this a classic 'American' dish.

beef stir-fry with oyster sauce

¼ cup bottled oyster sauce

¼ cup dry sherry or water

2 teaspoons sesame oil, divided

½ pound broccoli florets

½ pound lean beef (tenderloin, sirloin, strip, flank, or skirt) cut into stir-fry strips (2 x ½-inches)

1½ cup sliced water chestnuts

Salt and freshly ground black pepper to taste

Combine the oyster sauce, sherry, and 1 teaspoon of the sesame oil in a small bowl. Make sure all the ingredients are prepped and ready for stir-frying. Heat the remaining teaspoon of sesame oil in a nonstick wok or skillet until smoking. Add the broccoli and stir-fry for 3 minutes. Add the beef, water chestnuts, and sauce. Stir fry for 2 more minutes. Season with salt and pepper to taste and serve over brown rice.

> One serving: 470 calories, 47g protein, 37g carbohydrate, 15g fat (5g saturated), 102mg cholesterol, 675mg sodium, 8g fiber

brown rice

½ cup brown rice

8 scallions, sliced (about 1 cup)

2 teaspoons sesame oil

Salt and freshly ground black pepper to taste

Fill a large saucepan with about 2–3 quarts of water and bring to the boil. Place the rice in a strainer and rinse under cold water. Add to the saucepan, stir once or twice, and boil for 30 minutes. Alternatively, follow the cooking instructions on the package. Drain, leaving about 3 tablespoons water on the rice. Toss the scallions and sesame oil with the rice. Season with salt and pepper to taste.

Makes 2 servings.

> One serving: 140 calories, 3g protein, 20g carbohydrate, 5g fat (1g saturated), 0mg cholesterol, 2mg sodium, 1g fiber

minted tangerines

1 cup no-sugar-added lemon-
lime or citrus-flavored
seltzer, chilled

2 sprigs fresh mint

2 (.035-ounce) envelopes
sugar substitute

2 medium tangerines, peeled and
divided into segments

Pour the seltzer into a small bowl and add the mint sprigs, sugar substitute, and tangerine segments. Stir to dissolve the sugar substitute. Let the tangerine segments marinate for 15 minutes, then remove and arrange on 2 small plates. Pour a little of the marinade over the segments and garnish with a sprig of mint before serving.

One serving: 37 calories, 0.5g protein, 10g carbohydrate, 0.2g fat (0g saturated), 0mg cholesterol, 1mg sodium, 0g fiber

countdown

- Start rice.
- Marinate tangerines.
- Prepare beef ingredients.
- Stir-fry beef.
- Finish rice.

shopping list

TO BUY:

½ pound lean beef
(tenderloin, sirloin,
strip, flank, or skirt)

1 can sliced water chestnuts
(12 ounces needed)

1 bottle oyster sauce

1 small bottle sesame oil

1 small package brown rice

1 small bottle no-sugar-
added lemon-lime or
citrus-flavored seltzer
(8 ounces needed)

1 small bottle dry sherry

½ pound broccoli florets

1 small bunch scallions
(8 needed)

1 small bunch fresh mint

2 medium tangerines

STAPLES:

Sugar substitute

Salt

Black peppercorns

pork and peach salsa

For best results, the peaches should be ripe. Look for tree-ripened peaches, which have more flavor. ● *Both the pork and pasta salad can be served warm or at room temperature.*

helpful hints

● *If peaches are not available, use fresh pear or papaya.*
● *Shop-bought salsa can be used instead of fresh peach salsa. Make sure there is no sugar added.*

countdown

● *Preheat oven to 400 degrees .*
● *Start pork.*
● *Start pasta.*
● *Make salsa.*
● *Finish pasta.*

shopping list

TO BUY:

½ *pound pork tenderloin*
1 *box whole wheat fusilli or macaroni pasta (2 ounces needed)*
½ *pound zucchini*
2 *jalapeño peppers*
1 *small bunch fresh cilantro*
2 *ripe peaches*
1 *lime*
1 *cantaloupe*

STAPLES:

Carrots
Olive oil
Olive oil spray
Dried oregano
Ground cumin
Sugar substitute
Salt
Black peppercorns

pork and peach salsa

½ pound pork tenderloin
Olive oil spray
½ teaspoon dried oregano
½ teaspoon ground cumin
2 ripe peaches, washed, halved, and pitted
2 teaspoons freshly squeezed lime juice
2 (.035-ounce) envelopes sugar substitute
2 tablespoons chopped fresh cilantro
2 jalapeño peppers, seeded, and chopped (2 tablespoons)
Salt and freshly ground black pepper to taste

Preheat the oven to 400 degrees. Line a baking tray with foil. Remove any visible fat from the pork, place on the foil, and spray both sides with olive oil. Sprinkle the pork with the oregano and cumin. Place in the oven and roast for 25 minutes.

While the pork roasts, dice the peaches. Combine the lime juice and sugar substitute in a small bowl. Add the peaches, cilantro, and jalapeños. Toss well and season with salt and pepper to taste.

When the pork is cooked, slice and serve immediately, or let cool to room temperature and then slice. Serve with the salsa on the side.
Makes 2 servings.

One serving: 278 calories, 35g protein, 19g carbohydrate, 8g fat (3g saturated), 106mg cholesterol, 83mg sodium, 1g fiber

pasta salad

½ cup whole wheat fusilli or macaroni pasta (2 ounces)
2 cups sliced carrots
2 cups sliced zucchini
4 teaspoons olive oil
Salt and freshly ground black pepper to taste

Fill a large saucepan with water and bring to the boil. Add the pasta and boil for 7 minutes. Add the carrots and zucchini. Continue to boil for 2 minutes, or until the pasta is cooked through but firm. Drain the pasta and vegetables and toss with the olive oil. Season with salt and pepper to taste. Serve with the pork.
Makes 2 servings.

One serving: 285 calories, 9g protein, 40g carbohydrate, 10g fat (2g saturated), 0mg cholesterol, 51mg sodium, 7g fiber

melon

1 cantaloupe, cubed (4 cups)

Divide the cantaloupe between 2 dessert bowls.
Makes 2 servings.

One serving: 77 calories, 2g protein, 18g carbohydrate, 1g fat (0g saturated), 0mg cholesterol, 20mg sodium, 2g fiber

desserts

introduction

With this chapter to hand, there's no need to abandon your healthy eating lifestyle when you want a special treat or have guests for dinner.

Most desserts, unfortunately, are laden with carbohydrates. I created these recipes for those times when you want something sweet at the end of a meal, while staying within the guidelines of a good-carb lifestyle.

Desserts have not been included as part of the Quick Start section, but the Strawberry Pecan Whip and Coffee Latte Whip are two desserts that you can enjoy during the Quick Start phase (and subsequent phases). They're satisfying at the end of a meal and have limited carbohydrate content. A few desserts are included in the Which Carb section because they fit the nutritional guidelines for that menu. But most desserts have been included in the Right Carb meals.

I have created some additional temptations as alternatives to a simple fruit dessert. The Mocha Fudge Soufflé and the Raspberry Parfait are winners and can be served to guests with pride.

dessert index

strawberry pecan whip

'Whipped Jell-O' was a favorite of mine when I was young. Here is an updated version that fits perfectly into a low-carb lifestyle—and can be eaten in Quick Start, Which Carbs, and Right Carbs.

strawberry pecan whip

1 (0.3-ounce) package sugar-free, low-calorie strawberry Jell-O gelatin

1 cup boiling water

1 cup cold water

1 teaspoon vanilla extract

2 tablespoons pecan pieces, toasted

¼ cup part-skim ricotta cheese

Dissolve the Jell-O in boiling water, stirring for 2 minutes. Add the cold water and place in the refrigerator to set for 1½ hours. Stir the vanilla extract and pecans into the ricotta cheese. Whip into the partially set Jell-O with an electric beater. Divide between 4 dessert bowls. Refrigerate to set once more before serving. *Makes 4 servings.*

One serving: 147 calories, 8g protein, 3g carbohydrate, 11g fat (3g saturated), 15mg cholesterol, 45mg sodium, 1g fiber

helpful hints

- *Any fruit-flavored, sugar-free Jell-O gelatin can be used.*
- *Be careful toasting pecans, as they burn easily.*

countdown

- *Set water to boil.*
- *Make recipe.*

shopping list

TO BUY:

1 (0.3-ounce) package sugar-free, low-calorie strawberry Jell-O gelatin

1 small carton part-skim ricotta cheese

1 small package pecan pieces

STAPLES:

Vanilla extract

apricot almond custard

Good quality dried apricots add more flavor to this dish. Once reconstituted, they should look like fresh apricots. This dessert can be eaten during Right Carbs.

apricot almond custard

6 dried apricots
½ cup skim milk
1 (.035-ounce) envelope
  sugar substitute
¼ teaspoon almond extract
1 egg
1 tablespoon slivered almonds

Preheat the oven to 350 degrees. Bring a small saucepan of water to a boil and add the apricots. Boil for 3–4 minutes to reconstitute, then drain, and coarsely chop. Combine the apricots, milk, sugar substitute, almond extract, and egg in a small bowl. Divide between 2 ovenproof ramekins or a bowl (3 x 1¾ inches deep). Sprinkle the almonds on top. Bake for 30 minutes, or until the custard is firm.

Makes 2 servings.

One serving: 143 calories, 8g protein,
17g carbohydrate, 6g fat (1g saturated),
108mg cholesterol, 64mg sodium, 3g fiber

countdown

- *Preheat oven to 350 degrees.*
- *Set a small saucepan of water to boil.*
- *Complete recipe.*

shopping list

TO BUY:
  1 package dried apricots
    (6 needed)
  1 small bottle almond extract
  1 small package slivered
    almonds (about ½ ounce
    needed)
STAPLES:
  Skim milk
  Sugar substitute
  Egg

coffee latte whip

This recipe was created for the Quick Start phase but can be used during any phase.

coffee latte whip

1 tablespoon gelatine (1 envelope or ¼ ounce)

¼ cup cold water

½ cup boiling water

3 (.035-ounce) envelopes sugar substitute

½ tablespoon unsweetened cocoa powder

¼ cup strong, decaffeinated, black coffee

2 tablespoons heavy whipping cream

Soak the gelatine in the cold water for 5 minutes. Pour the boiling water into the cold water-gelatine mixture to dissolve the gelatine. Stir in the sugar substitute, cocoa powder, and coffee. Pour into a bowl and refrigerate for 1 hour to set. Remove the gelatine from the refrigerator and whip with an electric beater. Add the whipping cream and continue to whip until fluffy. Pour into 2 dessert dishes and refrigerate to set, about 15 minutes.
Makes 2 servings.

One serving: **74 calories**, 4g protein, 3g carbohydrate, 6g fat (4g saturated), 21mg cholesterol, 12mg sodium, 0.5g fiber

mocha fudge cake

Melting the chocolate in a microwave takes only minutes.

mocha fudge cake

2 ounces bittersweet or plain
chocolate

1 tablespoon strong,
decaffeinated, black coffee

2 (.035-ounce) envelopes
sugar substitute

4 egg whites

Preheat the oven to 350 degrees. Place the chocolate in a microwave-safe bowl and microwave on high for 2 minutes to melt. Stir in the coffee and sugar substitute.

Beat the egg whites until stiff peaks form. Fold into the chocolate mixture. Spoon into 2 soufflé dishes (each 1 1/3 high x 4 inches in diameter), or a single Pyrex bowl, (3 inches high x 6 inches in diameter). Bake in the oven for 8 minutes and serve warm.

Makes 2 servings.

One serving: 169 calories, 11g protein,
9g carbohydrate, 15g fat (9g saturated),
0mg cholesterol, 111mg sodium, 0g fiber

helpful hints

● *Buy high-quality chocolate for best results.*

● *Instant coffee can be used.*

countdown

● *Preheat oven to 350 degrees.*

● *Melt chocolate.*

● *Whip egg whites.*

● *Complete recipe.*

shopping list

TO BUY:

2 ounces bittersweet or plain chocolate

STAPLES:

Eggs

Decaffeinated coffee

Sugar substitute

index

notes

acknowledgments

Many, many thanks go to my husband, Harold. He has been the main force behind this book. Since his decision nine years ago to adopt a low-carb lifestyle, he has stood by my work and by my side. He encouraged me to create the recipes, helped to test and taste them and edited every word.

I'd like to thank my assistant, Jackie Murrill, for her patience and help in testing these recipes. She spent hours on her feet working with me—and always with a smile.

Many thanks go to Martha Hopkins, my editor, who worked night and day to meet our tight schedule.

I'd also like to thank my family who embraced the project and supported me through it. My son James, his wife Patty and their son Zachary, who all came for dinner with a smile knowing they would be recipe-tasting guinea pigs. My son Charles and his girlfriend Lori who tested recipes via email. My son John, his wife Jill and their son Jeffrey, who cheered me on. My sister Roberta and brother-in-law Robert, who helped to edit my thoughts and words.

Thanks go to Kathy Martin, my editor at the Miami Herald, who has been a friend and booster for my columns and books.

Producing and hosting a weekly radio program has been a delight as well as an enormous amount of work. Thanks to the management and staff at WLRN 91.3 FM, public radio for South Florida, for their friendship and help.

I'd like to thank the many readers and students who correspond with me from all over the US to say how much they enjoy the recipes and how much better they feel. This kind of encouragement makes the lonely time in front of the computer worthwhile.

Most importantly, I'd like to thank all of you who read this book and prepare the meals. I hope you enjoy them and reap the benefits as much as I've enjoyed creating the recipes and watching the wonderful results.